THE NEW FOLGER LIBRARY
SHAKESPEARE

Designed to make Shakespeare's great plays available to all readers, the New Folger Library edition of Shakespeare's plays provides accurate texts in modern spelling and punctuation, as well as scene-by-scene action summaries, full explanatory notes, many pictures clarifying Shakespeare's language, and notes recording all significant departures from the early printed versions. Each play is prefaced by a brief introduction, by a guide to reading Shakespeare's language, and by accounts of his life and theater. Each play is followed by an annotated list of further readings and by a "Modern Perspective" written by an expert on that particular play.

Barbara A. Mowat is Director of Academic Programs at the Folger Shakespeare Library, Editor of *Shakespeare Quarterly*, Chair of the Folger Institute, and author of *The Dramaturgy of Shakespeare's Romances* and of essays on Shakespeare's plays and on the editing of the plays.

Paul Werstine is Professor of English at King's College and the Graduate School of the University of Western Ontario, Canada. He is author of many papers and articles on the printing and editing of Shakespeare's plays.

The Folger Shakespeare Library

The Folger Shakespeare Library in Washington, D.C., a privately funded research library dedicated to Shakespeare and the civilization of early modern Europe, was founded in 1932 by Henry Clay and Emily Jordan Folger. In addition to its role as the world's preeminent Shakespeare collection and its emergence as a leading center for Renaissance studies, the Folger Library offers a wide array of cultural and educational programs and services for the general public.

.THE NEW.
FOLGER LIBRARY
SHAKESPEARE

LOVE'S LABOR'S LOST

BY

WILLIAM SHAKESPEARE

WASHINGTON SQUARE PRESS
PUBLISHED BY POCKET BOOKS

New York   London   Toronto   Sydney   Tokyo   Singapore

A WASHINGTON SQUARE PRESS *Original* Publication

WSP

A Washington Square Press Publication of
POCKET BOOKS, a division of Simon & Schuster Inc.
1230 Avenue of the Americas, New York, NY 10020

ISBN: 0-671-72274-3

Washington Square Press New Folger Edition November 1996

10 9 8 7 6 5 4 3 2 1

Cover art by Kinuko Y. Craft

Printed in the U.S.A.

From the Director of the Library

For over thirty-five years, the Folger Library General Reader's Shakespeare has provided accurate and accessible texts of the plays and poems to students, teachers, and hundreds of thousands of other interested readers. Today, in an age often impatient with the past, the passion for Shakespeare continues to grow. No author speaks more powerfully to the human condition, in all its variety, than this actor/playwright from a minor sixteenth-century English village.

Over three decades, much has changed in the way Shakespeare's works are edited, performed, studied, and taught. It is time to replace the earlier Folger Shakespeare with an entirely new version, one that incorporates the best and most current thinking concerning both the texts and their interpretation. Professors Barbara Mowat and Paul Werstine are uniquely qualified to produce this New Folger Shakespeare for a new generation of readers. The Library is grateful for the learning, clarity, and imagination they have brought to this ambitious project.

Werner Gundersheimer, Director
The Folger Shakespeare Library

Contents

Editors' Preface

In recent years, ways of dealing with Shakespeare's texts and with the interpretation of his plays have been undergoing significant change. This edition, while retaining many of the features that have always made the Folger Shakespeare so attractive to the general reader, at the same time reflects these current ways of thinking about Shakespeare. For example, modern readers, actors, and teachers have become interested in the differences between, on the one hand, the early forms in which Shakespeare's plays were first published and, on the other hand, the forms in which editors through the centuries have presented them. In response to this interest, we have based our edition on what we consider the best early printed version of a particular play (explaining our rationale in a section called "An Introduction to This Text") and have marked our changes in the text—unobtrusively, we hope, but in such a way that the curious reader can be aware that a change has been made and can consult the "Textual Notes" to discover what appeared in the early printed version.

Current ways of looking at the plays are reflected in our brief prefaces, in many of the commentary notes, in the annotated lists of "Further Reading," and especially in each play's "Modern Perspective," an essay written by an outstanding scholar who brings to the reader his or her fresh assessment of the play in the light of today's interests and concerns.

As in the Folger Library General Reader's Shakespeare, which this edition replaces, we include explanatory notes designed to help make Shakespeare's language clearer to a modern reader, and we place the notes on the page facing the text that they explain. We also follow the earlier edition in including illustrations —of objects, of clothing, of mythological figures—from books and manuscripts in the Folger Library collection. We provide fresh accounts of the life of Shakespeare, of the publishing of his plays, and of the theaters in which his plays were performed, as well as an introduction to the text itself. We also include a section called "Reading Shakespeare's Language," in which we try to help readers learn to "break the code" of Elizabethan poetic language.

For each section of each volume, we are indebted to a host of generous experts and fellow scholars. The "Reading Shakespeare's Language" sections, for example, could not have been written had not Arthur King, of Brigham Young University, and Randal Robinson, author of *Unlocking Shakespeare's Language,* led the way in untangling Shakespearean language puzzles and generously shared their insights and methodologies with us. "Shakespeare's Life" profited by the careful reading given it by the late S. Schoenbaum, "Shakespeare's Theater" was read and strengthened by Andrew Gurr and John Astington, and "The Publication of Shakespeare's Plays" is indebted to the comments of Peter W. M. Blayney. Among earlier editions of the play, we particularly valued the late George Hibbard's (1990). We, as editors, take sole responsibility for any errors in our editions.

We are grateful to the authors of the "Modern Perspectives"; to Leeds Barroll and David Bevington for their generous encouragement; to the Huntington and Newberry Libraries for fellowship support; to King's College for the grants it has provided to Paul Werstine; to the Social Sciences and Humanities Research Council of Canada, which provided him with a Research Time Stipend for 1990–91; to R. J. Shroyer of the University of

Western Ontario for essential computer support; and to the Folger Institute's Center for Shakespeare Studies for its fortuitous sponsorship of a workshop on "Shakespeare's Texts for Students and Teachers" (funded by the National Endowment for the Humanities and led by Richard Knowles of the University of Wisconsin), a workshop from which we learned an enormous amount about what is wanted by college and high-school teachers of Shakespeare today.

Our biggest debt is to the Folger Shakespeare Library —to Werner Gundersheimer, Director of the Library, who made possible our edition; to Deborah Curren-Aquino, who provides extensive editorial and production support; to Jean Miller, the Library's Art Curator, who combs the Library holdings for illustrations, and to Julie Ainsworth, Head of the Photography Department, who carefully photographs them; to Peggy O'Brien, former Director of Education at the Folger and now Director of Education Programs at the Corporation for Public Broadcasting, and her assistant at the Folger, Molly Haws, who gave us expert advice about the needs being expressed by Shakespeare teachers and students (and to Martha Christian and other "master teachers" who used our texts in manuscript in their classrooms); to Jessica Hymowitz, who provided expert computer support; to the staff of the Academic Programs Division, especially Amy Adler, Mary Tonkinson, Lena Cowen Orlin, Linda Johnson, Kathleen Lynch, and Carol Brobeck; and, finally, to the staff of the Library Reading Room, whose patience and support are invaluable.

Barbara A. Mowat and Paul Werstine

Map of France, Spain, and Navarre.
From Giovanni Botero,
Le relationi vniuersali . . . (1618).

Shakespeare's *Love's Labor's Lost*

The story told in Shakespeare's early comedy *Love's Labor's Lost* seems, at first glance, to offer little outside of easy laughter. Four young men (one of them, admittedly, a king) decide to withdraw from the world for three years. They take an oath that, most importantly, forbids them to have anything to do with women in that space of time. Warned by Berowne, the most skeptical of the lords, that the oath will inevitably be broken, the King of Navarre is immediately put in an impossible situation: the Princess of France and her attending ladies are on their way to Navarre on an embassy. Fighting to keep his oath, the King lodges the Princess outside the gates of his court, but that ungracious strategy fails to head off the inevitable, as all four men fall immediately in love with the French ladies, abandoning their oaths and setting out to win the ladies' hands.

The laughter triggered by this simple story—usually at the expense of the misguided young men—is augmented by subplots involving a braggart soldier, a clever page, illiterate servants, a parson, a schoolmaster, and a constable so dull that he is named Dull. Letters and poems are misdelivered, confessions are overheard, entertainments are presented, and language is played with (and misused) by the ignorant and learned alike. This is a play that entertains and amuses.

At a deeper level, though, *Love's Labor's Lost* also teases the mind. It seems to begin with the premise that women either are to be feared and avoided as seductresses who tempt young men away from heroic endeavor, or are instead to be worshiped as goddesses who are men's sole guide to wisdom. The play soon makes it clear, however, that while this split vision of woman is what the men in the play accept, the reality of male-female relations is something other.

Our first major clue that the men's view of women is not to be trusted comes at the end of Act 3 (which, in this play, with its strange and misleading act divisions, is actually quite early in the action). Berowne confesses to himself (and the audience) that he has fallen in love with Rosaline. He is angry with himself—he who has so scoffed at love, now to be marching in love's army!—but his self-contempt gives him little excuse for the things he says about Rosaline. He has barely met her: in the previous scene he has had to ask her name. Yet he now accuses her of being the "worst" of the four women, a "wanton" who "will do the deed / Though Argus were her eunuch and her guard." This bitter attack on Rosaline as a wild sexual creature is preceded by a more general comment on "woman"—"like a German clock, . . . ever out of frame," "never going aright, being a watch, / But being watched that it may still go right." This is the same speaker who will shortly describe Rosaline as "the sun that maketh all things shine" and praise women's eyes as "the books, the arts, the academes / That show, contain, and nourish all the world."

Because we see Rosaline for ourselves, we see that both poles of Berowne's responses to her are incredible exaggerations. She is neither whore nor goddess. But Berowne's attitude toward her is of a piece with male views and expectations of women throughout the play. Lodged in the fields as potential seductresses, the women quickly become the focus of a military-style campaign of seduction themselves—"Advance your standards, and upon them, lords. / Pell-mell, down with them." The men will argue that, under the power of the ladies' eyes, they have been transformed and that their courtship, though seeming "ridiculous," has expressed genuine love; the women will answer that the men's gestures have been taken as "pleasant jest," "as bombast and as lining to the time," as "a merriment." The women seem quite bewildered by the men's belief that the women should, because the men want them, immediately give themselves in marriage.

Much of the action of *Love's Labor's Lost* turns on the discrepancy between, on the one hand, what the men think about the women and, on the other, how the women see themselves (and see the men). That women are not identical to men's images of them is a common theme in Shakespeare's plays. In *Love's Labor's Lost* it receives one of its most pressing examinations. Thus, while the play amuses, it also gives us much to ponder.

After you have read the play, we invite you to turn to the back of this book to read *"Love's Labor's Lost:* A Modern Perspective" by Professor William C. Carroll of Boston University.

Reading Shakespeare's Language: *Love's Labor's Lost*

For many people today, reading Shakespeare's language can be a problem—but it is a problem that can be solved. Those who have studied Latin (or even French or German or Spanish), and those who are used to reading poetry, will have little difficulty understanding the language of Shakespeare's poetic drama. Others, though, need to develop the skills of untangling unusual sentence structures and of recognizing and understanding poetic compressions, omissions, and wordplay. And even those skilled in reading unusual sentence structures may have occasional trouble with Shakespeare's words. Four hundred years of "static" intervene between his speaking and our hearing. Most of his immense vocabulary is still in use, but a few of his words are not, and, worse, some of his words now have meanings quite different from those they had in the sixteenth century. In the theater, most of these difficulties are solved for us by actors who study the language and articulate it for us so that the essential meaning is heard—or, when combined with stage action, is at least felt. When reading on one's own, one must do what each actor does: go over the lines (often with a dictionary close at hand) until the puzzles are solved and the lines yield up their poetry and the characters speak in words and phrases that are, suddenly, rewarding and wonderfully memorable.

Shakespeare's Words

As you begin to read the opening scenes of a play by Shakespeare, you may notice occasional unfamiliar words. Some are unfamiliar simply because we no longer use them. In the opening scenes of *Love's Labor's Lost*, for example, you will find the words *wight* (person), *farborough* (petty constable), *welkin* (heavens), and *yclept* (called). Words of this kind are explained in notes to the text and will become familiar the more of Shakespeare's plays you read.

In *Love's Labor's Lost*, as in all of Shakespeare's writing, more problematic are the words that we still use but that we use with a different meaning. In the opening scenes of *Love's Labor's Lost*, for example, the word *passed* has the meaning of "spoken," *stops* is used where we would say "obstructions," *envious* is used where we would say "malicious," *lie* where we would say "reside," and *quick* where we would say "lively." Such words will be explained in the notes to the text, but they, too, will become familiar as you continue to read Shakespeare's language.

Shakespeare's Sentences

In an English sentence, meaning is quite dependent on the place given each word. "The dog bit the boy" and "The boy bit the dog" mean very different things, even though the individual words are the same. Because English places such importance on the positions of words in sentences, on the way words are arranged, unusual arrangements can puzzle a reader. Shakespeare frequently shifts his sentences away from "normal" English arrangements—often to create the rhythm he seeks, sometimes to use a line's poetic rhythm to emphasize a particular word, sometimes to give a character his or her own speech patterns or to allow the character to speak in a special way. When we attend a good performance of the play, the actors will have worked out the sentence structures and will articulate the sentences so that the meaning is clear. In reading for yourself, do as the actor does. That is, when you become puzzled by a character's speech, check to see if words are being presented in an unusual sequence.

Look first for the placement of subject and verb. Shakespeare often rearranges verbs and subjects (e.g., instead of "He goes" we find "Goes he"). In *Love's Labor's Lost*, when Berowne says "Or vainly comes th' admirèd princess hither," he is using such a construction. (The "normal" arrangement would be "th' admirèd princess comes.") And so is the King of Navarre when he says "Nor shines the silver moon one-half so bright." Shakespeare also frequently places the object before the subject and verb (e.g., instead of "I hit him" we might find "Him I hit"). Dumaine's "The grosser manner of these world's delights / He throws upon the gross world's baser slaves" is an example of such an inversion (the normal arrangement would be "he throws the grosser manner of these world's delights upon . . ."), as is Berowne's "So much, dear liege, I have already sworn."

Inversions are not the only unusual sentence structures in Shakespeare's language. Often in his sentences words that would normally appear together are separated from each other. (Again, this is often done to create a particular rhythm or to stress a particular word.) Take, for example, the play's first two lines: "Let fame, that all hunt after in their lives, / Live registered upon our brazen tombs." Here, a subject ("fame") is separated from its verb ("live") by the clause "that all hunt after in their lives." Or take Maria's lines: "The only soil of his fair virtue's gloss, / If virtue's gloss will stain with any soil, / Is a sharp wit matched with too blunt a will." Here, the "normal" construction "The only soil is a sharp wit" is interrupted by the insertion of a phrase ("of his fair virtue's gloss") and then a clause ("If virtue's gloss will stain with any soil"). In order to create for yourself sentences that seem more like the English of everyday speech, you may wish to rearrange the words, putting together the word clusters (e.g., "Let fame live registered upon our brazen tombs"). You will usually find that the sentence will gain in clarity but will lose its rhythm or shift its emphasis.

In some of his plays (*Hamlet* is a good example), rather than separating basic sentence elements, Shakespeare simply holds them back, delaying them until other material to which he wants to give greater emphasis has been presented. While there are not nearly so many examples of this construction in *Love's Labor's*

Lost as there are in *Hamlet*, this kind of sentence is, nevertheless, evident in, for example, the Princess's words to the King of Navarre, near the end of the play:

> If this austere insociable life
> Change not your offer made in heat of blood;
> If frosts and fasts, hard lodging, and thin weeds
> Nip not the gaudy blossoms of your love,
> But that it bear this trial, and last love;
> Then, at the expiration of the year,
> Come challenge me, challenge me by these deserts.

Here the verbs ("Come challenge . . . challenge") in this imperative sentence are delayed until the Princess can present in vivid detail her conditions for granting any further hearing to the King's expressions of love.

In many of Shakespeare's plays, sentences are sometimes complicated not because of unusual structures or interruptions but because Shakespeare omits words that English sentences normally require. (In conversation, we, too, often omit words. We say "Heard from him yet?" and our hearer supplies the missing "Have you.") Frequent reading of Shakespeare—and of other poets— trains us to supply such missing words. In his later plays, Shakespeare uses omissions both of verbs and of nouns to great dramatic effect. In *Love's Labor's Lost* omissions are rare and seem to be used primarily for the sake of speech rhythm. For example, when Berowne mockingly responds to Dumaine's praise of Katherine's beauty ("As fair as day)," Berowne says "Ay, as some days, but then no sun must shine." In Berowne's speech the omission of the words "as fair" before "as some days" produces a regular iambic pentameter line. Or, to take another example, Berowne's line "Nothing so sure, and thereby all forsworn" is both rhythmical and elliptical. It would lose much of its expressive force if its omissions were repaired: "Nothing is so sure, and thereby we are all forsworn."

Shakespearean Wordplay

Shakespeare plays with language so often and so variously that entire books are written on the topic. Indeed the wordplay in *Love's Labor's Lost* alone is a topic that has been examined at book length. Here we will discuss only two kinds of wordplay, puns and metaphors. A pun is a play on words that sound the same but that have different meanings (or on a single word that has more than one meaning). Much of the humor of *Love's Labor's Lost* depends on puns and related kinds of wordplay, a great deal of it to be found in the rapid exchanges of wit among its speakers. Take, for example, this verbal skirmish between Berowne and Rosaline:

> ROSALINE Is the fool sick?
> BEROWNE Sick at the heart.
> ROSALINE Alack, let it blood.
> BEROWNE Would that do it good?
> ROSALINE My physic says "ay."
> BEROWNE Will you prick 't with your eye?
> ROSALINE No point, with my knife.

There are two different kinds of puns in these lines. The one on *ay* and *eye* is an example of a pun using two words that sound the same but have different meanings. When Rosaline says "ay" to Berowne, he puns on the word to tell her, in a subtle and playful way, that he loves her. That is, he invites her to pierce his heart with her *eye*, an invitation that arises from a belief (about which much was written in Shakespeare's time) that lovers' eyes emitted beams that entered each other's eyes and, through the eyes, penetrated to each other's hearts. Rosaline declines Berowne's overture with another kind of pun, one that plays bilingually on two different meanings of the same word. When Rosaline says "No point," she can be understood doubly to deny Berowne because "no point" means both "not at all" (the meaning in French of *non point)* and "my eye has no point."

To give only one other example of hundreds available in this play:

KATHERINE
　You sheep and I pasture. Shall that finish the jest?
BOYET
　So you grant pasture for me. ⌈*He tries to kiss her.*⌉
KATHERINE　　　　　　　　　　Not so, gentle beast.
　My lips are no common, though several they be.
BOYET
　Belonging to whom?
KATHERINE　　　　　　　To my fortunes and me.

To refuse Boyet the kiss for which he is angling, Katherine is given one of the more complicated of the play's puns, one that exploits three meanings of the word *several.* One of the meanings of *several* is opposite to that of *common.* While *common* refers to pasture where anyone may graze stock, *several* is pasture that is privately owned and enclosed. Not just any sheep, and particularly, in this case, not Boyet, may feed on Katherine's several lips, which are also several because they are "more than one" and because they are "parted," rather than together, as she verbally fends off Boyet.

Closely related to puns are two other kinds of wordplay that are widespread in *Love's Labor's Lost,* namely, polyptoton and (what we now call) malapropism. Polyptoton is simply the use, in rapid succession, of two words with the same root. The play's third line exemplifies the scheme polyptoton: "And then *grace* us in the *disgrace* of death." Dumaine's first speech soon offers another instance: "The *grosser* manner of these world's delights / He throws upon the *gross* world's baser slaves." While polyptoton showcases a character's mastery of language and invites the audience to delight in such mastery, malapropism usually calls attention to a character's inability to achieve even standard expression and invites the audience to ridicule the character for mistaking one word for another. Dull, for instance, tells us that he "reprehends" (instead of "represents") the Duke. In *Love's Labor's Lost*, however, Shakespeare puts into the speeches of some of his characters malapropisms that may evoke from an audience rather more delight than ridicule. When Costard tells us that the "contempts" (rather than "contents") of Armado's first letter concern him, an audience may laugh at Costard's blunder, but once the audience hears Armado's letter describe Costard as "that low-spirited swain, that base minnow of thy mirth," the audience may recognize that in Costard's blunder lies an accurate assessment of Armado's tone. Costard's reference to "the sinplicity [not "simplicity," or foolishness] of man to hearken after the flesh" has seemed to some readers another malapropism that is more than a mere blunder. The puns, polyptoton, and malapropisms of *Love's Labor's Lost* display wonderful agility and encourage the reader to approach the play with an attentive ear and a lively imagination.

Metaphors are plays on words in which one object or idea is expressed as if it were something else, something with which it shares common features. The King of Navarre's opening speech in the play is thick with metaphors:

KING
　　Let fame, that all hunt after in their lives,
　　Live registered upon our brazen tombs,
　　And then grace us in the disgrace of death,
　　When, spite of cormorant devouring time,
　　Th' endeavor of this present breath may buy　　5
　　That honor which shall bate his scythe's keen edge
　　And make us heirs of all eternity.
　　Therefore, brave conquerors, for so you are
　　That war against your own affections
　　And the huge army of the world's desires,　　10
　　Our late edict shall strongly stand in force.

In the first line's metaphor, the King compares fame to quarry that all of us, as hunters, seek. Then, in line 4, time is metaphorically transformed into a cormorant, that is, a greedy, rapacious bird from whose scavenging it is a struggle to protect anything. But time does not remain a figurative bird. Instead, in a metaphor in line 6, it becomes a mower with a sharp scythe, cutting down the living. In yet another metaphor that extends across lines 8 to 11, the King figures his fellow scholars as brave conquerors, triumphing alone over a huge army that, again metaphorically, represents their own passions (affections) and worldly desires.

　　Since *Love's Labor's Lost* is so concerned with language, it may be appropriate to cite some of its metaphors that compare language itself to other things.

　　Taffeta phrases, silken terms precise,
　　　　Three-piled hyperboles, spruce affectation,
　　Figures pedantical—these summer flies
　　　　Have blown me full of maggot ostentation.
　　I do forswear them, and I here protest
　　　　By this white glove—how white the hand,
　　　　　　God knows!—

> Henceforth my wooing mind shall be expressed
>   In russet yeas and honest kersey noes.
> And to begin: Wench, so God help me, law,
> My love to thee is sound, sans crack or flaw.

In this speech is a series of metaphors comparing different orders of language to different kinds of cloth. Elaborate, ornate language, or "figures pedantical" (scholarly figures of speech), are represented as taffeta, silk, and velvet of the highest quality, whose pile is three times normal thickness. Plain, even vulgar, language is russet and kersey—that is, coarse homespun cloth, worn by peasants. Part of the fun in reading this speech is observing Berowne's inability to maintain the distinction he himself has created, as in the last two lines he mixes plain language (e.g., "crack," "flaw," "wench," and "God save me, law") with the ornate and pedantic use of a word from a foreign language ("sans," which is French for "without").

Implied Stage Action

Finally, in reading Shakespeare's plays we should always remember that what we are reading is a performance script. The dialogue is written to be spoken by actors who, at the same time, are moving, gesturing, picking up objects, weeping, shaking their fists. Some stage action is described in what are called "stage directions"; some is suggested within the dialogue itself. We must learn to be alert to such signals as we stage the play in our imaginations. At the beginning of the play, when the King of Navarre instructs his lords to "subscribe your names" and Longaville and Dumaine voice agreement, it is reasonably clear from this dialogue that they do indeed sign their names, and we provide stage directions to this effect. Again, a little later in the same scene when Constable Dull addresses the King with the words "This letter will tell you more" and the King remarks "A letter from the magnificent Armado," it is fairly certain that this dialogue is accompanied by the transfer of a letter from Dull to the King. And so again we provide a stage direction that says as much: "He [i.e., Dull] gives the letter to the King." At other points in the play, the action to be staged in conjunction with the dialogue is not quite so easy to imagine. In 4.3 Berowne is onstage alone as the King enters. Berowne notes the approach of the King with the words "Here comes one with a paper." Then the First Quarto reads "He [i.e., Berowne] stands aside." In one way, this stage direction is consistent with the action that follows: Berowne does escape the King's notice, for the King speaks as if he were alone onstage. Yet in another way, the First Quarto's stage direction is inconsistent with a later remark by Berowne, who observes several lines later, "Like a demigod here sit I in the sky, / And wretched fools' secrets heedfully o'ereye." These words suggest that he did not simply "stand aside," as the First Quarto said, but climbed up above the King in some manner, perhaps scaling a stage-property tree. Here we, as editors, have chosen only to comment on the apparent inconsistency between the First Quarto's stage direction and its later dialogue; we have not intervened to regularize it one way or the other, but have left the matter to readers, directors, and actors to ponder.

In 5.2 there appears a First Quarto stage direction that continues to present, after centuries of guesswork, a significant interpretive challenge to editors and readers. Just after Armado, who is playing the role of Hector in a pageant of the Nine Worthies, has begged the Princess to "bestow on me the sense of hearing [i.e., to listen to me]," the First Quarto prints the stage direction

"Berowne steps forth." Whatever the significance of Berowne's stepping forward, the dialogue between Armado and the Princess goes on uninterrupted as the Princess replies "Speak, brave Hector." Six lines after the stage direction, however, Costard interrupts Armado's delivery of Hector's speech in the pageant with the news that Jaquenetta is pregnant. Some editors attempt to connect "Berowne steps forth" to Costard's later announcement by adding to the First Quarto's stage direction words prescribing that Berowne whisper to Costard, but there is nothing in the First Quarto upon which to ground any such connection. We, therefore, have simply presented our readers with the First Quarto's words so that our readers can engage with the interpretive issue themselves. Elsewhere, as editors, we have added stage directions (marked with brackets) when we feel reasonably sure our suggestions are valid, but readers, directors, and actors will need to use their own imaginations and their own understandings of the play for their individual stagings.

It is immensely rewarding to work carefully with Shakespeare's language so that the words, the sentences, the wordplay, and the implied stage action all become clear—as readers for the past four centuries have discovered. It may be more pleasurable to attend a good performance of a play—though not everyone has thought so. But the joy of being able to stage one of Shakespeare's plays in one's imagination, to return to passages that continue to yield further meanings (or further questions) the more one reads them—these are pleasures that, for many, rival (or at least augment) those of the performed text, and certainly make it worth considerable effort to "break the code" of Elizabethan poetic drama and let free the remarkable language that makes up a Shakespeare text.

Shakespeare's Life

Surviving documents that give us glimpses into the life of William Shakespeare show us a playwright, poet, and actor who grew up in the market town of Stratford-upon-Avon, spent his professional life in London, and returned to Stratford a wealthy landowner. He was born in April 1564, died in April 1616, and is buried inside the chancel of Holy Trinity Church in Stratford.

We wish we could know more about the life of the world's greatest dramatist. His plays and poems are testaments to his wide reading—especially to his knowledge of Virgil, Ovid, Plutarch, Holinshed's *Chronicles*, and the Bible—and to his mastery of the English language, but we can only speculate about his education. We know that the King's New School in Stratford-upon-Avon was considered excellent. The school was one of the English "grammar schools" established to educate young men, primarily in Latin grammar and literature. As in other schools of the time, students began their studies at the age of four or five in the attached "petty school," and there learned to read and write in English, studying primarily the catechism from the Book of Common Prayer. After two years in the petty school, students entered the lower form (grade) of the grammar school, where they began the serious study of Latin grammar and Latin texts that would occupy most of the remainder of their school days. (Several Latin texts that Shakespeare used repeatedly in writing his plays and poems were texts that schoolboys memorized and recited.) Latin comedies were introduced early in the lower form; in the upper form, which the boys

CATECHISMVS

paruus pueris primùm Latinè qui ediscatur, proponendus in Scholis.

LONDINI
Apud Iohannem Dayum Typographum. An. 1573.

Cum Priuilegio Regiæ Maiestatis.

Title page of a 1573 Latin and Greek catechism for children.

entered at age ten or eleven, students wrote their own Latin orations and declamations, studied Latin historians and rhetoricians, and began the study of Greek using the Greek New Testament.

Since the records of the Stratford "grammar school" do not survive, we cannot prove that William Shakespeare attended the school; however, every indication (his father's position as an alderman and bailiff of Stratford, the playwright's own knowledge of the Latin classics, scenes in the plays that recall grammar-school experiences—for example, *The Merry Wives of Windsor,* 4.1) suggests that he did. We also lack generally accepted documentation about Shakespeare's life after his schooling ended and his professional life in London began. His marriage in 1582 (at age eighteen) to Anne Hathaway and the subsequent births of his daughter Susanna (1583) and the twins Judith and Hamnet (1585) are recorded, but how he supported himself and where he lived are not known. Nor do we know when and why he left Stratford for the London theatrical world, nor how he rose to be the important figure in that world that he had become by the early 1590s.

We do know that by 1592 he had achieved some prominence in London as both an actor and a playwright. In that year was published a book by the playwright Robert Greene attacking an actor who had the audacity to write blank-verse drama and who was "in his own conceit [i.e., opinion] the only Shake-scene in a country." Since Greene's attack includes a parody of a line from one of Shakespeare's early plays, there is little doubt that it is Shakespeare to whom he refers, a "Shake-scene" who had aroused Greene's fury by successfully competing with university-educated dramatists like Greene himself. It was also in 1592 that Shakespeare became a published poet. In that year he published his long narrative poem *Venus and Adonis;* in 1593, he followed it with *The Rape of Lucrece.* Both poems were dedicated to the young earl of Southampton (Henry Wriothesley), who may have become Shakespeare's patron.

It seems no coincidence that Shakespeare wrote these narrative poems in years in which the theaters were closed because of the plague, a contagious epidemic disease that devastated the population of London. When the theaters reopened late in 1594, Shakespeare apparently resumed his double career of actor and playwright and began his long (and seemingly profitable) service as an acting-company shareholder. Records from the fall of 1594 show him to be a leading member of the Lord Chamberlain's Men. It was this company of actors, later named the King's Men, for whom he would be a principal actor, dramatist, and shareholder for the rest of his career.

So far as we can tell, that career spanned about twenty years. In the 1590s, he wrote his plays on English history as well as several comedies and at least two tragedies (*Titus Andronicus* and *Romeo and Juliet*). These histories, comedies, and tragedies are the plays credited to him in 1598 in a work, *Palladis Tamia,* that in one chapter compares English writers with "Greek, Latin, and Italian Poets." There the author, Francis Meres, claims that Shakespeare is comparable to the Latin dramatists Seneca for tragedy and Plautus for comedy, and calls him "the most excellent in both kinds for the stage." He also names him "Mellifluous and honey-tongued Shakespeare": "I say," writes Meres, "that the Muses would speak with Shakespeare's fine filed phrase, if they would speak English." Since Meres also mentions Shakespeare's "sugared sonnets among his private friends," it is assumed that many of Shakespeare's sonnets (not published until 1609) were also written in the 1590s.

In 1599, Shakespeare's company built a theater for themselves across the river from London, naming it the Globe. The plays that are considered by many to be Shakespeare's major tragedies (*Hamlet, Othello, King Lear,* and *Macbeth*) were written while the company was resident in this theater, as were such comedies as *Twelfth Night* and *Measure for Measure.* Many of Shakespeare's plays were performed at court (both for Queen Elizabeth I and, after her death in 1603, for King James I), some were presented at the Inns of Court (the residences of London's legal societies), and some were doubtless performed in other towns, at the universities, and at great houses when the King's Men went on tour; otherwise, his plays from 1599 to 1608 were, so far as we know, performed only at the Globe. Between 1608 and 1612, Shakespeare wrote several plays—among them *The Winter's Tale* and *The Tempest*—presumably for the company's new indoor Blackfriars theater, though the plays seem to have been performed also at the Globe and at court. Surviving documents describe a performance of *The Winter's Tale* in 1611 at the Globe, for example, and performances of *The Tempest* in 1611 and 1613 at the royal palace of Whitehall.

Shakespeare wrote very little after 1612, the year in which he probably wrote *King Henry VIII.* (It was at a performance of *Henry VIII* in 1613 that the Globe caught fire and burned to the ground.) Sometime between 1610 and 1613 he seems to have returned to live in Stratford-upon-Avon, where he owned a large house and considerable property, and where his wife and his two daughters and their husbands lived. (His son Hamnet had died in 1596.) During his professional years in London, Shakespeare had presumably derived income from the acting

A stylized representation of the Globe theater.
From Claes Jansz Visscher, *Londinum florentissima Britanniae urbs* . . . (c. 1625).

company's profits as well as from his own career as an actor, from the sale of his play manuscripts to the acting company, and, after 1599, from his shares as an owner of the Globe. It was presumably that income, carefully invested in land and other property, which made him the wealthy man that surviving documents show him to have become. It is also assumed that William Shakespeare's growing wealth and reputation played some part in inclining the crown, in 1597, to grant John Shakespeare, William's father, the coat of arms that he had so long sought. William Shakespeare died in Stratford on April 23, 1616 (according to the epitaph carved under his bust in Holy Trinity Church) and was buried on April 25. Seven years after his death, his collected plays were published as *Mr. William Shakespeares Comedies, Histories, & Tragedies* (the work now known as the First Folio).

The years in which Shakespeare wrote were among the most exciting in English history. Intellectually, the discovery, translation, and printing of Greek and Roman classics were making available a set of works and worldviews that interacted complexly with Christian texts and beliefs. The result was a questioning, a vital intellectual ferment, that provided energy for the period's amazing dramatic and literary output and that fed directly into Shakespeare's plays. The Ghost in *Hamlet*, for example, is wonderfully complicated in part because he is a figure from Roman tragedy—the spirit of the dead returning to seek revenge—who at the same time inhabits a Christian hell (or purgatory); Hamlet's description of humankind reflects at one moment the Neoplatonic wonderment at mankind ("What a piece of work is a man!") and, at the next, the Christian disparagement of human sinners ("And yet, to me, what is this quintessence of dust?").

As intellectual horizons expanded, so also did geographical and cosmological horizons. New worlds—both North and South America—were explored, and in them were found human beings who lived and worshiped in ways radically different from those of Renaissance Europeans and Englishmen. The universe during these years also seemed to shift and expand. Copernicus had earlier theorized that the earth was not the center of the cosmos but revolved as a planet around the sun. Galileo's telescope, created in 1609, allowed scientists to see that Copernicus had been correct; the universe was not organized with the earth at the center, nor was it so nicely circumscribed as people had, until that time, thought. In terms of expanding horizons, the impact of these discoveries on people's beliefs—religious, scientific, and philosophical—cannot be overstated.

London, too, rapidly expanded and changed during the years (from the early 1590s to around 1610) that Shakespeare lived there. London—the center of England's government, its economy, its royal court, its overseas trade—was, during these years, becoming an exciting metropolis, drawing to it thousands of new citizens every year. Troubled by overcrowding, by poverty, by recurring epidemics of the plague, London was also a mecca for the wealthy and the aristocratic, and for those who sought advancement at court, or power in government or finance or trade. One hears in Shakespeare's plays the voices of London—the struggles for power, the fear of venereal disease, the language of buying and selling. One hears as well the voices of Stratford-upon-Avon—references to the nearby Forest of Arden, to sheep herding, to small-town gossip, to village fairs and markets. Part of the richness of Shakespeare's work is the influence felt there of the various

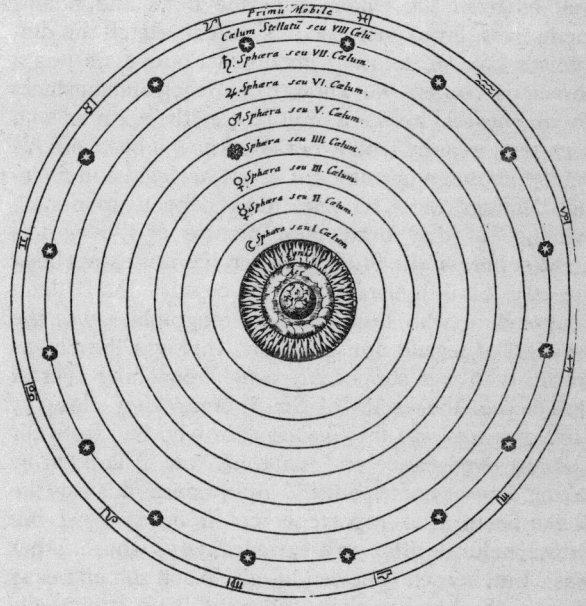

Ptolemaic universe.
From Marcus Manilius, *The sphere of . . .* (1675).

worlds in which he lived: the world of metropolitan London, the world of small-town and rural England, the world of the theater, and the worlds of craftsmen and shepherds.

That Shakespeare inhabited such worlds we know from surviving London and Stratford documents, as well as from the evidence of the plays and poems themselves. From such records we can sketch the dramatist's life. We know from his works that he was a voracious reader. We know from legal and business documents that he was a multifaceted theater man who became a wealthy landowner. We know a bit about his family life and a fair amount about his legal and financial dealings. Most scholars today depend upon such evidence as they draw their picture of the world's greatest playwright. Such, however, has not always been the case. Until the late eighteenth century, the William Shakespeare who lived in most biographies was the creation of legend and tradition. This was the Shakespeare who was supposedly caught poaching deer at Charlecote, the estate of Sir Thomas Lucy close by Stratford; this was the Shakespeare who fled from Sir Thomas's vengeance and made his way in London by taking care of horses outside a playhouse; this was the Shakespeare who reportedly could barely read but whose natural gifts were extraordinary, whose father was a butcher who allowed his gifted son sometimes to help in the butcher shop, where William supposedly killed calves "in a high style," making a speech for the occasion. It was this legendary William Shakespeare whose Falstaff (in *1* and *2 Henry IV*) so pleased Queen Elizabeth that she demanded a play about Falstaff in love, and demanded that it be written in fourteen days (hence the existence of *The Merry Wives of Windsor*). It was this legendary Shakespeare who reached the top of his acting career in the roles of the Ghost in *Hamlet* and old Adam in *As You Like It*—and who died of a fever contracted by drinking too hard at "a merry meeting" with the poets Michael Drayton and Ben Jonson. This legendary Shakespeare is a rambunctious, undisciplined man, as attractively "wild" as his plays were seen by earlier generations to be. Unfortunately, there is no trace of evidence to support these wonderful stories.

Perhaps in response to the disreputable Shakespeare of legend—or perhaps in response to the fragmentary and, for some, all-too-ordinary Shakespeare documented by surviving records—some people since the mid-nineteenth century have argued that William Shakespeare could not have written the plays that bear his name. These persons have put forward some dozen names as more likely authors, among them Queen Elizabeth, Sir Francis Bacon, Edward de Vere (earl of Oxford), and Christopher Marlowe. Such attempts to find what for these people is a more believable author of the plays is a tribute to the regard in which the plays are held. Unfortunately for their claims, the documents that exist that provide evidence for the facts of Shakespeare's life tie him inextricably to the body of plays and poems that bear his name. Unlikely as it seems to those who want the works to have been written by an aristocrat, a university graduate, or an "important" person, the plays and poems seem clearly to have been produced by a man from Stratford-upon-Avon with a very good "grammar-school" education and a life of experience in London and in the world of the London theater. How this particular man produced the works that dominate the cultures of much of the world almost four hundred years after his death is one of life's mysteries—and one that will continue to tease our imaginations as we continue to delight in his plays and poems.

Shakespeare's Theater

The actors of Shakespeare's time are known to have performed plays in a great variety of locations. They played at court (that is, in the great halls of such royal residences as Whitehall, Hampton Court, and Greenwich); they played in halls at the universities of Oxford and Cambridge, and at the Inns of Court (the residences in London of the legal societies); and they also played in the private houses of great lords and civic officials. Sometimes acting companies went on tour from London into the provinces, often (but not only) when outbreaks of bubonic plague in the capital forced the closing of theaters to reduce the possibility of contagion in crowded audiences. In the provinces the actors usually staged their plays in churches (until around 1600) or in guildhalls. While surviving records show only a handful of occasions when actors played at inns while on tour, London inns were important playing places up until the 1590s.

The building of theaters in London had begun only shortly before Shakespeare wrote his first plays in the 1590s. These theaters were of two kinds: outdoor or public playhouses that could accommodate large numbers of playgoers, and indoor or private theaters for much smaller audiences. What is usually regarded as the first London outdoor public playhouse was called simply the Theatre. James Burbage—the father of Richard Burbage, who was perhaps the most famous actor in Shakespeare's company—built it in 1576 in an area north of the city of London called Shoreditch. Among the more famous of the other public playhouses that capitalized on the new fashion were the Curtain and the

Fortune (both also built north of the city), the Rose, the Swan, the Globe, and the Hope (all located on the Bankside, a region just across the Thames south of the city of London). All these playhouses had to be built outside the jurisdiction of the city of London because many civic officials were hostile to the performance of drama and repeatedly petitioned the royal council to abolish it.

The theaters erected on the Bankside (a region under the authority of the Church of England, whose head was the monarch) shared the neighborhood with houses of prostitution and with the Paris Garden, where the blood sports of bearbaiting and bullbaiting were carried on. There may have been no clear distinc- tion between playhouses and buildings for such sports, for we know that the Hope was used for both plays and baiting and that Philip Henslowe, owner of the Rose and, later, partner in the ownership of the Fortune, was also a partner in a monopoly on baiting. All these forms of entertainment were easily accessible to Lon- doners by boat across the Thames or over London Bridge.

Evidently Shakespeare's company prospered on the Bankside. They moved there in 1599. Threatened by difficulties in renewing the lease on the land where their first theater (the Theatre) had been built, Shakespeare's company took advantage of the Christmas holiday in 1598 to dismantle the Theatre and transport its timbers across the Thames to the Bankside, where, in 1599, these timbers were used in the building of the Globe. The weather in late December 1598 is recorded as having been especially harsh. It was so cold that the Thames was "nigh [nearly] frozen," and there was heavy snow. Perhaps the weather aided Shakespeare's compa- ny in eluding their landlord, the snow hiding their activity and the freezing of the Thames allowing them to slide the timbers across to the Bankside without paying tolls for repeated trips over London Bridge. Attractive as this narrative is, it remains just as likely that the heavy snow hampered transport of the timbers in wagons through the London streets to the river. It also must be remembered that the Thames was, according to report, only "nigh frozen" and therefore as impassable as it ever was. Whatever the precise circumstances of this fascinating event in English theater history, Shakespeare's company was able to begin playing at their new Globe theater on the Bankside in 1599. After the first Globe burned down in 1613 during the staging of Shakespeare's *Henry VIII* (its thatch roof was set alight by cannon fire called for by the performance), Shakespeare's company immediately rebuilt on the same location. The second Globe seems to have been a grander structure than its predecessor. It remained in use until the beginning of the English Civil War in 1642, when Parliament officially closed the theaters. Soon thereafter it was pulled down.

The public theaters of Shakespeare's time were very different buildings from our theaters today. First of all, they were open-air playhouses. As recent excavations of the Rose and the Globe confirm, some were polygonal or roughly circular in shape; the Fortune, however, was square. The most recent estimates of their size put the diameter of these buildings at 72 feet (the Rose) to 100 feet (the Globe), but we know that they held vast audiences of two or three thousand, who must have been squeezed together quite tightly. Some of these spectators paid extra to sit or stand in the two or three levels of roofed galleries that extended, on the upper levels, all the way around the theater and surrounded an open space. In this space were the stage and, perhaps, the tiring house (what we would call dressing rooms), as well as the so-called yard. In the yard stood the spectators who chose to pay less, the ones whom Hamlet contemptuously called "groundlings." For a roof they had only the sky, and so they were exposed to all kinds of weather. They stood on a floor that was sometimes made of mortar and sometimes of ash mixed with the shells of hazelnuts. The latter provided a porous and therefore dry footing for the crowd, and the shells may have been more comfortable to stand on because they were not as hard as mortar. Availability of shells may not have been a problem if hazelnuts were a favorite food for Shakespeare's audiences to munch on as they watched his plays. Archaeologists who are today unearthing the remains of theaters from this period have discovered quantities of these nutshells on theater sites.

Unlike the yard, the stage itself was covered by a roof. Its ceiling, called "the heavens," is thought to have been elaborately painted to depict the sun, moon, stars, and planets. Just how big the stage was remains hard to determine. We have a single sketch of part of the interior of the Swan. A Dutchman named Johannes de Witt visited this theater around 1596 and sent a sketch of it back to his friend, Arend van Buchel. Because van Buchel found de Witt's letter and sketch of interest, he copied both into a book. It is van Buchel's copy, adapted, it seems, to the shape and size of the page in his book, that survives. In this sketch, the stage appears to be a large rectangular platform that thrusts far out into the yard, perhaps even as far as the center of the circle formed by the surrounding galleries. This drawing, combined with the specifications for the size of the stage in the building contract for the Fortune, has led scholars to conjecture that the stage on which Shakespeare's plays were performed must have measured approximately 43 feet in width and 27 feet in depth, a vast acting area. But the digging up of a large part of the Rose by archaeologists has provided evidence of a quite different stage design. The Rose stage was a platform tapered at the corners and much shallower than what seems to be depicted in the van Buchel sketch. Indeed, its measurements seem to be about 37.5 feet across at its widest point and only 15.5 feet deep. Because the surviving indications of stage size and design differ from each other so much, it is possible that the stages in other theaters, like the Theatre, the Curtain, and the Globe (the outdoor playhouses where we know that Shakespeare's plays were performed), were different from those at both the Swan and the Rose.

After about 1608 Shakespeare's plays were staged not only at the Globe but also at an indoor or private playhouse in Blackfriars. This theater had been constructed in 1596 by James Burbage in an upper hall of a former Dominican priory or monastic house. Although Henry VIII had dissolved all English monasteries in the 1530s (shortly after he had founded the Church of England), the area remained under church, rather than hostile civic, control. The hall that Burbage had purchased and renovated was a large one in which Parliament had once met. In the private theater that he constructed, the stage, lit by candles, was built across the narrow end of the hall, with boxes flanking it. The rest of the hall offered seating room only. Because there was no provision for standing room, the largest audience it could hold was less than a thousand, or about a quarter of what the Globe could accommodate. Admission to Blackfriars was correspondingly more expensive. Instead of a penny to stand in the yard at the Globe, it cost a minimum of sixpence to get into Blackfriars. The best seats at the Globe (in the Lords' Room in the gallery above and behind the stage) cost sixpence; but the boxes flanking the stage at Blackfriars were half a crown, or five times sixpence. Some spectators who were particularly interested in displaying themselves paid even more to sit on stools on the Blackfriars stage.

Whether in the outdoor or indoor playhouses, the stages of Shakespeare's time were different from ours. They were not separated from the audience by the dropping of a curtain between acts and scenes. Therefore the playwrights of the time had to find other ways of signaling to the audience that one scene (to be imagined as occurring in one location at a given time) had ended and the next (to be imagined at perhaps a different location at a later time) had begun. The customary way used by Shakespeare and many of his contemporaries was to have everyone onstage exit at the end of one scene and have one or more different characters enter to begin the next. In a few cases, where characters remain onstage from one scene to another, the dialogue or stage action makes the change of location clear, and the characters are generally to be imagined as having moved from one place to another. For example, in *Romeo and Juliet*, Romeo and his friends remain onstage in Act 1 from scene 4 to scene 5, but they are represented as having moved between scenes from the street that leads to Capulet's house into Capulet's house itself. The new location is signaled in part by the appearance onstage of Capulet's servingmen carrying napkins, something they would not take into the streets. Playwrights had to be quite resourceful in the use of hand properties, like the napkin, or in the use of dialogue to specify where the action was taking place in their plays because, in contrast to most of today's theaters, the playhouses of Shakespeare's time did not use movable scenery to dress the stage and make the setting precise. As another consequence of this difference, however, the playwrights of Shakespeare's time did not have to specify exactly where the action of their plays was set when they did not choose to do so, and much of the action of their plays is tied to no specific place.

Usually Shakespeare's stage is referred to as a "bare stage," to distinguish it from the stages of the last two or three centuries with their elaborate sets. But the stage in Shakespeare's time was not completely bare. Philip Henslowe, owner of the Rose, lists in his inventory of stage properties a rock, three tombs, and two mossy banks. Stage directions in plays of the time also call for such things as thrones (or "states"), banquets (presumably tables with plaster replicas of food on them), and beds and tombs to be pushed onto the stage. Thus the stage often held more than the actors.

The actors did not limit their performing to the stage alone. Occasionally they went beneath the stage, as the Ghost appears to do in the first act of *Hamlet*. From there they could emerge onto the stage through a trapdoor. They could retire behind the hangings across the back of the stage (or the front of the tiring house), as, for example, the actor playing Polonius does when he hides behind the arras. Sometimes the hangings could be drawn back during a performance to "discover" one or more actors behind them. When performance required that an actor appear "above," as when Juliet is imagined to stand at the window of her chamber in the famous and misnamed "balcony scene," then the actor probably climbed the stairs to the gallery over the back of the stage and temporarily shared it with some of the spectators. The stage was also provided with ropes and winches so that actors could descend from, and reascend to, the "heavens."

Perhaps the greatest difference between dramatic performances in Shakespeare's time and ours was that in Shakespeare's England the roles of women were played by boys. (Some of these boys grew up to take male roles in their maturity.) There were no women in the acting companies, only in the audience. It had not always been so in the history of the English stage. There are records of women on English stages in the thirteenth and fourteenth centuries, two hundred years before Shakespeare's plays were performed. After the accession of James I in 1603, the queen of England and her ladies took part in entertainments at court called masques, and with the reopening of the theaters in 1660 at the restoration of Charles II, women again took their place on the public stage.

The chief competitors for the companies of adult actors such as the one to which Shakespeare belonged and for which he wrote were companies of exclusively boy actors. The competition was most intense in the early 1600s. There were then two principal children's companies: the Children of Paul's (the choirboys from St. Paul's Cathedral, whose private playhouse was near the cathedral); and the Children of the Chapel Royal (the choirboys from the monarch's private chapel, who performed at the Blackfriars theater built by Burbage in 1596, which Shakespeare's company had been stopped from using by local residents who objected to crowds). In *Hamlet* Shakespeare writes of "an aerie [nest] of children, little eyases [hawks], that cry out on the top of question and are most tyrannically clapped for 't. These are now the fashion and . . . berattle the common stages [attack the public theaters]." In the long run, the adult actors prevailed. The Children of Paul's dissolved around 1606. By about 1608 the Children of the Chapel Royal had been forced to stop playing at the Blackfriars theater, which was then taken over by the King's Men, Shakespeare's own troupe.

Acting companies and theaters of Shakespeare's time were organized in different ways. For example, Philip Henslowe owned the Rose and leased it to companies of actors, who paid him from their takings. Henslowe would act as manager of these companies, initially paying playwrights for their plays and buying properties, recovering his outlay from the actors. Shakespeare's company, however, managed itself, with the principal actors, Shakespeare among them, having the status of "sharers" and the right to a share in the takings, as well as the responsibility for a part of the expenses. Five of the sharers themselves, Shakespeare among them, owned the Globe. As actor, as sharer in an acting company and in ownership of theaters, and as playwright, Shakespeare was about as involved in the theatrical industry as one could imagine. Although Shakespeare and his fellows prospered, their status under the law was conditional upon the protection of powerful patrons. "Common players"—those who did not have patrons or masters—were classed in the language of the law with "vagabonds and sturdy beggars." So the actors had to secure for themselves the official rank of servants of patrons. Among the patrons under whose protection Shakespeare's company worked were the lord chamberlain and, after the accession of King James in 1603, the king himself.

We are now perhaps on the verge of learning a great deal more about the theaters in which Shakespeare and his contemporaries performed—or at least of opening up new questions about them. Already about 70 percent of the Rose has been excavated, as has about 10 percent of the second Globe, the one built in 1614. It is to be hoped that soon more will be available for study. These are exciting times for students of Shakespeare's stage.

The Publication of Shakespeare's Plays

Eighteen of Shakespeare's plays found their way into print during the playwright's lifetime, but there is nothing to suggest that he took any interest in their publication. These eighteen appeared separately in editions called quartos. Their pages were not much larger than the one you are now reading, and these little books were sold unbound for a few pence. The earliest of the quartos that still survive were printed in 1594, the year that both *Titus Andronicus* and a version of the play now called *2 King Henry VI* became available. While almost every one of these early quartos displays on its title page the name of the acting company that performed the play, only about half provide the name of the playwright, Shakespeare. The first quarto edition to bear the name Shakespeare on its title page is *Love's Labor's Lost* of 1598. A few of these quartos were popular with the book-buying public of Shakespeare's lifetime; for example, quarto *Richard II* went through five editions between 1597 and 1615. But most of the quartos were far from best-sellers; *Love's Labor's Lost* (1598), for instance, was not reprinted in quarto until 1631. After Shakespeare's death, two more of his plays appeared in quarto format: *Othello* in 1622 and *The Two Noble Kinsmen*, coauthored with John Fletcher, in 1634.

In 1623, seven years after Shakespeare's death, *Mr. William Shakespeares Comedies, Histories, & Tragedies* was published. This printing offered readers in a single book thirty-six of the thirty-eight plays now thought to have been written by Shakespeare, including eighteen that had never been printed before. And it offered them in a style that was then reserved for serious literature and scholarship. The plays were arranged in double columns on pages nearly a foot high. This large page size is called "folio," as opposed to the smaller "quarto," and the 1623 volume is usually called the Shakespeare First Folio. It is reputed to have sold for the lordly price of a pound. (One copy at the Folger Library is marked fifteen shillings—that is, three-quarters of a pound.)

In a preface to the First Folio entitled "To the great Variety of Readers," two of Shakespeare's former fellow actors in the King's Men, John Heminge and Henry Condell, wrote that they themselves had collected their dead companion's plays. They suggested that they had seen his own papers: "we have scarce received from him a blot in his papers." The title page of the Folio declared that the plays within it had been printed "according to the True Original Copies." Comparing the Folio to the quartos, Heminge and Condell disparaged the quartos, advising their readers that "before you were abused with divers stolen and surreptitious copies, maimed, and deformed by the frauds and stealths of injurious impostors." Many Shakespeareans of the eighteenth and nineteenth centuries believed Heminge and Condell and regarded the Folio plays as superior to anything in the quartos.

Once we begin to examine the Folio plays in detail, it becomes less easy to take at face value the word of Heminge and Condell about the superiority of the Folio texts. For example, of the first nine plays in the Folio (one quarter of the entire collection), four were essentially reprinted from earlier quarto printings that Heminge and Condell had disparaged; and four have now been identified as printed from copies written in the hand of a professional scribe of the 1620s named Ralph Crane; the ninth, *The Comedy of Errors*, was apparently also printed from a manuscript, but one whose origin cannot be readily identified. Evidently then, eight of the first nine plays in the First Folio were not printed, in spite of what the Folio title page announces, "according to the True Original Copies," or Shakespeare's own papers, and the source of the ninth is unknown. Since today's editors have been forced to treat Heminge and Condell's pronouncements with skepticism, they must choose whether to base their own editions upon quartos or the Folio on grounds other than Heminge and Condell's story of where the quarto and Folio versions originated.

Editors have often fashioned their own narratives to explain what lies behind the quartos and Folio. They have said that Heminge and Condell meant to criticize only a few of the early quartos, the ones that offer much shorter and sometimes quite different, often garbled, versions of plays. Among the examples of these are the 1600 quarto of *Henry V* (the Folio offers a much fuller version) or the 1603 *Hamlet* quarto (in 1604 a different, much longer form of the play got into print as a quarto). Early in this century editors speculated that these questionable texts were produced when someone in the audience took notes from the plays' dialogue during performances and then employed "hack poets" to fill out the notes. The poor results were then sold to a publisher and presented in print as Shakespeare's plays. More recently this story has given way to another in which the shorter versions are said to be recreations from memory of Shakespeare's plays by actors who wanted to stage them in the provinces but lacked manuscript copies. Most of the quartos offer much better texts than these so-called bad quartos. Indeed, in

most of the quartos we find texts that are at least equal to
or better than what is printed in the Folio. Many of this
century's Shakespeare enthusiasts have persuaded
themselves that most of the quartos were set into type
directly from Shakespeare's own papers, although there
is nothing on which to base this conclusion except the
desire for it to be true. Thus speculation continues about
how the Shakespeare plays got to be printed. All that we
have are the printed texts.

The book collector who was most successful in bringing together copies of the quartos and the First Folio was
Henry Clay Folger, founder of the Folger Shakespeare
Library in Washington, D.C. While it is estimated that
there survive around the world only about 230 copies of
the First Folio, Mr. Folger was able to acquire more than
seventy-five copies, as well as a large number of frag-
ments, for the library that bears his name. He also
amassed a substantial number of quartos. For example,
only fourteen copies of the First Quarto of *Love's Labor's
Lost* are known to exist, and three are at the Folger
Shakespeare Library. As a consequence of Mr. Folger's
labors, twentieth-century scholars visiting the Folger
Library have been able to learn a great deal about
sixteenth- and seventeenth-century printing and, particularly, about the printing of Shakespeare's plays. And
Mr. Folger did not stop at the First Folio, but collected
many copies of later editions of Shakespeare, beginning
with the Second Folio (1632), the Third (1663–64), and
the Fourth (1685). Each of these later folios was based
on its immediate predecessor and was edited anony-
mously. The first editor of Shakespeare whose name we
know was Nicholas Rowe, whose first edition came out
in 1709. Mr. Folger collected this edition and many,
many more by Rowe's successors.

An Introduction to This Text

The earliest surviving printed version of *Love's Labor's Lost* (usually called the "First Quarto") dates from 1598. However, scholars have long suspected that this printing is not the earliest printed version of the play. The title page of the First Quarto reads in part: "Loues labors lost. . . . Newly corrected and augmented. . . ." This language is closely similar to what is found on the title page of the Second Quarto of *Romeo and Juliet* (1599), which reads in part: "Romeo and Iuliet. . . . Newly corrected, augmented, and emended." This Second Quarto of *Romeo and Juliet* replaced the *Romeo and Juliet* First Quarto of 1597 (which survives); and both the Second Quarto of *Romeo and Juliet* and the First Quarto of *Love's Labor's Lost* were published by the same bookseller, Cuthbert Burby. On these grounds, scholars have come to believe that the "First Quarto" of *Love's Labor's Lost* replaces an earlier printed version of its play (now lost), just as the Second Quarto of *Romeo and Juliet* did.

Only recently, however, has the further possibility arisen that such an earlier lost printed version may have had a role to play in the printing not only of the *Love's Labor's Lost* First Quarto but also of the First Folio version of 1623. The traditional account of the printing of these two early versions says that the First Quarto of *Love's Labor's Lost* was printed directly from a manuscript and that the First Folio version was printed from a copy of the First Quarto that had been lightly annotated with reference to another manuscript, perhaps, in the opinion of some scholars, a playhouse manuscript. The suggestion about the kind of manuscript that might have

li

been consulted in the printing of the Folio has now been questioned, since study of surviving manuscripts of non-Shakespearean plays indicates that there are no distinctive features peculiar to all playhouse manuscripts; this fact casts doubt on the possibility of identifying what kind of manuscript the printer of the First Folio might have consulted.

More significantly, recent research has called the traditional account of the play's Quarto and Folio versions into question in a more fundamental way. Detailed, computer-assisted examination of typesetters' spelling habits in the printing houses in which the First Folio and the Love's Labor's Lost First Quarto were set into type indicates that both these early printed versions may have been printed from copies of the lost printed text thought to have predated the First Quarto (1598). (For a preliminary report of this research, see Paul Werstine's "The Editorial Usefulness of Printing House and Compositor Studies," pp. 35–64 in Play-texts in Old-spelling: Papers from the Glendon Conference [New York: AMS Press, 1984].)

If such is the case, as we believe, then the First Folio and the First Quarto have equal authority as witnesses to the text of the play, since both stand at the same remove from an earlier lost printed version. It may therefore seem to make as much sense to base an edition of Love's Labor's Lost on the First Folio as it does to base it on the First Quarto, as we do in this edition (and as has usually been done in this century). It is important to remember, though, that the First Quarto version is much closer to the time of the play's first production and its possible earlier printing than is the Folio version printed a quarter of a century later. There is, therefore, a greater likelihood that the Quarto may preserve features of the first production's (and, possibly, first printing's) language that became out-of-date by the time the Folio was printed in 1623. It is for this reason that the present edition is based directly on the Quarto printing of the play.* But the present edition differs from other late-twentieth-century editions of the play in accepting several more Folio readings, since we believe that the Folio may stand at the same remove from an earlier lost printing as does the Quarto.

Love's Labor's Lost presents still further challenges to an editor. Both the Quarto and the Folio contain many brief passages and words in corrupt Latin. Editors are hard pressed to determine how to treat these corruptions. Are they to be understood as jokes at the expense of the characters in whose speeches the corruptions occur—jokes that may have been appreciated by playgoers and readers of the time who had a Latin grammar-school education? Or are they printers' (or perhaps scribes') errors that editors should correct? We differ from many other editors in regarding quite a few of the corruptions as jokes, and so have not corrected them. (For a rationale of this editorial policy, see Paul Werstine's "Variants in the First Quarto of *Love's Labor's Lost*," *Shakespeare Studies* 12 [1979]: 25–34 and J. W. Binns's "Shakespeare's Latin Citations: The Editorial Problem," *Shakespeare Survey* 35 [1982]: 119–28.) There is also, in the opinion of most editors of the play, considerable confusion in the First Quarto, and, only slightly less often, in the First Folio, in the identification of particular roles both in speech prefixes and in dialogue. These are the roles of Rosaline and Katherine and of Holofernes and Nathaniel. For detailed discussion of

---

*We have also consulted the computerized text of the First Quarto provided by the Text Archive of the Oxford University Computing Centre, to which we are grateful.

our handling of this issue, see the longer notes to 2.1.41 and to 4.2.82 on pages 230–32 and 235–36.

For the convenience of the reader, we have modernized the punctuation and the spelling of the Quarto. Sometimes we go so far as to modernize certain old forms of words; for example, when *a* means "he," we change it to *he;* we change *mo* to *more* and *ye* to *you.* But it has not been our editorial practice in any of the plays to modernize some words that sound distinctly different from modern forms. For example, when the early printed texts read *sith* or *apricokes* or *porpentine*, we have not modernized to *since, apricots, porcupine.* When the forms *an, and*, or *and if* appear instead of the modern form *if*, we have reduced *and* to *an* but have not changed any of these forms to their modern equivalent, *if*.

Whenever we change the wording of the Quarto or add anything to its stage directions, we mark the change by enclosing it in pointed brackets (⟨ ⟩) if the source of the change is the First Folio, or in superior half-brackets (⌐⌐) if the source of the change is an edition of the play after the First Folio, or if the change originates with the current edition. We want our readers to be immediately aware when we have intervened. (Only when we correct an obvious typographical error in the Quarto does the change not get marked.) Whenever we change the Quarto's wording or change its punctuation so that meaning changes, we list the change in the textual notes at the back of the book, even if all we have done is fix an obvious error.

We, like a great many editors before us, regularize a number of the proper names. In *Love's Labor's Lost*, one of the characters is called both "Costard" and "Costart" in the First Quarto; in our edition he is called simply "Costard." We expand the often severely abbreviated forms of names used as speech headings in early printed texts into the full names of the characters. Variations in the speech headings of the early printed texts are recorded in the textual notes.

Whenever it is reasonably certain, in our view, that a speech is accompanied by a particular action, we provide a stage direction describing the action. (Occasional exceptions to this rule occur when the action is so obvious that to add a stage direction would insult the reader.) Stage directions for the entrances of characters in mid-scene are, with rare exceptions, placed so that they immediately precede the characters' participation in the scene, even though these entrances may appear somewhat earlier in the early printed texts. Whenever we move a stage direction, we record this change in the textual notes. Latin stage directions (e.g., *Exeunt)* are translated into English (e.g., *They exit).*

In the present edition, as well, we mark with a dash any change of address within a speech, unless a stage direction intervenes. When the *-ed* ending of a word is to be pronounced, we mark it with an accent. Like editors for the past two centuries we print metrically linked lines in the following way:

DUMAINE
  How follows that?
  BEROWNE　　　　　　　Fit in his place and time.

However, when there are a number of short verse-lines that can be linked in more than one way, we do not, with rare exceptions, indent any of them.

The Explanatory Notes

The notes that appear on the pages facing the text are designed to provide readers with the help they may need to enjoy the play. Whenever the meaning of a word in the text is not readily accessible in a good contemporary dictionary, we offer the meaning in a note. Sometimes we provide a note even when the relevant meaning is to be found in the dictionary but when the word has acquired since Shakespeare's time other potentially confusing meanings, or when the word has a highly specialized meaning. In our notes, we try to offer modern synonyms for Shakespeare's words. We also try to indicate to the reader the connection between the word in the play and the modern synonym. For example, Shakespeare sometimes uses the word *head* to mean "source," but, for modern readers, there may be no connection evident between these two words. We provide the connection by explaining Shakespeare's usage as follows: "**head:** fountainhead, source." On some occasions, a whole phrase or clause needs explanation. Then, if space allows, we rephrase in our own words the difficult passage, and add at the end synonyms for individual words in the passage. When scholars have been unable to determine the meaning of a word or phrase, we acknowledge the uncertainty.

LOVE'S
LABOR'S
LOST

Characters in the Play

KING of Navarre, also known as Ferdinand

BEROWNE
LONGAVILLE } *lords attending the King*
DUMAINE

The PRINCESS of France

ROSALINE
MARIA } *ladies attending the Princess*
KATHERINE
BOYET, a lord attending the Princess

ARMADO, the BRAGGART, also known as Don Adriano de
    Armado
BOY, Armado's PAGE, also known as MOTE
JAQUENETTA, the WENCH
COSTARD, the CLOWN or SWAIN
DULL, the CONSTABLE
HOLOFERNES, the PEDANT, or schoolmaster
NATHANIEL, the CURATE

FORESTER
MONSIEUR MARCADE, a messenger from France

Lords, Blackamoors, Musicians

LOVE'S
LABOR'S
LOST

ACT 1

1.1 The King of Navarre and his lords vow to retire from the world (especially from women) and study for three years. One of the lords, Berowne, reminds the King that the Princess of France is coming and that they will thus have to break their oaths immediately. Constable Dull arrives with a letter from Don Armado accusing a servant, Costard, of already having broken the King's order about not consorting with women.

———

0 SD. **Navarre . . . Dumaine:** For a brief account of the historical individuals who bore these names, see longer note, page 227.

2. **brazen:** brass (See page 52.)

3. **disgrace of death:** (1) misfortune of dying; (2) disgracing of death (which is shamed when its victims win eternal fame)

4. **spite:** i.e., in spite; **cormorant:** greedy, rapacious (See page 16.)

5. **breath:** (1) perhaps, breathing time, i.e., life; (2) perhaps, speech

6. **bate:** blunt; **his . . . edge:** Time is represented here as a mower with a sharp scythe, cutting down the living. (See page 48.)

9. **affections:** passions

11. **late:** recent

12. **Navarre:** See longer note, page 228.

13. **academe:** academy

14. **Still:** (1) unperturbed, calm; (2) constant; **living art:** (1) possibly, the art of proper living (the Stoics' *ars vivendi*); (2) art or learning infused by vitality

(continued)

6

⟨ACT 1⟩

⌐Scene 1¬
Enter Ferdinand, King of Navarre, Berowne,
Longaville, and Dumaine.

KING
Let fame, that all hunt after in their lives,
Live registered upon our brazen tombs,
And then grace us in the disgrace of death,
When, spite of cormorant devouring time,
Th' endeavor of this present breath may buy   5
That honor which shall bate his scythe's keen edge
And make us heirs of all eternity.
Therefore, brave conquerors, for so you are
That war against your own affections
And the huge army of the world's desires,   10
Our late edict shall strongly stand in force.
Navarre shall be the wonder of the world;
Our court shall be a little academe,
Still and contemplative in living art.
You three, Berowne, Dumaine, and Longaville,   15
Have sworn for three years' term to live with me,
My fellow scholars, and to keep those statutes
That are recorded in this schedule here.
⌐*He holds up a scroll.*¬
Your oaths are passed, and now subscribe your
 names,   20
That his own hand may strike his honor down

7

18. **schedule:** (1) a scroll or strip of parchment or paper; (2) a statement of details appended to a legal document

19. **passed:** spoken

21. **hand:** i.e., handwriting

24. **deep:** solemn; **it:** i.e., what you subscribe to

26. **pine:** starve

27. **pates:** literally, heads, but here, by metonymy, referring to the brains

28. **bankrout:** bankrupt

29. **is mortified:** i.e., has brought his desires into subjection

30. **manner:** kind

33. **all these:** (1) possibly, the **love, wealth,** and **pomp** that he finds in **philosophy;** (2) possibly, his three companions

34. **say . . . over:** i.e., repeat

38. **not . . . woman:** Forbidding scholars in academies to associate with women was traced by sixteenth-century writers to Plato's academy in Athens.

39. **enrollèd:** written

44. **to wink . . . day:** i.e., to doze anytime during the day

45. **wont:** accustomed; **think . . . night:** Proverbial: "He that sleeps well thinks no harm."

48. **barren:** destitute of attraction or interest

That violates the smallest branch herein.
If you are armed to do as sworn to do,
Subscribe to your deep oaths, and keep it too.
LONGAVILLE
  I am resolved. 'Tis but a ⟨three⟩ years' fast.   25
The mind shall banquet though the body pine.
Fat paunches have lean pates, and dainty bits
Make rich the ribs but bankrout quite the wits.
                    ⌜*He signs his name.*⌝
DUMAINE
  My loving lord, Dumaine is mortified.
The grosser manner of these world's delights   30
He throws upon the gross world's baser slaves.
To love, to wealth, to ⟨pomp⟩ I pine and die,
With all these living in philosophy.
                    ⌜*He signs his name.*⌝
BEROWNE
  I can but say their protestation over.
So much, dear liege, I have already sworn,   35
That is, to live and study here three years.
But there are other strict observances:
As not to see a woman in that term,
Which I hope well is not enrollèd there;
And one day in a week to touch no food,   40
And but one meal on every day besides,
The which I hope is not enrollèd there;
And then to sleep but three hours in the night,
And not be seen to wink of all the day—
When I was wont to think no harm all night,   45
And make a dark night too of half the day—
Which I hope well is not enrollèd there.
O, these are barren tasks, too hard to keep,
Not to see ladies, study, fast, not sleep.
KING
  Your oath is passed to pass away from these.   50

51. **an if:** i.e., if

55. **By yea and nay:** i.e., I swore and I did not swear (a common oath based, irreverently, on Matthew 5.37, which prohibits such equivocation: "let your communication be Yea, yea; Nay, nay")

56. **end:** purpose, goal

61. **Come on:** Some editors hear a pun on **common** (line 58).

63, 65. **study:** think about intently

67. **too . . . oath:** i.e., an oath that is too hard to keep

68. **Study:** set out, endeavor; **troth:** pledge, oath

72. **stops:** impediments, obstructions

73. **train:** entice, allure; **vain:** foolish, worthless

75. **with pain purchased:** i.e., obtained through effort or suffering

76. **As:** Such as

77. **the while:** i.e., at the same time

Lady Fame. (1.1.1)
From August Casimir Redel, *Apophtegmata symbolica* . . . [n.d.].

BEROWNE
　Let me say no, my liege, an if you please.
　I only swore to study with your Grace
　And stay here in your court for three years' space.
LONGAVILLE
　You swore to that, Berowne, and to the rest.
BEROWNE
　By yea and nay, sir. Then I swore in jest.　　　　　55
　What is the end of study, let me know?
KING
　Why, that to know which else we should not know.
BEROWNE
　Things hid and barred, you mean, from common
　　　sense.
KING
　Ay, that is study's godlike recompense.　　　　　60
BEROWNE
　Come on, then, I will swear to study so,
　To know the thing I am forbid to know:
　As thus—to study where I well may dine,
　　When I to ⌜feast⌝ expressly am forbid;
　Or study where to meet some mistress fine　　　　　65
　　When mistresses from common sense are hid;
　Or having sworn too hard-a-keeping oath,
　Study to break it, and not break my troth.
　If study's gain be thus, and this be so,
　Study knows that which yet it doth not know.　　　　　70
　Swear me to this, and I will ne'er say no.
KING
　These be the stops that hinder study quite,
　And train our intellects to vain delight.
BEROWNE
　Why, all delights are vain, ⟨and⟩ that most vain
　Which with pain purchased doth inherit pain:　　　　　75
　As painfully to pore upon a book
　　To seek the light of truth, while truth the while

78. **falsely:** treacherously; **his:** i.e., the gazer's

79. **Light:** The eye, in gazing, was believed to emit its own beams of light. (The image is that of searching for light with a light.)

81. **eyes:** i.e., sight

82. **Study . . . how:** i.e., let me study how

83. **fairer eye:** i.e., the eye of a beautiful woman

84. **Who dazzling so:** i.e., when the gazer's eye loses steady vision from looking at so bright a light; **his heed:** i.e., what he heeds

85. **it:** i.e., his own eye

86–87. **Study . . . looks:** Proverbial: "He that gazes upon the sun shall at last be blind." **saucy:** insolent

88. **Small:** i.e., little

89. **Save:** except

90–91. **earthly godfathers . . . star:** i.e., astronomers, who name the stars (**Godfathers** name infants at baptism.) **fixèd star:** The "fixed stars" were those that appeared to hold fixed positions in the sky relative to each other (in contrast to the planets, or "wandering stars").

92. **of:** i.e., from; **shining:** i.e., starlit

93. **wot:** know

97. **Proceeded:** argued (with wordplay on "proceeding" in the sense of taking an academic degree)

98. **weeds the corn:** pulls up the wheat (as if it were weeds); **weeding:** weeds

99. **green geese:** geese hatched in the autumn (with the secondary sense of young, immature, gullible people)

101. **Fit:** appropriately; **his:** its

(continued)

12

Doth falsely blind the eyesight of his look.
　Light seeking light doth light of light beguile.
So, ere you find where light in darkness lies, 　80
Your light grows dark by losing of your eyes.
Study me how to please the eye indeed
　By fixing it upon a fairer eye,
Who dazzling so, that eye shall be his heed
　And give him light that it was blinded by. 　85
Study is like the heaven's glorious sun,
　That will not be deep-searched with saucy looks.
Small have continual plodders ever won,
　Save base authority from others' books.
These earthly godfathers of heaven's lights, 　90
　That give a name to every fixèd star,
Have no more profit of their shining nights
　Than those that walk and wot not what they are.
Too much to know is to know naught but fame,
And every godfather can give a name. 　95

KING
　How well he's read to reason against reading.

DUMAINE
　Proceeded well, to stop all good proceeding.

LONGAVILLE
　He weeds the corn, and still lets grow the weeding.

BEROWNE
　The spring is near when green geese are a-breeding.

DUMAINE
　How follows that? 　100

BEROWNE　　　　　　Fit in his place and time.

DUMAINE
　In reason nothing.

BEROWNE　　　　　　Something then in rhyme.

KING
　Berowne is like an envious sneaping frost
　That bites the firstborn infants of the spring. 　105

102–3. **reason . . . rhyme:** wordplay on the proverb "Neither rhyme nor reason"

104. **envious:** malicious; **sneaping:** nipping; **frost:** Navarre plays on Berowne's **rhyme** in the sense of "rime" or frost.

105. **infants:** i.e., buds

106. **proud:** punning on "proud" as luxuriant

108. **abortive:** premature

111. **like of:** i.e., like

113. **Climb . . . gate:** i.e., behave absurdly

116, 117. **for:** i.e., in favor of

118. **keep:** adhere to, fulfill

119. **bide:** abide, endure; **each . . . day:** i.e., each day in the three years

123. **Item:** Latin for "likewise" (used to introduce each article in a formal list)

128. **Marry:** i.e., indeed (originally an oath on the name of the Virgin Mary)

131. **gentility:** politeness, good manners

134. **possible:** i.e., possibly

BEROWNE

  Well, say I am. Why should proud summer boast
    Before the birds have any cause to sing?
  Why should I joy in any abortive birth?
  At Christmas I no more desire a rose
  Than wish a snow in May's new-fangled shows,   110
  But like of each thing that in season grows.
  So you, to study now it is too late,
  Climb o'er the house to unlock the little gate.

KING

  Well, sit you out. Go home, Berowne. Adieu.

BEROWNE

  No, my good lord, I have sworn to stay with you.   115
  And though I have for barbarism spoke more
    Than for that angel knowledge you can say,
  Yet, confident, I'll keep what I have sworn
    And bide the penance of each three years' day.
  Give me the paper. Let me read the same,   120
  And to the strictest decrees I'll write my name.

KING

  How well this yielding rescues thee from shame.

BEROWNE ⌐*reads*¬ *Item, That no woman shall come with-*
  in a mile of my court. Hath this been proclaimed?

LONGAVILLE   Four days ago.   125

BEROWNE   Let's see the penalty. ⌐*Reads:*¬ *On pain of*
  losing her tongue. Who devised this penalty?

LONGAVILLE   Marry, that did I.

BEROWNE   Sweet lord, and why?

LONGAVILLE

  To fright them hence with that dread penalty.   130

⌐BEROWNE¬

  A dangerous law against gentility.
  ⌐*Reads:*¬ *Item, If any man be seen to talk with a*
  woman within the term of three years, he shall endure
  such public shame as the rest of the court can possible
  devise.   135

139. **complete:** perfect (pronounced com'plete)
140. **Aquitaine:** a province in southwest France
145. **overshot:** off the mark, going over the target
149. **with fire:** i.e., set on fire during their capture
150. **of force:** perforce, of necessity
151. **lie:** stay, reside; **mere:** utter, absolute
152. **forsworn:** perjured
155. **affects:** emotions, passions
159. **at large:** as a whole
161. **in attainder of:** sentenced or condemned to
162. **Suggestions . . . me:** i.e., I am as susceptible to temptations as the next man
164. **I . . . oath:** an equivocation: I, who am giving my oath last, will (1) be the one who keeps it longest; (2) be the least likely, or the last, to keep it.
165. **quick:** lively; **recreation:** amusement

A cormorant. (1.1.4)
From Ulisse Aldrovandi, . . . *Ornithologiae* . . . (1599–1603).

This article, my liege, yourself must break,
  For well you know here comes in embassy
The French king's daughter with yourself to speak—
  A maid of grace and complete majesty—
About surrender up of Aquitaine   140
  To her decrepit, sick, and bedrid father.
Therefore this article is made in vain,
  Or vainly comes th' admirèd princess hither.

KING
What say you, lords? Why, this was quite forgot.

BEROWNE
So study evermore is overshot.   145
While it doth study to have what it would,
It doth forget to do the thing it should.
And when it hath the thing it hunteth most,
'Tis won as towns with fire—so won, so lost.

KING
We must of force dispense with this decree.   150
She must lie here on mere necessity.

BEROWNE
Necessity will make us all forsworn
  Three thousand times within this three years'
    space;
For every man with his affects is born,   155
  Not by might mastered, but by special grace.
If I break faith, this word shall speak for me:
I am forsworn on mere necessity.
So to the laws at large I write my name,
  And he that breaks them in the least degree   160
Stands in attainder of eternal shame.
  Suggestions are to other as to me,
But I believe, although I seem so loath,
I am the last that will last keep his oath.
              ⌜*He signs his name.*⌝
But is there no quick recreation granted?   165

168. **planted:** established

170. **who:** i.e., whom

172. **compliments:** ceremonious distinctions and observances

173. **mutiny:** discord

174. **child:** i.e., creature; **fancy:** fantasticalness; caprice; **Armado:** a 1580s English spelling of "armada" (See longer note, page 228.); **hight:** is called

175. **For interim . . . studies:** i.e., as an interlude (i.e., something light and humorous) between periods of study

176. **high-born:** noble

177. **world's debate:** i.e., wars throughout the world

180. **minstrelsy:** i.e., entertainment

181. **wight:** person

182. **fire-new words:** i.e., brand new words

183. **Costard:** This character's name is both the name of a large apple and a term for the head. **swain:** rustic laborer

185. **Duke's own person:** i.e., Ferdinand, King of Navarre, who is also later called Duke by the visiting Princess and by Armado

187. **reprehend:** The proper word is "represent." Much of the play's humor arises from the rustic characters' verbal blunders; this form of humor is now called malapropism.

188. **farborough:** i.e., thirdborough, or petty constable

191. **commends you:** The proper form would be "commends himself to you."

194. **contempts:** malapropism for "contents," but "contempts" accurately anticipates Armado's tone regarding Costard; **touching:** i.e., concerning

KING
  Ay, that there is. Our court, you know, is haunted
    With a refinèd traveler of Spain,
  A man in all the world's new fashion planted,
    That hath a mint of phrases in his brain;
  One who the music of his own vain tongue   170
    Doth ravish like enchanting harmony,
  A man of compliments, whom right and wrong
    Have chose as umpire of their mutiny.
  This child of fancy, that Armado hight,
    For interim to our studies shall relate   175
  In high-born words the worth of many a knight
    From tawny Spain lost in the world's debate.
  How you delight, my lords, I know not, I,
  But I protest I love to hear him lie,
  And I will use him for my minstrelsy.   180
BEROWNE
  Armado is a most illustrious wight,
  A man of fire-new words, fashion's own knight.
LONGAVILLE
  Costard the swain and he shall be our sport,
  And so to study three years is but short.

Enter ⌜Dull,⌝ a Constable, with a letter, ⌜and⌝ Costard.

DULL Which is the Duke's own person?   185
BEROWNE This, fellow. What wouldst?
DULL I myself reprehend his own person, for I am his
    Grace's farborough. But I would see his own
    person in flesh and blood.
BEROWNE This is he.   190
DULL, ⌜*to King*⌝ Signior Arm-, Arm-, commends you.
    There's villainy abroad. This letter will tell you
    more.   ⌜*He gives the letter to the King.*⌝
COSTARD Sir, the contempts thereof are as touching
    me.   195
KING A letter from the magnificent Armado.

197. **matter:** subject matter

199. **low heaven:** i.e., a heaven that offers only high words, and thus a **low heaven** compared to the Christian one

204–5. **style . . . climb:** Berowne puns on **style** as "stile," a set of steps built over a fence.

206. **is to:** i.e., applies to

207. **manner of it:** state of the case

207–8. **taken . . . manner:** i.e., caught in the act **manner:** from law—French *mainour*, originally meaning "handwork," then "stolen goods," and later any crime

210. **In manner . . . following:** a legal formula

212. **form:** bench

218. **correction:** punishment

218–19. **God . . . right:** formal prayer of a knight before trial by combat

222. **sinplicity:** While there are many typographical errors in the First Quarto, this spelling is so apt that it may not be an error. **hearken after:** i.e., heed the desires of; seek

224. **the welkin's vicegerent:** heaven's deputy

225. **dominator:** ruler

230. **but so:** i.e., not worth much

BEROWNE   How low soever the matter, I hope in God
for high words.

LONGAVILLE   A high hope for a low heaven. God grant
us patience!   200

BEROWNE   To hear, or forbear hearing?

LONGAVILLE   To hear meekly, sir, and to laugh moderately, or to forbear both.

BEROWNE   Well, sir, be it as the style shall give us cause
to climb in the merriness.   205

COSTARD   The matter is to me, sir, as concerning
Jaquenetta. The manner of it is, I was taken with
the manner.

BEROWNE   In what manner?

COSTARD   In manner and form following, sir, all those   210
three. I was seen with her in the manor house,
sitting with her upon the form, and taken following
her into the park, which, put together, is "in manner and form following." Now, sir, for the manner.
It is the manner of a man to speak to a woman. For   215
the form—in some form.

BEROWNE   For the "following," sir?

COSTARD   As it shall follow in my correction, and God
defend the right.

KING   Will you hear this letter with attention?   220

BEROWNE   As we would hear an oracle.

COSTARD   Such is the sinplicity of man to hearken after
the flesh.

KING ⌐*reads*⌐   *Great deputy, the welkin's vicegerent and
sole dominator of Navarre, my soul's earth's god, and*   225
body's fost'ring patron—

COSTARD   Not a word of Costard yet.

KING ⌐*reads*⌐   *So it is—*

COSTARD   It may be so, but if he say it is so, he is, in
telling true, but so.   230

KING   Peace.

COSTARD   Be to me, and every man that dares not fight.

234. **secrets:** personal matters

235–36. **sable-colored melancholy, black ... humor:** i.e., the disease of melancholy, which was believed to be caused by an excess of black bile in the body

236–37. **commend ... to:** commit ... to the care of

237. **physic:** medicine

239. **time when:** this parody of legal language continues with **ground which, place where,** etc.

243. **yclept:** called; **park:** A park was an expanse of land stocked with game.

245. **obscene:** repulsive, loathsome

246. **snow-white pen:** i.e., goose quill; **ebon-colored:** ebony, black

249–50. **curious-knotted garden:** formal knot garden, or one in which the flower beds are laid out in intricately symmetrical patterns (See page 46.)

250. **low-spirited:** base

253. **unlettered:** illiterate

255. **vassal:** (1) a man holding land from a feudal lord; (2) servile person

257. **hight:** is called

259. **sorted and consorted:** associated, accompanied

260. **continent canon:** i.e., decree requiring sexual abstinence

261. **passion:** sorrow, grieve

263. **wench:** young woman; rustic woman; female servant

266. **pricks:** incites, urges

267. **meed:** reward

KING   No words.

COSTARD   Of other men's secrets, I beseech you.

KING ⌜*reads*⌝   *So it is, ⟨besieged⟩ with sable-colored mel-* 235
ancholy, I did commend the black oppressing humor
to the most wholesome physic of thy health-giving air;
and, as I am a gentleman, betook myself to walk. The
time when? About the sixth hour, when beasts most
graze, birds best peck, and men sit down to that 240
nourishment which is called supper. So much for the
time when. Now for the ground which—which, I
mean, I walked upon. It is yclept thy park. Then for the
place where—where, I mean, I did encounter that
obscene and most prepost'rous event that draweth 245
from my snow-white pen the ebon-colored ink, which
here thou viewest, beholdest, surveyest, or seest. But to
the place where. It standeth north-north-east and by
east from the west corner of thy curious-knotted
garden. There did I see that low-spirited swain, that 250
base minnow of thy mirth,—

COSTARD   Me?

KING ⌜*reads*⌝   *that unlettered, small-knowing soul,—*

COSTARD   Me?

KING ⌜*reads*⌝   *that shallow vassal,—*   255

COSTARD   Still me?

KING ⌜*reads*⌝   *which, as I remember, hight Costard,—*

COSTARD   O, me!

KING ⌜*reads*⌝   *sorted and consorted, contrary to thy*
established proclaimed edict and continent canon, 260
which with—O with—but with this I passion to say
wherewith—

COSTARD   With a wench.

KING ⌜*reads*⌝   *with a child of our grandmother Eve, a*
female; or, for thy more sweet understanding, a 265
woman: him, I, as my ever-esteemed duty pricks
me on, have sent to thee, to receive the meed of
punishment by thy sweet Grace's officer, Anthony

270. **estimation:** consequence

271. **an 't:** i.e., if it

272. **weaker vessel:** i.e., woman (See 1 Peter 3.7.)

274. **vessel . . . fury:** perhaps an allusion to Romans 9.22: "vessels of wrath fitted to destruction"

275. **at . . . notice:** i.e., as soon as I am notified of your orders

281. **best, for the worst:** i.e., the best example of something very bad

282. **sirrah:** term of address to a male social inferior

286. **marking of it:** paying attention to it

294. **so varied too:** i.e., the proclamation also covers that variation

298. **serve your turn:** i.e., suit your purpose (of exonerating yourself)

299. **serve my turn:** i.e., provide for my sexual needs

302–3. **mutton and porridge:** mutton broth (with probable wordplay on **mutton** as prostitute and on **mutton and porridge** as sex)

    Dull, a man of good repute, carriage, bearing, and
    estimation. 270
DULL Me, an 't shall please you. I am Anthony Dull.
KING ⌐*reads*⌐ *For Jaquenetta—so is the weaker vessel*
    called which I apprehended with the aforesaid
    swain—I keep her as a vessel of thy law's fury, and
    shall, at the least of thy sweet notice, bring her to trial. 275
    Thine, in all compliments of devoted and heartburn-
    ing heat of duty,

              Don Adriano de Armado.

BEROWNE This is not so well as I looked for, but the
    best that ever I heard. 280
KING Ay, the best, for the worst. ⌐*To Costard.*⌐ But,
    sirrah, what say you to this?
COSTARD Sir, I confess the wench.
KING Did you hear the proclamation?
COSTARD I do confess much of the hearing it, but little 285
    of the marking of it.
KING It was proclaimed a year's imprisonment to be
    taken with a wench.
COSTARD I was taken with none, sir. I was taken with a
    damsel. 290
KING Well, it was proclaimed "damsel."
COSTARD This was no damsel neither, sir. She was a
    virgin.
BEROWNE It is so varied too, for it was proclaimed
    "virgin." 295
COSTARD If it were, I deny her virginity. I was taken
    with a maid.
KING This "maid" will not serve your turn, sir.
COSTARD This maid will serve my turn, sir.
KING Sir, I will pronounce your sentence: you shall 300
    fast a week with bran and water.
COSTARD I had rather pray a month with mutton and
    porridge.

304. **keeper:** jailer

308. **lay . . . to:** i.e., bet . . . against; **goodman's:** farmer's; householder's (The higher the rank, the grander the hat; a farmer's hat would be little better than a cap.)

313–14. **prosperity:** malapropism for "adversity" (**Affliction** seems also to be a malapropism, but it is unclear what word is intended.)

1.2 Armado confides first to his page Mote and then to Jaquenetta herself that he is in love with Jaquenetta. He is given responsibility for the imprisoned Costard.

—————

0 SD. **Mote:** See longer note, page 229.

1–2. **what . . . melancholy:** The expected answer to this question is "This man's in love." (Compare Ovid's *Ars Amatoria*, or Art of Love: "By looking melancholy you will prove / Successful; all will say, 'This man's in love'" [1661 translation].)

5. **imp:** child (literally, a young shoot of a plant or tree)

7. **part . . . and:** distinguish . . . from

8. **juvenal:** (1) i.e., juvenile; (2) the name of a Roman satirist of the first century A.D.

9. **familiar:** readily intelligible; **working:** operation

10. **signior:** i.e., sir, or master (with a pun on "senior")

14. **epitheton:** epithet, adjective

15. **nominate:** name

KING And Don Armado shall be your keeper.
  My Lord Berowne, see him delivered o'er,   305
  And go we, lords, to put in practice that
    Which each to other hath so strongly sworn.
          ⌐*King, Longaville, and Dumaine exit.*⌐

BEROWNE
  I'll lay my head to any goodman's hat,
    These oaths and laws will prove an idle scorn.
  Sirrah, come on.   310

COSTARD I suffer for the truth, sir; for true it is I was
    taken with Jaquenetta, and Jaquenetta is a true
    girl. And therefore welcome the sour cup of pros-
    perity. Affliction may one day smile again, and till
    then, sit thee down, sorrow.   315
                       They exit.

⌐Scene 2⌐
Enter Armado and Mote, his page.

ARMADO Boy, what sign is it when a man of great spirit
    grows melancholy?

BOY A great sign, sir, that he will look sad.

ARMADO Why, sadness is one and the selfsame thing,
    dear imp.   5

BOY No, no. O Lord, sir, no!

ARMADO How canst thou part sadness and melan-
    choly, my tender juvenal?

BOY By a familiar demonstration of the working, my
    tough signior.   10

ARMADO Why "tough signior"? Why "tough signior"?

BOY Why "tender juvenal"? Why "tender juvenal"?

ARMADO I spoke it "tender juvenal" as a congruent
    epitheton appertaining to thy young days, which
    we may nominate "tender."   15

16. **appurtenant:** fitting
25. **condign:** deserved
27. **ingenious:** intelligent
28. **quick:** quick-moving (The statement is proverbial.)
32. **crossed:** contradicted
33. **mere contrary:** i.e., exactly the opposite (of the truth); **crosses:** i.e., coins stamped with crosses (See picture below.)
39. **told:** counted
40. **ill:** i.e., unskilled
43. **varnish:** adornment, embellishment
46. **deuce-ace:** in dice, a throw of a deuce and an ace
48. **vulgar:** common people
50. **piece:** masterpiece
51. **wink:** blink

A "cross." (1.2.33)
From Edward Hawkins,
The silver coins of England . . . (1841).

BOY And I "tough signior" as an appurtenant title to
your old time, which we may name "tough."

ARMADO Pretty and apt.

BOY How mean you, sir? I pretty and my saying apt, or
I apt and my saying pretty? 20

ARMADO Thou pretty because little.

BOY Little pretty, because little. Wherefore apt?

ARMADO And therefore apt, because quick.

BOY Speak you this in my praise, master?

ARMADO In thy condign praise. 25

BOY I will praise an eel with the same praise.

ARMADO What, that an eel is ingenious?

BOY That an eel is quick.

ARMADO I do say thou art quick in answers. Thou
heat'st my blood. 30

BOY I am answered, sir.

ARMADO I love not to be crossed.

BOY, ⌐*aside*⌐ He speaks the mere contrary; crosses love
not him.

ARMADO I have promised to study three years with the 35
Duke.

BOY You may do it in an hour, sir.

ARMADO Impossible.

BOY How many is one thrice told?

ARMADO I am ill at reckoning. It fitteth the spirit of a 40
tapster.

BOY You are a gentleman and a gamester, sir.

ARMADO I confess both. They are both the varnish of a
complete man.

BOY Then I am sure you know how much the gross 45
sum of deuce-ace amounts to.

ARMADO It doth amount to one more than two.

BOY Which the base vulgar do call "three."

ARMADO True.

BOY Why, sir, is this such a piece of study? Now here is 50
"three" studied ere you'll thrice wink. And how

53. dancing horse: perhaps a reference to Master Banks's famous horse Morocco, which had been taught to beat out numbers with its hoof (See page 162.)

55. figure: (1) figure of speech; (2) numeral

58. base: reprehensible, despicable

59. base wench: lowly servant

60. humor of affection: i.e., inclination to love

62. for: i.e., in exchange for

63. curtsy: bow; **think scorn:** scorn

64. outswear: (1) overcome by swearing; (2) forswear

66. Hercules: in Greek mythology, a hero of extraordinary strength and courage (See page 120.)

67. authority: i.e., references (to great men who have loved)

68. sweet my child: i.e., my sweet child

69. carriage: bearing, manners

70–72. Samson . . . porter: In Judges 16.3, the biblical hero Samson is described as carrying off the gates of Gaza. (See page 74.)

73. well-knit: strongly and compactly built

78. complexion: (1) temperament; (2) coloring

79. all the four: i.e., all four of the humors, whose relative proportions in the human body determined both temperament and appearance, according to the Greek medical writer Galen

82. green: perhaps, as if suffering from adolescent anemia, or greensickness

85. Green . . . lovers: perhaps an allusion to poetic associations of love with the greenery of spring.

87. affected: loved

88. wit: intelligence

easy it is to put "years" to the word "three" and study "three years" in two words, the dancing horse will tell you.

ARMADO A most fine figure.   55

BOY, ⌜*aside*⌝ To prove you a cipher.

ARMADO I will hereupon confess I am in love; and as it is base for a soldier to love, so am I in love with a base wench. If drawing my sword against the humor of affection would deliver me from the 60 reprobate thought of it, I would take desire prisoner and ransom him to any French courtier for a new-devised curtsy. I think scorn to sigh; methinks I should outswear Cupid. Comfort me, boy. What great men have been in love?   65

BOY Hercules, master.

ARMADO Most sweet Hercules! More authority, dear boy, name more; and, sweet my child, let them be men of good repute and carriage.

BOY Samson, master; he was a man of good carriage, 70 great carriage, for he carried the town gates on his back like a porter, and he was in love.

ARMADO O, well-knit Samson, strong-jointed Samson; I do excel thee in my rapier as much as thou didst me in carrying gates. I am in love too. Who was 75 Samson's love, my dear Mote?

BOY A woman, master.

ARMADO Of what complexion?

BOY Of all the four, or the three, or the two, or one of the four.   80

ARMADO Tell me precisely of what complexion.

BOY Of the sea-water green, sir.

ARMADO Is that one of the four complexions?

BOY As I have read, sir, and the best of them too.

ARMADO Green indeed is the color of lovers. But to 85 have a love of that color, methinks Samson had small reason for it. He surely affected her for her wit.

89. green: immature

91. maculate: spotted, impure (from *macula*, Latin for "spot")

97. pathetical: stirring, touching

102. to blame: i.e., blameworthy, guilty

103. this: i.e., her complexion

104. still: always; **the same:** i.e., the same red and white

105. native: naturally; **owe:** own

106. A dangerous: an injurious

106–7. the reason . . . red: See longer note, page 229.

108–9. "The King . . . Beggar": In 4.1.72–88, Armado tells a story of King Cophetua in love with a beggar maid. Shakespeare alludes to this story in *Romeo and Juliet* as well, but no surviving version of the ballad dates from earlier than 1612.

111. since: ago

112–13. neither serve . . . tune: i.e., neither the words nor the tune would serve your purpose

115. example: justify; **digression:** moral deviation

117. rational hind: i.e., rustic boor endowed with reason

119. To be whipped: i.e., she deserves to be whipped (Whipping was a punishment for vagrants and prostitutes.)

121. heavy: i.e., sad, melancholy

122. light: unchaste

BOY   It was so, sir, for she had a green wit.
ARMADO   My love is most immaculate white and red.   90
BOY   Most maculate thoughts, master, are masked
   under such colors.
ARMADO   Define, define, well-educated infant.
BOY   My father's wit and my mother's tongue, assist
   me.   95
ARMADO   Sweet invocation of a child, most pretty and
   pathetical.
BOY
      If she be made of white and red,
         Her faults will ne'er be known,
      For ⌐blushing⌐ cheeks by faults are bred,   100
         And fears by pale white shown.
      Then if she fear, or be to blame,
         By this you shall not know,
      For still her cheeks possess the same
         Which native she doth owe.   105
   A dangerous rhyme, master, against the reason of
   white and red.
ARMADO   Is there not a ballad, boy, of "The King and
   the Beggar"?
BOY   The world was very guilty of such a ballad some   110
   three ages since, but I think now 'tis not to be found;
   or if it were, it would neither serve for the writing
   nor the tune.
ARMADO   I will have that subject newly writ o'er, that I
   may example my digression by some mighty prece-   115
   dent. Boy, I do love that country girl that I took in
   the park with the rational hind Costard. She deserves well.
BOY, ⌐*aside*⌐   To be whipped—and yet a better love than
   my master.   120
ARMADO   Sing, boy. My spirit grows heavy in love.
BOY, ⌐*aside*⌐   And that's great marvel, loving a light
   wench.

127. **suffer:** allow

128. **penance:** malapropism, perhaps for "pleasance," or pleasure

129. **For:** i.e., as for

130. **allowed . . . dey-woman:** i.e., permitted to function as the dairymaid

135. **lodge:** perhaps, a hunting lodge; or, perhaps, a cottage at the entrance of the park

136. **hereby:** i.e., near by

140, 142. **With that face, So I heard you say:** expressions of disbelief

144. **Fair . . . you:** a proverbial response to **farewell**

146. **Villain:** (1) peasant; (2) scoundrel

148–49. **on a full stomach:** (1) with courage; (2) according to the proverb "The belly that is full may well fast"

151. **fellows:** servants

ARMADO   I say sing.

BOY   Forbear till this company be past.   125

*Enter Clown (⌐Costard,¬) Constable (⌐Dull,¬) and Wench
(⌐Jaquenetta.¬)*

DULL, ⌐*to Armado*¬   Sir, the Duke's pleasure is that you
    keep Costard safe, and you must suffer him to take
    no delight, nor no penance, but he must fast three
    days a week. For this damsel, I must keep her at the
    park. She is allowed for the dey-woman. Fare you   130
    well.

ARMADO, ⌐*aside*¬   I do betray myself with blushing.—
    Maid.

JAQUENETTA   Man.

ARMADO   I will visit thee at the lodge.   135

JAQUENETTA   That's hereby.

ARMADO   I know where it is situate.

JAQUENETTA   Lord, how wise you are.

ARMADO   I will tell thee wonders.

JAQUENETTA   With that face?   140

ARMADO   I love thee.

JAQUENETTA   So I heard you say.

ARMADO   And so, farewell.

JAQUENETTA   Fair weather after you.

⌐DULL¬   Come, Jaquenetta, away.   145
                           ⌐*Dull and Jaquenetta*¬ *exit.*

ARMADO, ⌐*to Costard*¬   Villain, thou shalt fast for thy
    offenses ere thou be pardoned.

COSTARD   Well, sir, I hope when I do it I shall do it on
    a full stomach.

ARMADO   Thou shalt be heavily punished.   150

COSTARD   I am more bound to you than your fellows,
    for they are but lightly rewarded.

ARMADO, ⌐*to Boy*¬   Take away this villain. Shut him up.

BOY   Come, you transgressing slave, away.

157. **fast and loose:** i.e., a confidence man's trick

160. **desolation:** malapropism, perhaps for "jubilation" or for "consolation"

164. **words:** possibly with a pun on "wards," or cells

167. **affect:** love

170. **argument:** proof

171–72. **falsely attempted:** i.e., pursued at the cost of oath-breaking

172. **familiar:** attendant spirit, demon

174. **Solomon:** For Solomon's amorousness, see 1 Kings 11.1–3.

175. **wit:** intelligence

175–76. **Cupid's butt-shaft:** the unbarbed arrow of Cupid, the Roman god of love

176. **Hercules' club:** Hercules is often pictured wielding or leaning on a mighty club. See illustrations, pages 60 and 120.

177. **odds for:** i.e., advantage over

177–78. **first . . . cause:** In 1590s books about dueling, the reasons for fighting a duel were (1) being accused of a crime punishable by death; (2) having one's honor insulted.

179. **passado:** a fencing step forward with a thrust; **he:** i.e., Cupid; **duello:** dueling code

182. **manager:** master

183. **extemporal . . . rhyme:** i.e., god of extemporaneous verse

184. **turn sonnet:** perhaps, fashion a love poem (A sonnet could be any love poem, not just the fourteen-line poem to which the name is now restricted.)

185. **folio:** See "The Publication of Shakespeare's Plays," page xlviii.

COSTARD, ⌈*to Armado*⌉ Let me not be pent up, sir. I will 155
fast being loose.

BOY No, sir, that were fast and loose. Thou shalt to
prison.

COSTARD Well, if ever I do see the merry days of
desolation that I have seen, some shall see. 160

BOY What shall some see?

COSTARD Nay, nothing, Master Mote, but what they
look upon. It is not for prisoners to be too silent in
their words, and therefore I will say nothing. I thank
God I have as little patience as another man, and 165
therefore I can be quiet.

⌈*Costard and Boy*⌉ *exit.*

ARMADO I do affect the very ground (which is base)
where her shoe (which is baser) guided by her foot
(which is basest) doth tread. I shall be forsworn
(which is a great argument of falsehood) if I love. 170
And how can that be true love which is falsely
attempted? Love is a familiar; love is a devil. There is
no evil angel but love, yet was Samson so tempted,
and he had an excellent strength; yet was Solomon
so seduced, and he had a very good wit. Cupid's 175
butt-shaft is too hard for Hercules' club, and therefore too much odds for a Spaniard's rapier. The first
and second cause will not serve my turn; the
passado he respects not, the *duello* he regards not.
His disgrace is to be called "boy," but his glory is to 180
subdue men. Adieu, valor; rust, rapier; be still,
drum, for your manager is in love. Yea, he loveth.
Assist me, some extemporal god of rhyme, for I am
sure I shall turn sonnet. Devise wit, write pen, for I
am for whole volumes in folio. 185

He exits.

LOVE'S LABOR'S LOST

ACT 2

2.1 The Princess of France and her ladies arrive at Navarre. The King greets them but refuses to admit them into his court, forcing them to stay in tents in the fields. Navarre's lords each show an interest in one of the Princess's ladies.

———

1. **dearest spirits:** best energies or powers
3. **embassy:** message
4. **held:** regarded as
5. **inheritor:** possessor
6. **owe:** own
7. **Matchless Navarre:** i.e., the peerless king of Navarre; **plea:** i.e., the substance of the plea, or claim
9. **dear:** precious
10. **dear:** rare, and therefore valuable
11. **general world besides:** i.e., rest of the world
12. **them all:** i.e., all the graces
13. **mean:** ordinary
14. **flourish:** decoration
16. **uttered by:** i.e., offered for; **of chapmen's:** i.e., by merchants'
17. **tell:** (1) count; (2) talk about
20. **tasker:** i.e., taskmaster, the one setting the tasks

⟨ACT 2⟩

*Enter the Princess of France, with three attending
Ladies (⌜Rosaline, Maria, and Katherine), Boyet⌝
and ⌜other⌝ Lords.*

BOYET
Now, madam, summon up your dearest spirits.
Consider who the King your father sends,
To whom he sends, and what's his embassy.
Yourself, held precious in the world's esteem,
To parley with the sole inheritor   5
Of all perfections that a man may owe,
Matchless Navarre; the plea of no less weight
Than Aquitaine, a dowry for a queen.
Be now as prodigal of all dear grace
As nature was in making graces dear   10
When she did starve the general world besides
And prodigally gave them all to you.

PRINCESS
Good Lord Boyet, my beauty, though but mean,
Needs not the painted flourish of your praise.
Beauty is bought by judgment of the eye,   15
Not uttered by base sale of chapmen's tongues.
I am less proud to hear you tell my worth
Than you much willing to be counted wise
In spending your wit in the praise of mine.
But now to task the tasker: good Boyet,   20

41

21. **fame:** rumor

23. **outwear:** i.e., wear out

25. **to 's:** to us, i.e., to me (Here the Princess, whom the Quarto often calls a queen, uses the "royal we.")

27. **in that behalf:** i.e., for that purpose, toward that end

28. **Bold:** sure; **single:** select

29. **best-moving:** most persuasive; **fair:** i.e., fair-minded; **solicitor:** agent, representative

32. **Importunes:** begs (pronounced impor'tunes); **conference:** conversation

33. **attend:** await

34. **suitors:** petitioners; **his high will:** i.e., the expression of his royal intentions

37. **votaries:** those bound by special oath

38. **vow-fellows:** i.e., colleagues in taking this vow

39. **Longaville:** The final syllable of this name seems sometimes to rhyme with "will" and sometimes with "vile."

41 SP. **Maria:** For the editorial and production choices presented in this scene by the Quarto speech prefixes, see longer note, page 230.

43. **solemnizèd:** accents on second and fourth syllables

45. **parts:** personal qualities

46. **fitted in arts:** i.e., prepared with learning; **glorious in arms:** i.e., having won glory in battle

47. **would:** i.e., wishes to be or to do

48. **soil of:** stain on

51. **Whose edge:** i.e., the edge of whose wit; **still:** always

52. **It:** i.e., his wit; **his:** its

You are not ignorant all-telling fame
Doth noise abroad Navarre hath made a vow,
Till painful study shall outwear three years,
No woman may approach his silent court.
Therefore to 's seemeth it a needful course, 25
Before we enter his forbidden gates,
To know his pleasure, and in that behalf,
Bold of your worthiness, we single you
As our best-moving fair solicitor.
Tell him the daughter of the King of France 30
On serious business craving quick dispatch,
⟨Importunes⟩ personal conference with his Grace.
Haste, signify so much, while we attend,
Like ⟨humble-visaged⟩ suitors, his high will.

BOYET
Proud of employment, willingly I go. 35

PRINCESS
All pride is willing pride, and yours is so.
                                        Boyet exits.
Who are the votaries, my loving lords,
That are vow-fellows with this virtuous duke?

⌜A⌝ LORD
⌜Lord⌝ Longaville is one.

PRINCESS   Know you the man? 40

⌜MARIA⌝
I know him, madam. At a marriage feast
Between Lord Perigort and the beauteous heir
Of Jaques Falconbridge, solemnizèd
In Normandy, saw I this Longaville.
A man of sovereign ⟨parts⟩ he is esteemed, 45
Well fitted in arts, glorious in arms.
Nothing becomes him ill that he would well.
The only soil of his fair virtue's gloss,
If virtue's gloss will stain with any soil,
Is a sharp wit matched with too blunt a will, 50
Whose edge hath power to cut, whose will still wills
It should none spare that come within his power.

53. **belike:** probably

54. **humors:** moods

55. **Such . . . grow:** Compare the proverb: "Soon ripe, soon rotten."

58. **Of:** i.e., by

59. **Most . . . ill:** i.e., knowing little of evil, he can do much harm

60–61. **For he . . . no wit:** i.e., his intelligence would compensate for lack of beauty, and his beauty would make up for lack of intelligence

62. **Duke Alanson's:** i.e., duke of Alençon's

63–64. **much too little . . . worthiness:** i.e., my report of the goodness I observed in him falls far short of conveying his great personal worth   **to:** i.e., compared to

67. **but a merrier man:** The contrast drawn here between Berowne's name and his merry nature can be explained if, as some suggest, the name sounds like "brown" (i.e., "gloomy, serious"). Later in the play, however, his name is made to rhyme with "moon."

69. **withal:** with

73. **conceit's expositor:** expounder of witty notions

75. **play truant:** i.e., abandon the serious interests of the aged

80. **bedecking:** adorning

PRINCESS
   Some merry mocking lord, belike. Is 't so?
⌜MARIA⌝
   They say so most that most his humors know.
PRINCESS
   Such short-lived wits do wither as they grow. 55
   Who are the rest?
⌜KATHERINE⌝
   The young Dumaine, a well-accomplished youth,
   Of all that virtue love for virtue loved.
   Most power to do most harm, least knowing ill;
   For he hath wit to make an ill shape good, 60
   And shape to win grace though he had no wit.
   I saw him at the Duke Alanson's once,
   And much too little of that good I saw
   Is my report to his great worthiness.
⟨ROSALINE⟩
   Another of these students at that time 65
   Was there with him, if I have heard a truth.
   Berowne they call him, but a merrier man,
   Within the limit of becoming mirth,
   I never spent an hour's talk withal.
   His eye begets occasion for his wit, 70
   For every object that the one doth catch
   The other turns to a mirth-moving jest,
   Which his fair tongue, conceit's expositor,
   Delivers in such apt and gracious words
   That agèd ears play truant at his tales, 75
   And younger hearings are quite ravishèd,
   So sweet and voluble is his discourse.
PRINCESS
   God bless my ladies, are they all in love,
   That every one her own hath garnishèd
   With such bedecking ornaments of praise? 80
⌜A⌝ LORD
   Here comes Boyet.

82. **what admittance:** perhaps, what permission to enter (is granted me)

83. **your fair approach:** i.e., the approach of you, who are beautiful

84. **competitors:** associates

85. **addressed:** prepared

87. **in the field:** i.e., out of doors

90. **unpeopled house:** i.e., house understaffed with servants

94. **The roof . . . court:** i.e., the sky

100. **Our Lady:** i.e., the Virgin Mary

101. **by my will:** an oath

102. **will:** desire

Pattern for a "curious-knotted garden." (1.1.249–50)
From Charles Estienne, *Maison rustique* . . . (1606).

Enter Boyet.

PRINCESS   Now, what admittance, lord?
BOYET
Navarre had notice of your fair approach,
And he and his competitors in oath
Were all addressed to meet you, gentle lady,   85
Before I came. Marry, thus much I have learned:
He rather means to lodge you in the field,
Like one that comes here to besiege his court,
Than seek a dispensation for his oath
To let you enter his ⌜unpeopled⌝ house.   90

*Enter ⌜King of⌝ Navarre, Longaville, Dumaine, and
Berowne.*

Here comes Navarre.
KING   Fair Princess, welcome to the court of Navarre.
PRINCESS   "Fair" I give you back again, and "wel-
come" I have not yet. The roof of this court is too
high to be yours, and welcome to the wide fields too   95
base to be mine.
KING
You shall be welcome, madam, to my court.
PRINCESS
I will be welcome, then. Conduct me thither.
KING
Hear me, dear lady. I have sworn an oath.
PRINCESS
Our Lady help my lord! He'll be forsworn.   100
KING
Not for the world, fair madam, by my will.
PRINCESS
Why, will shall break it, will and nothing else.
KING
Your Ladyship is ignorant what it is.

105. **Where:** i.e., whereas

106. **sworn out housekeeping:** abjured or given up hospitality

109. **sudden:** impetuously

110. **ill beseemeth:** i.e., is not appropriate for

112. **suddenly . . . me:** promptly deliver your answer; **suit:** petition

114. **You will . . . away:** i.e., you will do it faster in order to get me to leave

116. **Brabant:** a duchy in western Europe now incorporated in Belgium and Holland

117 SP. **Rosaline:** See longer note to 2.1.41 SP.

121. **quick:** (1) hot-tempered; (2) sharp, caustic

122. **long:** i.e., because; **that spur me:** who urges me on, as a horse is urged with spurs (Rosaline's answer takes Berowne's **quick** in its sense of "hasty, fast-moving." Lines 123-24 continue the horseback riding image.)

127. **fair befall:** i.e., good luck to

Father Time with his scythe. (1.1.6)
From Jean de Serres, *A generall historie of France . . .* (1611).

PRINCESS
  Were my lord so, his ignorance were wise,
  Where now his knowledge must prove ignorance.   105
  I hear your Grace hath sworn out housekeeping.
  'Tis deadly sin to keep that oath, my lord,
  And sin to break it.
  But pardon me, I am too sudden bold.
  To teach a teacher ill beseemeth me.   110
  Vouchsafe to read the purpose of my coming,
  And suddenly resolve me in my suit.
             ⌜*She gives him a paper.*⌝

KING
  Madam, I will, if suddenly I may.
PRINCESS
  You will the sooner that I were away,
  For you'll prove perjured if you make me stay.   115
  ⌜*They walk aside while the King reads the paper.*⌝
BEROWNE, ⌜*to Rosaline*⌝
  Did not I dance with you in Brabant once?
⟨ROSALINE⟩
  Did not I dance with you in Brabant once?
BEROWNE
  I know you did.
⟨ROSALINE⟩   How needless was it then
  To ask the question.   120
BEROWNE   You must not be so quick.
⟨ROSALINE⟩
  'Tis long of you that spur me with such questions.
BEROWNE
  Your wit's too hot, it speeds too fast; 'twill tire.
⟨ROSALINE⟩
  Not till it leave the rider in the mire.
BEROWNE
  What time o' day?   125
⟨ROSALINE⟩   The hour that fools should ask.
BEROWNE   Now fair befall your mask.

128. **fall:** i.e., befall

130. **so:** i.e., provided that

132. **intimate:** state

134. **entire:** pronounced en'tire

135. **Disbursèd . . . his wars:** i.e., paid out for wars fought by the King of France

136. **he:** my father; **we:** i.e., I (The king here uses the formal "royal we.")

139. **bound:** subject

140. **Although . . . worth:** i.e., even though its value is less than the sum owed

142. **unsatisfied:** not settled by payment

145. **little purposeth:** has little intention (of doing)

150. **had depart withal:** i.e., would part with

154–55. **make / A yielding:** i.e., make me give in to persuasion

159. **In so unseeming to:** perhaps, in so unbecomingly failing to; or perhaps, in thus seeming not to

⟨ROSALINE⟩ Fair fall the face it covers.
BEROWNE And send you many lovers.
⟨ROSALINE⟩ Amen, so you be none. 130
BEROWNE Nay, then, will I be gone.
KING, ⌈*coming forward with the Princess*⌉
    Madam, your father here doth intimate
    The payment of a hundred thousand crowns,
    Being but the one half of an entire sum
    Disbursèd by my father in his wars. 135
    But say that he or we, as neither have,
    Received that sum, yet there remains unpaid
    A hundred thousand more, in surety of the which
    One part of Aquitaine is bound to us,
    Although not valued to the money's worth. 140
    If then the King your father will restore
    But that one half which is unsatisfied,
    We will give up our right in Aquitaine,
    And hold fair friendship with his Majesty.
    But that, it seems, he little purposeth; 145
    For here he doth demand to have repaid
    A hundred thousand crowns, and not demands,
    On payment of a hundred thousand crowns,
    To have his title live in Aquitaine—
    Which we much rather had depart withal, 150
    And have the money by our father lent,
    Than Aquitaine, so gelded as it is.
    Dear Princess, were not his requests so far
    From reason's yielding, your fair self should make
    A yielding 'gainst some reason in my breast, 155
    And go well satisfied to France again.
PRINCESS
    You do the King my father too much wrong,
    And wrong the reputation of your name,
    In so unseeming to confess receipt
    Of that which hath so faithfully been paid. 160

164. **arrest:** take as security

167. **Charles his father:** i.e., Charles, Navarre's father (One of the historical Navarre's most famous rulers was Charles II, 1349–87.)

170. **specialties:** special contracts

173. **All liberal reason:** i.e., any reasonable argument

176. **Make tender of:** i.e., tender, offer

178. **without:** outside; **received:** welcomed

179. **As:** i.e., that

183. **consort:** accompany

187. **do my commendations:** i.e., offer it my respects, compliments

"Brazen tombs." (1.1.2)
From Sir William Dugdale, *The antiquities of Warwickshire . . .* (1656).

KING
  I do protest I never heard of it;
  And if you prove it, I'll repay it back
  Or yield up Aquitaine.
PRINCESS   We arrest your word.—
  Boyet, you can produce acquittances   165
  For such a sum from special officers
  Of Charles his father.
KING   Satisfy me so.
BOYET
  So please your Grace, the packet is not come
  Where that and other specialties are bound.   170
  Tomorrow you shall have a sight of them.
KING
  It shall suffice me; at which interview
  All liberal reason I will yield unto.
  Meantime receive such welcome at my hand
  As honor (without breach of honor) may   175
  Make tender of to thy true worthiness.
  You may not come, fair princess, within my gates,
  But here without you shall be so received
  As you shall deem yourself lodged in my heart,
  Though so denied fair harbor in my house.   180
  Your own good thoughts excuse me, and farewell.
  Tomorrow shall we visit you again.
PRINCESS
  Sweet health and fair desires consort your Grace.
KING
  Thy own wish wish I thee in every place.
                    He exits ⌜*with Dumaine,*
                    Longaville, and Attendants.⌝
BEROWNE, ⌜*to Rosaline*⌝ Lady, I will commend you to   185
  my ⟨own⟩ heart.
ROSALINE Pray you, do my commendations. I would
  be glad to see it.
BEROWNE I would you heard it groan.

190. fool: while primarily a term of ridicule, sometimes a term of pity or of endearment

192. let it blood: i.e., have it bled by a surgeon (Blood-letting was a method used to treat the sick.)

194. physic: medical knowledge

195. eye: with a pun on **ay**

196. No point: (1) not at all (French *non point*); (2) i.e., my eye has no point

199. stay thanksgiving: i.e., wait around to thank you

204. an: i.e., if

205. light in the light: i.e., unchaste when rightly perceived

213. choler: anger

A marriage feast. (2.1.41)
From Theodor Graminaeus,
Beschreibung derer . . . Hochzeit . . . (1587).

ROSALINE	Is the fool sick?	190
BEROWNE	Sick at the heart.	
ROSALINE	Alack, let it blood.	
BEROWNE	Would that do it good?	
ROSALINE	My physic says "ay."	
BEROWNE	Will you prick 't with your eye?	195
ROSALINE	No point, with my knife.	
BEROWNE	Now God save thy life.	
ROSALINE	And yours from long living.	
BEROWNE	I cannot stay thanksgiving.	*He exits.*

Enter Dumaine.

DUMAINE, ⌜*to Boyet*⌝
  Sir, I pray you, a word. What lady is that same? 200
BOYET
  The heir of Alanson, ⌜Katherine⌝ her name.
DUMAINE
  A gallant lady, monsieur. Fare you well. *He exits.*

Enter Longaville.

LONGAVILLE, ⌜*to Boyet*⌝
  I beseech you, a word. What is she in the white?
BOYET
  A woman sometimes, an you saw her in the light.
LONGAVILLE
  Perchance light in the light. I desire her name. 205
BOYET
  She hath but one for herself; to desire that were a
    shame.
LONGAVILLE Pray you, sir, whose daughter?
BOYET Her mother's, I have heard.
LONGAVILLE God's blessing on your beard! 210
BOYET Good sir, be not offended. She is an heir of
    Falconbridge.
LONGAVILLE Nay, my choler is ended. She is a most
    sweet lady.

215. **unlike:** i.e., unlikely

217. **by good hap:** i.e., by chance (used here probably for the sake of the rhyme)

218–19. **wedded . . . will:** Proverbial: "To be wedded to one's will."

221. **welcome to you:** Proverbial: "You are welcome to go."

227. **grapple, board:** In sea battles of the time, crews of opposing ships sought to fasten their ships together with grappling irons in order to board each other's ships and fight hand to hand.

231. **pasture:** with a pun on "pastor," Latin for "shepherd"

232. **So:** provided

234. **no common:** i.e., not common pasture, where anyone's stock may graze; **several:** (1) more than one; (2) privately owned, enclosed pasture; (3) parted

237. **jangling:** squabbling; **gentles:** gentlefolk

239. **bookmen:** students

BOYET   Not unlike, sir, that may be.   215
                              Longaville exits.

                    Enter Berowne.

BEROWNE, ⌈*to Boyet*⌉   What's her name in the cap?
BOYET   ⌈Rosaline,⌉ by good hap.
BEROWNE   Is she wedded or no?
BOYET   To her will, sir, or so.
BEROWNE   You are welcome, sir. Adieu.   220
BOYET   Farewell to me, sir, and welcome to you.
                              Berowne exits.

MARIA
  That last is Berowne, the merry madcap lord.
  Not a word with him but a jest.
BOYET   And every jest but
  a word.   225
PRINCESS
  It was well done of you to take him at his word.
BOYET
  I was as willing to grapple as he was to board.
KATHERINE
  Two hot sheeps, marry.
BOYET   And wherefore not ships?
  No sheep, sweet lamb, unless we feed on your lips. 230
⌈KATHERINE⌉
  You sheep and I pasture. Shall that finish the jest?
BOYET
  So you grant pasture for me.   ⌈*He tries to kiss her.*⌉
⌈KATHERINE⌉   Not so, gentle beast.
  My lips are no common, though several they be.
BOYET
  Belonging to whom?   235
⌈KATHERINE⌉   To my fortunes and me.
PRINCESS
  Good wits will be jangling; but, gentles, agree,
  This civil war of wits were much better used
  On Navarre and his bookmen, for here 'tis abused.

241. **By:** i.e., concerning; **still rhetoric:** i.e., dumb eloquence

244. **affected:** i.e., in love

246–47. **all . . . desire:** i.e., he could do nothing except gaze with longing **behaviors:** deportment, manners **retire:** withdrawal **thorough:** through

248. **agate:** i.e., a quartz crystal set in a ring, often carved with tiny figures; **with . . . impressed:** i.e., with your image on it

249. **Proud . . . form:** i.e., made proud because its form is the image of the Princess

250. **all impatient:** eagerly longing

252. **make their repair:** go

253. **looking:** i.e., through looking

254–58. **all . . . passed:** The King's senses are here represented as jewels encased in crystal glass, displaying themselves for the Princess to buy. **As:** i.e., as if they were **tend'ring:** offering **glassed:** encased in glass **point you:** direct your attention

259. **His face's . . . amazes:** The King's face here becomes a page in a book with his eyes the main text. The rest of his face is the margin **(margent)**, which directs attention to the wonder **(amazes)** in his eyes.

263. **disposed:** in a joking mood (Boyet responds as if she meant simply "inclined.")

264. **But:** i.e., merely, only

268. **lovemonger:** trafficker in love; **skillfully:** cleverly

BOYET
  If my observation, which very seldom lies,   240
  By the heart's still rhetoric, disclosèd wi' th' eyes,
  Deceive me not now, Navarre is infected.
PRINCESS   With what?
BOYET
  With that which we lovers entitle "affected."
PRINCESS   Your reason?   245
BOYET
  Why, all his behaviors did make their retire
  To the court of his eye, peeping thorough desire.
  His heart like an agate with your print impressed,
  Proud with his form, in his eye pride expressed.
  His tongue, all impatient to speak and not see,   250
  Did stumble with haste in his eyesight to be;
  All senses to that sense did make their repair,
  To feel only looking on fairest of fair.
  Methought all his senses were locked in his eye,
  As jewels in crystal for some prince to buy,   255
  Who, tend'ring their own worth from where they
    were glassed,
  Did point you to buy them along as you passed.
  His face's own margent did quote such amazes
  That all eyes saw his eyes enchanted with gazes.   260
  I'll give you Aquitaine, and all that is his,
  An you give him for my sake but one loving kiss.
PRINCESS, ⌜*to her Ladies*⌝
  Come, to our pavilion. Boyet is disposed.
BOYET
  But to speak that in words which his eye hath
    disclosed.   265
  I only have made a mouth of his eye
  By adding a tongue which I know will not lie.
⌜MARIA⌝
  Thou art an old lovemonger and speakest skillfully.

269. **of:** i.e., from

270. **Venus:** Roman goddess of love, and mother of the god Cupid

272. **Do you hear:** i.e., pay attention; **mad wenches:** wildly foolish young women

"Cupid's butt-shaft is too hard for Hercules' club."
(1.2.175–76)
From Georgius Camerarius, *Emblemata amatoria* . . . (1627).

⌜KATHERINE⌝
  He is Cupid's grandfather, and learns news of him.
⌜ROSALINE⌝
  Then was Venus like her mother, for her father is   270
    but grim.
BOYET
  Do you hear, my mad wenches?
⌜MARIA⌝   No.
BOYET   What then, do
    you see?   275
⌜MARIA⌝
  Ay, our way to be gone.
BOYET   You are too hard for me.
                                  They all exit.

LOVE'S
LABOR'S
LOST

ACT 3

3.1 Armado frees Costard and gives him a love letter to take to Jaquenetta. Berowne then enters. He gives Costard a letter to take to Rosaline. Berowne, alone, admits that he is in love.

---

1. **make passionate:** i.e., affect with the passion of love

3. **Concolinel:** This unknown word is perhaps the title of, or a word from, a song that the Boy sings. (The First Folio prints "Song" after *"Enter Braggart and Boy."*)

4. **air:** melody

5. **give enlargement to:** i.e., enlarge, set free

5–6. **the swain:** i.e., Costard

6. **festinately:** speedily

8–9. **French brawl:** a courtly dance that featured the male partner's skills

11–12. **jig . . . end:** i.e., sing a tune as a jig

12. **canary . . . feet:** i.e., dance to it as though you were dancing the canaries, a lively Spanish dance; **humor it:** adapt yourself to it

17–18. **with . . . eyes:** i.e., with your hat pulled down over your eyes (See illustration, page 70.) **penthouse:** a sloping, overhanging roof

19. **thin-belly doublet:** close-fitting jacket, tailored to feature your leanness

20. **after:** after the manner of, in imitation of

20–21. **old painting:** No particular painting has been identified.

21–22. **a snip and away:** i.e., a little bit of one tune and then on to another (Proverbial: "A snatch and away.")

(continued)

⟨ACT 3⟩

⌜Scene 1⌝
Enter Braggart ⌜Armado⌝ and his Boy.

ARMADO Warble, child, make passionate my sense of
hearing.

BOY ⌜*sings*⌝ Concolinel.

ARMADO Sweet air. Go, tenderness of years. ⌜*He hands
over a key.*⌝ Take this key, give enlargement to the   5
swain, bring him festinately hither. I must employ
him in a letter to my love.

BOY Master, will you win your love with a French
brawl?

ARMADO How meanest thou? Brawling in French?   10

BOY No, my complete master, but to jig off a tune at the
tongue's end, canary to it with your feet, humor it
with turning up your eyelids, sigh a note and sing a
note, sometimes through the throat ⌜as⌝ if you
swallowed love with singing love, sometimes   15
through ⌜the⌝ nose as if you snuffed up love by
smelling love; with your hat penthouse-like o'er the
shop of your eyes, with your arms crossed on your
⟨thin-belly⟩ doublet like a rabbit on a spit; or your
hands in your pocket like a man after the old   20
painting; and keep not too long in one tune, but a
snip and away. These are compliments, these are
humors; these betray nice wenches that would be
betrayed without these, and make them men of

22. **compliments:** ceremonies

23. **humors:** whims, caprices; **betray:** seduce; **nice:** foolish; coy; fastidious; unchaste

24-25. **men of note:** (1) men of distinction; (2) musical men

25. **do you note:** i.e., are you paying attention to

27. **purchased:** gained

28. **penny:** i.e., pennyworth

30. **The hobby-horse is forgot:** apparently part of a line from a lost song (Compare *Hamlet:* "For oh, for oh, the hobby-horse is forgot" 3.2.143-44.) **hobby-horse:** a character in morris dances (Armado, in his response, line 31, gives **hobby-horse** its meaning of "lustful person.") See page 82.

32. **colt:** (1) young horse; (2) lascivious fellow

33. **hackney:** (1) horse for hire; (2) prostitute

39. **prove:** demonstrate (When Armado repeats this word at line 40, the Boy pretends that it means "turn out to be.")

41-42. **and this . . . upon the instant:** i.e., and I will prove this . . . at this very moment

45. **out of heart:** disheartened, discouraged

50-51. **carry . . . letter:** i.e., deliver a letter for me

52. **sympathized:** matched; **horse:** like **ass,** an insulting term (Compare Falstaff in *Henry IV, Part 1:* "if I tell thee a lie, spit in my face, call me horse" [2.4.202-3].)

59. **ingenious:** i.e., intelligent one

note—do you note ⌜me?⌝—that most are affected 25
to these.

ARMADO How hast thou purchased this experience?

BOY By my ⌜penny⌝ of observation.

ARMADO But O— but O—.

BOY "The hobby-horse is forgot." 30

ARMADO Call'st thou my love "hobby-horse"?

BOY No, master. The hobby-horse is but a colt, ⌜*aside*⌝ and your love perhaps a hackney.—But have you forgot your love?

ARMADO Almost I had. 35

BOY Negligent student, learn her by heart.

ARMADO By heart and in heart, boy.

BOY And out of heart, master. All those three I will prove.

ARMADO What wilt thou prove? 40

BOY A man, if I live; and this "by, in, and without," upon the instant: "by" heart you love her, because your heart cannot come by her; "in" heart you love her, because your heart is in love with her; and "out" of heart you love her, being out of heart that 45 you cannot enjoy her.

ARMADO I am all these three.

BOY And three times as much more, ⌜*aside*⌝ and yet nothing at all.

ARMADO Fetch hither the swain. He must carry me a 50 letter.

BOY A message well sympathized—a horse to be ambassador for an ass.

ARMADO Ha? Ha? What sayest thou?

BOY Marry, sir, you must send the ass upon the horse, 55 for he is very slow-gaited. But I go.

ARMADO The way is but short. Away!

BOY As swift as lead, sir.

ARMADO ⟨Thy⟩ meaning, pretty ingenious?
Is not lead a metal heavy, dull, and slow? 60

61. **Minime:** absolutely not (Latin)

65. **smoke:** fumes of incense; or, less likely, fog or mist

66. **reputes:** considers

69. **Thump:** i.e., bang

70. **juvenal:** See note to 1.2.8.

71. **welkin:** sky

72. **gives thee place:** i.e., yields its place (in me) to you

75. **costard:** i.e., head; **broken:** cut (See lines 123–24 for Costard's account of how he cut his shin.)

76. **l'envoi:** literally, the action of sending off a poem, the poet's parting words (See Armado's definition at lines 86–87.)

77–78. **salve in the mail:** perhaps, ointment in the pack (The phrase perhaps refers to a mountebank's bag of fake remedies.) There is bilingual wordplay on **salve** beginning at line 83.

78. **plantain:** a weed whose leaves were used to stanch bleeding (See page 86.)

81. **my spleen:** i.e., (enforces) my laughter (The **spleen** was thought to be the seat of mirth, as well as of rage.)

83. **inconsiderate:** thoughtless (one); **salve:** (1) a Latin greeting, and in this sense the opposite of a farewell (**l'envoi**); (2) a salute also used in parting (the sense in which the Boy uses it in line 85.)

BOY
Minime, honest master, or rather, master, no.
ARMADO
I say lead is slow.
BOY   You are too swift, sir, to say so.
Is that lead slow which is fired from a gun?
ARMADO Sweet smoke of rhetoric!   65
He reputes me a cannon, and the bullet, that's
he.—
I shoot thee at the swain.
BOY   Thump, then, and I flee.
                        ⌜*He exits.*⌝

ARMADO
A most acute juvenal, voluble and free of grace.   70
By thy favor, sweet welkin, I must sigh in thy face.
Most rude melancholy, valor gives thee place.
My herald is returned.

            Enter ⌜*Boy*⌝ *and Clown* ⌜*Costard.*⌝

BOY   A wonder, master!
Here's a costard broken in a shin.   75
ARMADO
Some enigma, some riddle. Come, thy *l'envoi* begin.
COSTARD No egma, no riddle, no *l'envoi*, no salve in
    the mail, sir. O, sir, plantain, a plain plantain! No
    l'envoi, no *l'envoi*, no salve, sir, but a plantain.
ARMADO By virtue, thou enforcest laughter; thy silly 80
    thought, my spleen. The heaving of my lungs
    provokes me to ridiculous smiling. O pardon me,
    my stars! Doth the inconsiderate take *salve* for
    l'envoi, and the word *l'envoi* for a *salve?*
BOY
Do the wise think them other? Is not *l'envoi* a *salve?* 85
ARMADO
No, page, it is an epilogue or discourse to make plain

87. **precedence:** something that has already been said (as Armado explains); **sain:** said

88. **example it:** i.e., give an example of it

90. **still:** always; **at odds:** (1) quarreling; (2) an odd number

96. **stayed the odds:** (1) appeased the strife; (2) made the number even; **four:** i.e., a fourth

103. **ending in the goose:** i.e., ending in *oi* (The French word for "goose" is *oie*.)

105. **sold . . . bargain:** made a fool of him; **a goose:** i.e., a simpleton

107. **an:** i.e., if

108–9. **fast and loose:** See note to 1.2.157.

111. **argument:** debate, discussion

The melancholy lover. (3.1.17–19)
From [Robert Burton,] *The anatomy of melancholy . . .* (1638).

Some obscure precedence that hath tofore been sain.
I will example it:
>   The fox, the ape, and the humble-bee
>   Were still at odds, being but three.   90

There's the moral. Now the *l'envoi*.

BOY   I will add the *l'envoi*. Say the moral again.

ARMADO
>   The fox, the ape, and the humble-bee
>   Were still at odds, being but three.

BOY
>   Until the goose came out of door   95
>   And stayed the odds by adding four.

Now will I begin your moral, and do you follow with
my *l'envoi*.
>   The fox, the ape, and the humble-bee
>   Were still at odds, being but three.   100

ARMADO
>   Until the goose came out of door,
>   Staying the odds by adding four.

BOY   A good *l'envoi*, ending in the goose. Would you
desire more?

COSTARD
The boy hath sold him a bargain—a goose, that's   105
flat.—
Sir, your pennyworth is good, an your goose be fat.
To sell a bargain well is as cunning as fast and
loose.
Let me see: a fat *l'envoi*—ay, that's a fat goose.   110

ARMADO
Come hither, come hither. How did this argument
begin?

BOY
By saying that a costard was broken in a shin.
Then called you for the *l'envoi*.

117. **ended the market:** perhaps alluding to the proverb "Three women and a goose make a market"

118. **how:** i.e., in what sense

120. **sensibly:** so as to be easily understood (Costard, line 121, responds as if Mote meant "in a manner perceptible to the senses.")

126. **matter:** pus

132. **captivated:** captured

133–34. **purgation:** purgative, laxative (in response to Armado's use of **bound,** one meaning of which is "hard-bound" or "constipated")

135. **set:** convey; **durance:** imprisonment

137. **this significant:** i.e., the letter (literally, something that expresses a meaning)

139. **ward:** protection, safeguard

143. **incony Jew:** apparently a term of affection and admiration, whose more precise meaning is not known

146. **three farthings:** A three-farthing coin (worth three-quarters of a penny) was in use in the late sixteenth century.

COSTARD True, and I for a plantain. Thus came your 115
   argument in. Then the boy's fat *l'envoi*, the goose
   that you bought; and he ended the market.

ARMADO But tell me, how was there a costard broken
   in a shin?

BOY I will tell you sensibly. 120

COSTARD Thou hast no feeling of it, Mote. I will speak
   that *l'envoi*.
      I, Costard, running out, that was safely within,
      Fell over the threshold and broke my shin.

ARMADO We will talk no more of this matter. 125

COSTARD Till there be more matter in the shin.

ARMADO Sirrah Costard, I will enfranchise thee.

COSTARD O, marry me to one Frances! I smell some
   l'envoi, some goose, in this.

ARMADO By my sweet soul, I mean, setting thee at 130
   liberty, enfreedoming thy person. Thou wert im-
   mured, restrained, captivated, bound.

COSTARD True, true; and now you will be my purgation, and let me loose.

ARMADO I give thee thy liberty, set thee from durance, 135
   and, in lieu thereof, impose on thee nothing but
   this: bear this significant to the country maid
   Jaquenetta. (⌈*He gives him a paper.*⌉) There is remuneration (⌈*giving him a coin,*⌉) for the best ward of
   mine honor is rewarding my dependents.—Mote, 140
   follow.   ⌈*He exits.*⌉

BOY Like the sequel, I. Signior Costard, adieu.
                                          He exits.

COSTARD
   My sweet ounce of man's flesh, my incony Jew!
   Now will I look to his remuneration. ⌈*He looks at the*
   coin.⌉ "Remuneration"! O, that's the Latin word for 145
   three farthings. Three farthings—*remuneration.*

147. **inkle:** linen tape

148. **carries it:** wins the contest

149–50. **French crown:** (1) a coin; (2) perhaps, the head or crown of a man bald from syphilis (the "French disease")

150. **out of:** without (using)

151–84. **My . . . And:** See longer note, page 232.

153. **carnation:** flesh-colored

156. **halfpenny farthing:** i.e., the three-farthing coin given him by Armado

160. **good my knave:** i.e., my good fellow

167. **villain:** (1) peasant; (2) scoundrel

Samson carries "the town gates." (1.2.70–72)
From Gabriele Simeoni, *Figure de la Biblia* . . . (c.1577).

74

"What's the price of this inkle?" "One penny." "No,
I'll give you a remuneration." Why, it carries it!
Remuneration. Why, it is a fairer name than "French
crown." I will never buy and sell out of this word. 150

Enter Berowne.

BEROWNE My good knave Costard, exceedingly well
met.

COSTARD Pray you, sir, how much carnation ribbon
may a man buy for a remuneration?

BEROWNE What is a remuneration? 155

COSTARD Marry, sir, halfpenny farthing.

BEROWNE Why then, three farthing worth of silk.

COSTARD I thank your Worship. God be wi' you.
⌜*He begins to exit.*⌝

BEROWNE Stay, slave, I must employ thee.
As thou wilt win my favor, good my knave, 160
Do one thing for me that I shall entreat.

COSTARD When would you have it done, sir?

BEROWNE This afternoon.

COSTARD Well, I will do it, sir. Fare you well.

BEROWNE Thou knowest not what it is. 165

COSTARD I shall know, sir, when I have done it.

BEROWNE Why, villain, thou must know first.

COSTARD I will come to your Worship tomorrow
morning.

BEROWNE It must be done this afternoon. Hark, slave, 170
it is but this:
The Princess comes to hunt here in the park,
And in her train there is a gentle lady.
When tongues speak sweetly, then they name her
name, 175
And Rosaline they call her. Ask for her,
And to her white hand see thou do commend

178. **counsel:** private matter; **guerdon:** reward

183. **in print:** precisely, perfectly

184. **forsooth:** a mild oath; **love's:** Cupid's, the love god's

185. **beadle:** parish constable who punishes petty offenders; **humorous sigh:** i.e., sigh of love-longing

187. **pedant:** schoolmaster; **boy:** i.e., Cupid

188. **Than whom:** i.e., compared to whom is; **magnificent:** arrogantly ambitious

189. **wimpled:** blindfolded; **purblind:** completely blind (See illustration, page 78.)

190. **Signior Junior:** with a pun on senior-junior, or old-young (See longer note, page 232.) **Dan:** i.e., don (master or sir, from the Latin *dominus*)

191. **lord . . . arms:** See the description of the lover in 3.1.17–21 above.

192. **sovereign:** a three-syllable word here

193. **Liege:** i.e., liege-lord

194. **prince . . . codpieces:** i.e., controller of sexual engagements **plackets:** openings in petticoats or skirts; **codpieces:** showy appendages to the front of men's breeches

195. **imperator:** emperor, commander

196. **paritors:** apparitors, officers who summoned accused sexual offenders before the ecclesiastical courts

197. **corporal . . . field:** i.e., a field officer in his army

198. **colors:** regimental flag or standard; **tumbler's hoop:** i.e., acrobat's hoop festooned with bright ribbons or silks

199. **sue:** i.e., am a suitor to a woman

(continued)

This sealed-up counsel. There's thy guerdon. ⌜*He*
　gives him money.⌝ Go.
COSTARD　Gardon. ⌜*He looks at the money.*⌝ O sweet　180
　gardon! Better than remuneration, a 'levenpence
　farthing better! Most sweet gardon. I will do it, sir,
　in print. Gardon! Remuneration!　*He exits.*
BEROWNE
　And I forsooth in love! I that have been love's whip,
　A very beadle to a humorous sigh,　　　　　　　185
　A critic, nay, a nightwatch constable,
　A domineering pedant o'er the boy,
　Than whom no mortal so magnificent.
　This wimpled, whining, purblind, wayward boy,
　This Signior Junior, giant dwarf, Dan Cupid,　　190
　Regent of love rhymes, lord of folded arms,
　Th' anointed sovereign of sighs and groans,
　Liege of all loiterers and malcontents,
　Dread prince of plackets, king of codpieces,
　Sole imperator and great general　　　　　　195
　Of trotting paritors—O my little heart!
　And I to be a corporal of his field
　And wear his colors like a tumbler's hoop!
　What? I love, I sue, I seek a wife?
　A woman, that is like a German ⌜clock,⌝　　　200
　Still a-repairing, ever out of frame,
　And never going aright, being a watch,
　But being watched that it may still go right.
　Nay, to be perjured, which is worst of all.
　And, among three, to love the worst of all,　　205
　A whitely wanton with a velvet brow,
　With two pitch-balls stuck in her face for eyes.
　Ay, and by heaven, one that will do the deed
　Though Argus were her eunuch and her guard.
　And I to sigh for her, to watch for her,　　　210
　To pray for her! Go to. It is a plague

200. **German clock:** i.e., an elaborately constructed clock that broke down easily

201. **Still a-repairing:** i.e., always under repair; **frame:** order

202. **watch:** timepiece, clock face

203. **being watched:** i.e., in need of being watched

206. **whitely:** pale

209. **Argus:** a mythological creature with a hundred eyes (He was charged by Juno, queen of the gods, to keep watch over a woman to prevent Jove, king of the gods, from making love to this woman.)

210. **watch for her:** i.e., lose sleep because of her

211. **Go to:** an expression of impatience and frustration

215. **Joan:** Proverbial: "Joan is as good as my lady in the dark," with **Joan** as a name for a woman of the lower social order.

"This . . . purblind . . . boy, . . . Dan Cupid." (3.1.189–90)
From an anonymous engraving tipped into Jacques Callot,
[*La petite passion*, n.d.].

That Cupid will impose for my neglect
Of his almighty dreadful little might.
Well, I will love, write, sigh, pray, sue, groan.
Some men must love my lady, and some Joan. 215
⌈*He exits.*⌉

LOVE'S LABOR'S LOST

ACT 4

4.1 While hunting, the Princess, her ladies, and Boyet are visited by Costard, who, by mistake, delivers to them Armado's letter to Jaquenetta (rather than Berowne's letter to Rosaline).

---

4. **mounting mind:** wordplay on (1) intention to ascend and (2) ambition
5. **dispatch:** official dismissal given to an ambassador after completion of her mission
6. **Or:** before
9. **Hereby:** i.e., near by; **coppice:** thicket
10. **stand:** standing-place from which a hunter may shoot game; **fairest:** (1) best; (2) most beautiful (the sense that the Princess uses in lines 11–12)

A hobby-horse. (3.1.30–32)
From *The ancient English morris dance* [Anon., n.d.].

⟨ACT 4⟩

⌜Scene 1⌝

Enter the Princess, a Forester, her Ladies, ⌜Boyet⌝ and her ⌜other⌝ Lords.

PRINCESS
 Was that the King that spurred his horse so hard
 Against the steep uprising of the hill?
FORESTER
 I know not, but I think it was not he.
PRINCESS
 Whoe'er he was, he showed a mounting mind.—
 Well, lords, today we shall have our dispatch.   5
 Or Saturday we will return to France.—
 Then, forester, my friend, where is the bush
 That we must stand and play the murderer in?
FORESTER
 Hereby, upon the edge of yonder coppice,
 A stand where you may make the fairest shoot.   10
PRINCESS
 I thank my beauty, I am fair that shoot,
 And thereupon thou speakst "the fairest shoot."
FORESTER
 Pardon me, madam, for I meant not so.
PRINCESS
 What, what? First praise me, and again say no?
 O short-lived pride. Not fair? Alack, for woe!   15

17. **paint:** flatter

19. **good my glass:** i.e., my accurate looking glass, or mirror; **telling true:** i.e., telling the truth

21. **inherit:** possess

22. **merit:** (1) (my) excellence; (2) (my) giving a reward (The phrase **saved by merit** is a playful reference to the Catholic belief that good works were necessary to salvation; Protestants, who believed that faith alone was the way to salvation, regarded the Catholic belief as **heresy** [line 23].)

23. **fair:** i.e., beauty

27. **ill:** evil

28. **credit:** reputation

29. **Not wounding:** i.e., if I fail to hit the deer

32. **out of question:** beyond question, certainly

33. **Glory:** desire for fame, ambition; **detested:** odious

37. **that:** i.e., to which

38. **curst:** shrewish; **self:** same

FORESTER
　Yes, madam, fair.
PRINCESS　　　　　　　Nay, never paint me now.
　Where fair is not, praise cannot mend the brow.
　Here, good my glass, take this for telling true.
　　　　　　　　⌈*She gives him money.*⌉
　Fair payment for foul words is more than due.　　　20
FORESTER
　Nothing but fair is that which you inherit.
PRINCESS
　See, see, my beauty will be saved by merit.
　O heresy in fair, fit for these days!
　A giving hand, though foul, shall have fair praise.
　But come, the bow. ⌈*He hands her a bow.*⌉ Now　　25
　　mercy goes to kill,
　And shooting well is then accounted ill.
　Thus will I save my credit in the shoot:
　Not wounding, pity would not let me do 't;
　If wounding, then it was to show my skill,　　　30
　That more for praise than purpose meant to kill.
　And out of question so it is sometimes:
　Glory grows guilty of detested crimes,
　When for fame's sake, for praise, an outward part,
　We bend to that the working of the heart;　　　35
　As I for praise alone now seek to spill
　The poor deer's blood, that my heart means no ill.
BOYET
　Do not curst wives hold that self sovereignty
　Only for praise' sake when they strive to be
　Lords o'er their lords?　　　　　　　40
PRINCESS
　Only for praise; and praise we may afford
　To any lady that subdues a lord.

　　　　Enter Clown ⌈*Costard.*⌉

44. **God . . . den:** i.e., may God give you good even (i.e., afternoon)

52. **An:** i.e., if; **wit:** intelligence

62. **Break up this capon:** i.e., open this letter **Break up:** carve **capon:** (1) castrated cock; (2) love letter

64. **is mistook:** i.e., has been brought to the wrong person; **importeth:** concerns

67. **the neck . . . wax:** i.e., the letter's wax seal (with a possible play on the **neck** of the **capon**)

73. **illustrate:** i.e., illustrious

73–74. **King Cophetua . . . Zenelophon:** See note to 1.2.108–9.

73–74. **pernicious:** See longer note, page 232.

74. **indubitate:** undoubted, certain

75. **Veni, vidi, vici:** I came, I saw, I conquered (words attributed to Julius Caesar announcing a sudden military victory)

A plantain. (3.1.78)
From John Gerard, *The herball or generall historie of plantes . . .* (1597).

BOYET
Here comes a member of the commonwealth.

COSTARD   God dig-you-den all! Pray you, which is the
head lady?   45

PRINCESS   Thou shalt know her, fellow, by the rest that
have no heads.

COSTARD   Which is the greatest lady, the highest?

PRINCESS   The thickest and the tallest.

COSTARD
The thickest and the tallest: it is so, truth is   50
truth.

An your waist, mistress, were as slender as my wit,
One o' these maids' girdles for your waist should be
fit.

Are not you the chief woman? You are the thickest   55
here.

PRINCESS   What's your will, sir? What's your will?

COSTARD   I have a letter from Monsieur Berowne to
one Lady Rosaline.

PRINCESS
O, thy letter, thy letter! He's a good friend of mine.   60
Stand aside, good bearer.—Boyet, you can carve.
Break up this capon.

BOYET, ⌜*taking the letter*⌝   I am bound to serve.
This letter is mistook; it importeth none here.
It is writ to Jaquenetta.   65

PRINCESS   We will read it, I swear.
Break the neck of the wax, and everyone give ear.

BOYET *reads.   By heaven, that thou art fair is most
infallible, true that thou art beauteous, truth itself
that thou art lovely. More fairer than fair, beautiful*   70
*than beauteous, truer than truth itself, have commiser-
ation on thy heroical vassal. The magnanimous and
most illustrate King Cophetua set eye upon the pernicious and indubitate beggar Zenelophon; and he it
was that might rightly say "Veni, vidi, vici," which to*   75

76. **annothanize:** perhaps, "anatomize"; or, perhaps, "annotate"; or perhaps a combination of these words; **vulgar:** vernacular

77. **videlicet:** namely; **see:** Armado would be more correct to translate **vidi,** the Latin past tense, as "saw." "Came, saw, overcame" had become proverbial and it is the way Shakespeare normally cites the quotation. (See longer note, page 233.)

84. **catastrophe:** denouement, outcome

90. **exchange:** i.e., get in exchange; **Robes:** clothes signifying a person of high office or rank

96. **Nemean lion:** the ferocious lion killed by Hercules as the first of his twelve labors

98. **Submissive fall . . . before:** i.e., fall submissive before his . . . feet

99. **forage:** i.e., foraging, plundering

101. **repasture:** a repast, food

102. **plume of feathers:** i.e., fool; **indited:** composed

103. **vane:** i.e., weather vane, constantly changing with the wind

105. **but I:** i.e., if I do not

106. **Else:** otherwise; **going . . . erewhile:** i.e., since you just read it (with a pun on "stile," a set of steps built over a fence)

107. **keeps:** resides

annothanize in the vulgar (O base and obscure vulgar!) videlicet, "He came, see, and overcame: He
came, one; see, two; overcame, three. Who came? The
King. Why did he come? To see. Why did he see? To
overcome. To whom came he? To the beggar. What 80
saw he? The beggar. Who overcame he? The beggar.
The conclusion is victory. On whose side? The
⌈King's.⌉ The captive is enriched. On whose side? The
beggar's. The catastrophe is a nuptial. On whose side?
The King's—no, on both in one, or one in both. I am 85
the King, for so stands the comparison; thou the
beggar, for so witnesseth thy lowliness. Shall I command thy love? I may. Shall I enforce thy love? I could.
Shall I entreat thy love? I will. What shalt thou
exchange for rags? Robes. For tittles? Titles. For thyself? 90
Me. Thus expecting thy reply, I profane my lips on thy
foot, my eyes on thy picture, and my heart on thy every
part.
    Thine, in the dearest design of industry,
                Don Adriano de Armado. 95
Thus dost thou hear the Nemean lion roar
  'Gainst thee, thou lamb, that standest as his prey.
Submissive fall his princely feet before,
  And he from forage will incline to play.
But if thou strive, poor soul, what art thou then? 100
Food for his rage, repasture for his den.

PRINCESS
What plume of feathers is he that indited this letter?
What vane? What weathercock? Did you ever hear
    better?

BOYET
I am much deceived but I remember the style. 105

PRINCESS
Else your memory is bad, going o'er it erewhile.

BOYET
This Armado is a Spaniard that keeps here in court,

108. **phantasime:** perhaps, fantastic being; **Monarcho:** the title assumed by an insane Italian who lived at Elizabeth's court and represented himself as emperor of the world

108–10. **makes . . . To:** provides entertainment for

120. **mistaken:** i.e., made a mistake with

121. **put up this:** i.e., put this away

121–22. **'twill be thine:** i.e., it will be your turn; or, it will be of use to you

123. **shooter:** archer (with a pun on "suitor")

126. **continent:** container

128. **put off:** dismissed

129. **horns:** i.e., creatures with horns, deer

130. **if horns . . . miscarry:** i.e., if there are then no men with unfaithful wives (Such men, called "cuckolds," are often imaged as wearing horns.)

133. **deer:** with a pun on "dear"

A cuckold. (4.1.130, 5.1.68–70)
From *Bagford ballads* (printed in 1878).

A phantasime, a Monarcho, and one that makes
  sport
To the Prince and his bookmates. 110
PRINCESS, ⌜*to Costard*⌝ Thou, fellow, a word.
  Who gave thee this letter?
COSTARD I told you: my lord.
PRINCESS
  To whom shouldst thou give it?
COSTARD From my lord to my 115
  lady.
PRINCESS From which lord to which lady?
COSTARD
  From my Lord Berowne, a good master of mine,
  To a lady of France that he called Rosaline.
PRINCESS
  Thou hast mistaken his letter. Come, lords, away. 120
  ⌜*To Rosaline.*⌝ Here, sweet, put up this; 'twill be
  thine another day.
                    ⌜*The Princess, Katherine, Lords, and*
                        Forester exit. Boyet, Rosaline, Maria,
                            and Costard remain.⌝

BOYET
  Who is the shooter? Who is the shooter?
ROSALINE Shall I
  teach you to know? 125
BOYET
  Ay, my continent of beauty.
ROSALINE Why, she that bears the bow.
  Finely put off.
BOYET
  My lady goes to kill horns, but if thou marry,
  Hang me by the neck if horns that year miscarry. 130
  Finely put on.
ROSALINE
  Well, then, I am the shooter.
BOYET And who is your deer?

137. **brow:** the site of the cuckold's horns

139. **upon:** against (in a hostile way)

140. **King Pippen:** i.e., King Pepin (d. 768), father of Charlemagne

141. **hit it:** a reference to a popular song (See lines 145–48 for its lyrics.)

143. **Guinover:** i.e., Guinevere, queen to King Arthur, a perhaps legendary, perhaps historical, sixth-century king (See below.)

149. **did fit it:** harmonized

150. **mark:** target; **marvelous well shot:** i.e., hit with great accuracy

152. **mark but:** only take notice of

154. **prick:** bull's-eye (with a possible pun on "penis"); **mete:** aim

156. **o' the bow hand:** i.e., of the mark; **out:** (1) inaccurate; (2) out of practice

158. **clout:** target

King Arthur.
From [Sir Thomas Malory,] *The most ancient and famous history of . . . Arthur King of Britaine . . .* (1634).

ROSALINE
　If we choose by the horns, yourself come not near.
　Finely put on, indeed.　　　　　　　　　　　　　　135
MARIA
　You still wrangle with her, Boyet, and she strikes at
　　the brow.
BOYET
　But she herself is hit lower. Have I hit her now?
ROSALINE　Shall I come upon thee with an old saying,
　　that was a man when King Pippen of France was a　140
　　little boy, as touching the hit it?
BOYET　So I may answer thee with one as old, that was a
　　woman when Queen Guinover of Britain was a little
　　wench, as touching the hit it.
ROSALINE ⌜*sings*⌝
　　　　Thou canst not hit it, hit it, hit it,　　　　　145
　　　　　Thou canst not hit it, my good man.
BOYET ⌜*sings*⌝
　　　　　　An I cannot, cannot, cannot,
　　　　　　An I cannot, another can.
　　　　　　　　　　⌜*Rosaline*⌝ *exits.*
COSTARD
　By my troth, most pleasant. How both did fit it!
MARIA
　A mark marvelous well shot, for they both did hit　150
　　⌜it.⌝
BOYET
　A mark! O, mark but that mark. "A mark," says my
　　lady.
　Let the mark have a prick in 't to mete at, if it may
　　be.　　　　　　　　　　　　　　　　　　　155
MARIA
　Wide o' the bow hand! I' faith, your hand is out.
COSTARD
　Indeed, he must shoot nearer, or he'll ne'er hit the
　　clout.

159. **belike:** probably

160. **upshoot:** (1) upshot; (2) the best shot yet; **cleaving the pin:** splitting the peg in the center of the target

161. **greasily:** indecently

162. **pricks:** targets (See note to line 154.)

164. **rubbing:** In lawn bowling, the ball is said to "rub" when it strikes an impediment. (See page 216.)

165. **swain:** country bumpkin; **clown:** peasant

168. **incony:** See note to 3.1.143.

172. **Armado:** This sudden reference to Armado and to **his page** (line 176) is very puzzling.

176. **o' t' other:** i.e., on the other

177. **it:** i.e., the page Mote; **pathetical nit:** i.e., engaging little creature **nit:** gnat, small fly

177 SD. **within:** i.e., offstage

178. **Sola:** a cry that accompanied the blowing of horns in a hunt

4.2 The Pedant Holofernes, the Curate Nathaniel, and Constable Dull discuss the deer shot by the Princess. Costard and Jaquenetta enter with the letter from Berowne to Rosaline and are told to deliver it to the king.

———

0 SD. **Holofernes:** the name of the general slain by Judith in the Book of Judith, an apocryphal book of the Bible; **Pedant:** schoolmaster (See page 166.)

1. **reverend:** i.e., reverence-inspiring

1–2. **in the testimony:** with the approval

2. **testimony . . . conscience:** Nathaniel here loosely quotes 2 Corinthians 1.12.

BOYET, ⌜*to Maria*⌝
An if my hand be out, then belike your hand is in.
COSTARD
Then will she get the upshoot by cleaving the ⌜pin.⌝ 160
MARIA
Come, come, you talk greasily. Your lips grow foul.
COSTARD, ⌜*to Boyet*⌝
She's too hard for you at pricks, sir. Challenge her
to bowl.
BOYET
I fear too much rubbing. Good night, my good owl.
⌜*Boyet and Maria exit.*⌝
COSTARD
By my soul, a swain, a most simple clown. 165
Lord, Lord, how the ladies and I have put him
down.
O' my troth, most sweet jests, most incony vulgar
wit,
When it comes so smoothly off, so obscenely, as it 170
were, so fit.
Armado ⌜o' th' one⌝ side, O, a most dainty man!
To see him walk before a lady and to bear her fan.
To see him kiss his hand, and how most sweetly he
will swear. 175
And his page o' t' other side, that handful of wit!
Ah heavens, it is ⌜a⌝ most pathetical nit.
⌜*Shout* within.⌝
Sola, sola!
⌜*He exits.*⌝

⌜Scene 2⌝
Enter Dull ⌜*the Constable,*⌝ *Holofernes the Pedant, and*
Nathaniel ⌜*the Curate.*⌝

NATHANIEL   Very reverend sport, truly, and done in the
testimony of a good conscience.

3–4. **sanguis, in blood:** in full vigor (The speeches of Holofernes, a schoolmaster or pedant, are littered with Latin tags like **sanguis**, which he translates himself as **in blood.** See longer note, p. 234.)

4. **pomewater:** a large juicy apple (See page 170.)

6. **anon:** soon; **crab:** crab apple (See page 218.)

8. **epithets:** terms

9. **at the least:** i.e., to say the least

10. **of . . . head:** in its fifth year, when it grows its first full set of antlers

11. **Sir:** a proper form of address to a priest; **haud credo:** I cannot believe it (i.e., you're wrong)

12. **haud credo:** Dull seems to hear this Latin phrase as the English words "old gray doe." **pricket:** buck in its second year

13. **intimation:** i.e., pronouncement (See longer note, page 235.)

14. **insinuation:** (1) introduction; (2) indirect suggestion (See longer note to 4.2.13, page 235.)

15. **facere:** to make (Latin); **replication:** reply

16. **undressed:** inelegant

18. **unconfirmed:** uninstructed, ignorant

19. **insert . . . deer:** i.e., insert my Latin phrase (**haud credo**) back into our conversation as the name of a deer

22. **Twice-sod:** twice boiled (which is also the meaning of the Latin **bis coctus**)

27. **eat:** i.e., eaten

28. **replenished:** completed, perfected (by learning)

29. **sensible:** sensitive, aware

32. **Which:** i.e., as

33. **fructify:** bear fruit; **he:** i.e., in him

(continued)

96

HOLOFERNES   The deer was, as you know, *sanguis*, in
  blood, ripe as the pomewater, who now hangeth
  like a jewel in the ear of *caelo*, the sky, the welkin,   5
  the heaven, and anon falleth like a crab on the face
  of *terra*, the soil, the land, the earth.
NATHANIEL   Truly, Master Holofernes, the epithets are
  sweetly varied, like a scholar at the least. But, sir, I
  assure you, it was a buck of the first head.   10
HOLOFERNES   Sir Nathaniel, *haud credo*.
DULL   'Twas not a *haud credo*, 'twas a pricket.
HOLOFERNES   Most barbarous intimation! Yet a kind of
  insinuation, as it were, *in via*, in way, of explication;
  facere, as it were, replication, or rather, *ostentare*, to   15
  show, as it were, his inclination, after his undressed,
  unpolished, uneducated, unpruned, untrained, or
  rather unlettered, or ratherest, unconfirmed fash-
  ion, to insert again my *haud credo* for a deer.
DULL   I said the deer was not a *haud credo*, 'twas a   20
  pricket.
HOLOFERNES   Twice-sod simplicity, *bis coctus!*
  O thou monster ignorance, how deformed dost thou
    look!
NATHANIEL
  Sir, he hath never fed of the dainties that are bred   25
    in a book.
  He hath not eat paper, as it were; he hath not drunk
    ink. His intellect is not replenished. He is only an
    animal, only sensible in the duller parts.
  And such barren plants are set before us that we   30
    thankful should be—
  Which we ⌜of⌝ taste and feeling are—for those parts
    that do fructify in us more than he.
  For as it would ill become me to be vain, indiscreet,
    or a fool,   35
  So were there a patch set on learning, to see him in
    a school.

36. **patch . . . learning:** (1) fool made to attend classes; (2) spot or blemish set on scholarship

38. **omne bene:** all's well (Latin); **father's:** perhaps, (1) Church Father's; (2) old man's

41. **at Cain's birth:** i.e., in the time of Adam and Eve, the first humans in biblical history and Cain's parents

43. **Dictynna:** i.e., the moon (**Dictynna** is one name for the goddess of the moon, also called **Phoebe** and **Luna.** See page 114.); **goodman:** a title denoting a low social rank

45. **dictima:** a nonsense word

47–48. **was no more:** i.e., was no more than a month old

49. **raught:** reached

51. **allusion:** wordplay; **the exchange:** i.e., of Adam's name for Cain's

52. **collusion:** trickery (Dull's accusations about **collusion** and **pollution** [line 56] seem accurate.)

54. **comfort . . . capacity:** i.e., help your ability to understand

59–60. **extemporal:** extemporaneous

63. **Perge:** go on (Latin)

64. **abrogate:** do away with

65. **something . . . letter:** i.e., use some alliteration

66. **argues facility:** demonstrates an easy mastery (of language)

67. **preyful:** inclined to prey

69. **sore:** buck in its fourth year

69–70. **made sore:** i.e., wounded

But *omne bene*, say I, being of an old father's mind:
Many can brook the weather that love not the wind.

DULL
You two are bookmen. Can you tell me by your wit 40
What was a month old at Cain's birth that's not
five weeks old as yet?

HOLOFERNES Dictynna, goodman Dull, Dictynna,
goodman Dull.

DULL What is "dictima"? 45

NATHANIEL
A title to Phoebe, to Luna, to the moon.

HOLOFERNES
The moon was a month old when Adam was no
more.
And raught not to five weeks when he came to
fivescore. 50
Th' allusion holds in the exchange.

DULL 'Tis true indeed. The collusion holds in the
exchange.

HOLOFERNES God comfort thy capacity! I say, th' allusion holds in the exchange. 55

DULL And I say the pollution holds in the exchange, for
the moon is never but a month old. And I say besides
that, 'twas a pricket that the Princess killed.

HOLOFERNES Sir Nathaniel, will you hear an extemporal epitaph on the death of the deer? And, to humor 60
the ⌈ignorant, call I⌉ the deer the Princess killed a
pricket.

NATHANIEL *Perge*, good Master Holofernes, *perge*, so it
shall please you to abrogate scurrility.

HOLOFERNES I will something affect the letter, for it 65
argues facility.
The preyful princess pierced and pricked
a pretty pleasing pricket,
Some say a sore, but not a sore till now made
sore with shooting. 70

71. **sorel:** a buck in its third year

73. **Or . . . or:** either a wounded pricket, or

75. **If sore be sore:** i.e., if the deer is wounded; **L:** the roman numeral for fifty

80. **talent . . . claw: Talent** was a spelling of "talon."

80–81. **how he claws him:** i.e., how Nathaniel flatters, or fawns upon Holofernes

82 SP. **HOLOFERNES:** See longer note, page 235.

84–85. **motions:** impulses, stirrings of the soul

85. **revolutions:** considerations, reflections; **ventricle:** (1) belly; (2) one of the brain's cavities

86. **pia mater:** membrane enveloping the brain

92–93. **profit . . . you:** The obscene implication of these lines is repeated with a variation in lines 96–97.

95. **Mehercle:** perhaps, an oath "by Hercules" (the Greek mythological hero); **ingenious:** intelligent

96. **want:** lack

97–98. **Vir . . . loquitur:** A man is wise who says little (Latin). **sapis:** i.e., *sapit* (See longer note to 4.2.3–4, page 234.)

100. **Person:** Jaquenetta's pronunciation of "parson"

101. **quasi:** that is (Latin); **pierce:** This would seem to have been pronounced "purse."

103–4. **likeliest to:** i.e., most like

The dogs did yell. Put "l" to "sore," then sorel
  jumps from thicket,
  Or pricket sore, or else sorel. The people fall
  a-hooting.
If sore be sore, then "L" to "sore" makes fifty   75
  sores o' sorel.
Of one sore I an hundred make by adding but one
  more "L."

NATHANIEL A rare talent.

DULL, ⌜*aside*⌝ If a talent be a claw, look how he claws   80
  him with a talent.

⌜HOLOFERNES⌝ This is a gift that I have, simple, simple—a foolish extravagant spirit, full of forms,
  figures, shapes, objects, ideas, apprehensions, motions, revolutions. These are begot in the ventricle   85
  of memory, nourished in the womb of ⌜*pia mater*,⌝
  and delivered upon the mellowing of occasion. But
  the gift is good in those ⟨in⟩ whom it is acute, and I
  am thankful for it.

⌜NATHANIEL⌝ Sir, I praise the Lord for you, and so may   90
  my parishioners, for their sons are well tutored by
  you, and their daughters profit very greatly under
  you. You are a good member of the commonwealth.

⌜HOLOFERNES⌝ *Mehercle*, if their sons be ⌜ingenious,⌝   95
  they shall want no instruction; if their daughters be
  capable, I will put it to them. But *Vir sapis qui pauca
  loquitur.* A soul feminine saluteth us.

  Enter Jaquenetta and the Clown ⌜*Costard.*⌝

JAQUENETTA, ⌜*to Nathaniel*⌝ God give you good mor-
  row, Master Person.   100

⌜HOLOFERNES⌝ Master Person, *quasi* ⌜pierce one.⌝ And
  if one should be pierced, which is the one?

COSTARD Marry, Master Schoolmaster, he that is likeliest to a hogshead.

105. **hogshead:** (1) barrel (of beer or liquor); (2) blockhead (See page 172.)

105-6. **luster of conceit:** splendor of imagination

106. **turf:** clod; **fire . . . flint:** Proverbial: "In the coldest flint there is hot fire."

107. **pearl . . . swine:** Proverbial: "Cast not pearls before swine."

109. **as:** i.e., as to

112-13. **Facile . . . Ruminat:** "Easily, I pray, since you are making a mess of everything in the cool shade. It ruminates. . . ." These lines are a corrupt version of lines by **Mantuan** widely used for Latin instruction in Shakespeare's time. See longer note, page 236.

116-17. **Venetia . . . pretia:** An Italian proverb: "Venice, he that does not see thee does not praise thee."

119. **Ut:** do (in the musical scale "do, re, mi . . .")

121. **Horace:** classical Roman poet

124. **staff, verse:** synonyms for **stanza**

125. **Lege, domine:** read, sir (Latin)

126-43. **If . . . tongue:** See longer note, page 236.

126. **forsworn:** i.e., an oath-breaker

129. **oaks:** i.e., strong trees that bend to no wind; **osiers:** willows (which are flexible) See page 184.

131. **Study . . . leaves:** (1) study departs from its bent or tendency; (2) the student abandons his favorite book(s)

132. **art:** learning

134. **mark:** goal

⌐HOLOFERNES⌐ Of piercing a hogshead! A good luster   105
of conceit in a turf of earth; fire enough for a flint,
pearl enough for a swine. 'Tis pretty, it is well.
JAQUENETTA, ⌐*to Nathaniel*⌐ Good Master Parson, be so
good as read me this letter. It was given me by
Costard, and sent me from Don Armado. I beseech   110
you, read it.
⌐*She hands Nathaniel a paper, which he looks at.*⌐
⌐HOLOFERNES⌐
Facile precor gelida quando peccas omnia sub umbra.
Ruminat—
and so forth. Ah, good old Mantuan! I may speak of
thee as the traveler doth of Venice: 115
Venetia, Venetia,
Chi non ti vede, non ti pretia.
Old Mantuan, old Mantuan! Who understandeth
thee not, loves thee not. (⌐*He sings.*⌐) Ut, re, sol, la,
mi, fa. (⌐*To Nathaniel.*⌐)Under pardon, sir, what are   120
the contents? Or rather, as Horace says in his—
(⌐*Looking at the letter*⌐) What, my soul, verses?
⌐NATHANIEL⌐ Ay, sir, and very learned.
⌐HOLOFERNES⌐ Let me hear a staff, a stanza, a verse,
Lege, domine.   125
⌐NATHANIEL, *reads*⌐
If love make me forsworn, how shall I swear to love?
Ah, never faith could hold, if not to beauty vowed!
Though to myself forsworn, to thee I'll faithful prove.
Those thoughts to me were oaks, to thee like osiers
bowed.   130
Study his bias leaves and makes his book thine eyes,
Where all those pleasures live that art would
comprehend.
If knowledge be the mark, to know thee shall suffice.
Well-learnèd is that tongue that well can thee   135
commend.

138. **that I:** because I; **parts:** personal qualities

139. **Jove's lightning:** the lightning bolts thrown by the king of the Roman gods (See page 168.)

144. **find . . . apostrophus:** i.e., ignore the marks of elision **apostrophus:** apostrophe (See longer note, page 237.)

145. **supervise:** look over; **canzonet:** literally, a little song

146. **numbers ratified:** i.e., metrically correct verses

148. **caret:** it is omitted (Latin); **Ovidius Naso:** Ovid, the great Roman poet, whose family name **Naso** means "nose"

150. **fancy:** imagination; **jerks:** flashes; **Imitari:** to imitate

152. **damosella:** damsel (See page 174.)

154–55. **one . . . lords:** Actually, Berowne is one of the king's lords. **strange:** foreign

156. **overglance:** i.e., look at; **superscript:** superscription, or what is written above the poem

158. **intellect:** "Meaning" or "purport" is the sense that this word bore in Shakespeare's time, but the context of its use here suggests that Holofernes pedantically bends the word to mean "signature."

159. **nomination:** name

160–61. **all . . . employment:** i.e., whatever task you would like to set for me

162. **votaries:** those bound by a special vow

163. **sequent:** follower

165. **progression:** going forward, advance

166. **Trip and go:** These are words from a song in a morris dance.

(continued)

All ignorant that soul that sees thee without wonder;
  Which is to me some praise that I thy parts admire.
Thy eye Jove's lightning bears, thy voice his dreadful
      thunder, 140
  Which, not to anger bent, is music and sweet fire.
Celestial as thou art, O, pardon love this wrong,
That sings heaven's praise with such an earthly tongue.

HOLOFERNES You find not the apostrophus, and so
miss the accent. Let me supervise the ⌈canzonet.⌉ 145
⌈*He takes the paper.*⌉ Here are only numbers ratified,
but, for the elegancy, facility, and golden cadence of
poesy—*caret*. Ovidius Naso was the man. And why
indeed "Naso," but for smelling out the odoriferous
flowers of fancy, the jerks of invention? *Imitari* is 150
nothing: so doth the hound his master, the ape his
keeper, the tired horse his rider.—But damosella
virgin, was this directed to you?

JAQUENETTA Ay, sir, from one Monsieur Berowne, one
of the strange queen's lords. 155

⌈HOLOFERNES⌉ I will overglance the superscript: *"To
the snow-white hand of the most beauteous Lady
Rosaline."* I will look again on the intellect of the
letter for the nomination of the party ⌈writing⌉ to
the person written unto: *"Your Ladyship's in all* 160
desired employment, Berowne." Sir ⌈Nathaniel,⌉ this
Berowne is one of the votaries with the King, and
here he hath framed a letter to a sequent of the
stranger queen's: which accidentally, or by the way
of progression, hath miscarried. ⌈*To Jaquenetta.*⌉ 165
Trip and go, my sweet. Deliver this paper into the
royal hand of the King. It may concern much. Stay
not thy compliment. I forgive thy duty. Adieu.

JAQUENETTA Good Costard, go with me.—Sir, God
save your life. 170

COSTARD Have with thee, my girl.
                    ⌈*Costard and Jaquenetta*⌉ *exit.*

167. **concern much:** be of much consequence

167–68. **Stay . . . compliment:** i.e., do not stay to take formal leave of me

168. **forgive:** i.e., excuse you from observing

171. **Have:** i.e., I'll come along

173. **Father:** i.e., Father of the Church

175. **colorable colors:** specious pretexts (Holofernes plays with the proverb "I fear no colors," in which **colors** means battle flags or standards.)

177. **Marvelous:** i.e., marvelously; **for the pen:** i.e., as far as the penmanship was concerned

182. **undertake:** ensure; **ben venuto:** welcome (Italian)

185. **society:** company, fellowship

186–87. **the text:** a reference to some unidentified authority

188. **certes:** certainly

190. **Pauca verba:** few words (Latin) (Proverbial: "Few words are best."); **gentles:** nobles

191. **game:** (1) fun; (2) quarry, prey; **recreation:** (1) refreshment; (2) amusement

4.3 One after the other, the King and his lords enter and confess they are in love. Each, after he confesses, hides and eavesdrops on the next to enter. Then one after the other, they come forward and berate those they have overheard. After Berowne gives them a way of explaining away their perjury, the lords set off to entertain the ladies in the hope of winning their affections.

---

2. **coursing:** (1) chasing, hunting; (2) thrashing, drubbing; **pitched a toil:** i.e., set a trap for game

(continued)

⌈NATHANIEL⌉ Sir, you have done this in the fear of God
very religiously; and, as a certain Father saith—

HOLOFERNES Sir, tell not me of the Father. I do fear
colorable colors. But to return to the verses: did 175
they please you, Sir Nathaniel?

NATHANIEL Marvelous well for the pen.

HOLOFERNES I do dine today at the father's of a certain
pupil of mine, where if, before repast, it shall
please you to gratify the table with a grace, I will, 180
on my privilege I have with the parents of the
foresaid child or pupil, undertake your *ben venuto;*
where I will prove those verses to be very un-
learned, neither savoring of poetry, wit, nor invention. I beseech your society. 185

NATHANIEL And thank you too; for society, saith the
text, is the happiness of life.

HOLOFERNES And certes the text most infallibly concludes it. ⌈*To Dull.*⌉ Sir, I do invite you too. You shall
not say me nay. *Pauca verba.* Away! The gentles are 190
at their game, and we will to our recreation.

They exit.

⌈Scene 3⌉

Enter Berowne with a paper in his hand, alone.

BEROWNE The King, he is hunting the deer; I am
coursing myself. They have pitched a toil; I am
toiling in a pitch—pitch that defiles. Defile! A foul
word. Well, "set thee down, sorrow"; for so they
say the fool said, and so say I, and I the fool. Well 5
proved, wit. By the Lord, this love is as mad as Ajax.
It kills sheep, it kills me, I a sheep. Well proved
again, o' my side. I will not love. If I do, hang me. I'
faith, I will not. O, but her eye! By this light, but for
her eye I would not love her; yes, for her two eyes. 10

3. **toiling:** struggling; **a pitch:** a net used for trapping fish, with a pun on **pitch** as boiled-down tar; **pitch that defiles:** Proverbial: "He that touches pitch shall be defiled."

6. **as . . . Ajax:** proverbial

7. **It kills sheep:** When the Greek warrior Ajax went mad, he attacked sheep under the delusion that they were the enemy.

9. **By this light:** a mild oath; **but for:** i.e., were it not for

11–12. **lie in my throat:** i.e., am a complete liar

18. **if . . . in:** i.e., if only the other three were in love (or, in my dilemma)

19 SD. **He stands aside:** Later dialogue suggests that Berowne may here climb to a spot from which he looks down on the other characters. See lines 80–81.

22. **birdbolt:** blunt arrow (To be shot with Cupid's arrow is to fall in love.)

23. **under . . . pap:** i.e., in the heart; **In faith:** a mild oath

27. **night of dew:** perhaps, tears that I shed at night

37. **glasses:** looking glasses, mirrors

41. **shade:** partially conceal

Well, I do nothing in the world but lie, and lie in my
throat. By heaven, I do love, and it hath taught me to
rhyme, and to be melancholy. And here is part of my
rhyme, and here my melancholy. Well, she hath one
o' my sonnets already. The clown bore it, the fool   15
sent it, and the lady hath it. Sweet clown, sweeter
fool, sweetest lady. By the world, I would not care a
pin, if the other three were in. Here comes one with
a paper. God give him grace to groan.

He stands aside.

The King entereth ⌐with a paper.⌐

KING   Ay me!   20
BEROWNE, ⌐*aside*⌐ Shot, by heaven! Proceed, sweet
  Cupid. Thou hast thumped him with thy birdbolt
  under the left pap. In faith, secrets!
KING ⌐*reads*⌐
  So sweet a kiss the golden sun gives not
    To those fresh morning drops upon the rose   25
  As thy eyebeams, when their fresh rays have smote
    The night of dew that on my cheeks down flows.
  Nor shines the silver moon one-half so bright
    Through the transparent bosom of the deep
  As doth thy face, through tears of mine, give light.   30
    Thou shin'st in every tear that I do weep.
  No drop but as a coach doth carry thee;
    So ridest thou triumphing in my woe.
  Do but behold the tears that swell in me,
    And they thy glory through my grief will show.   35
  But do not love thyself; then thou ⟨wilt⟩ keep
  My tears for glasses, and still make me weep.
  O queen of queens, how far dost thou excel
  No thought can think, nor tongue of mortal tell.

How shall she know my griefs? I'll drop the paper.   40
Sweet leaves, shade folly. Who is he comes here?

43. **in thy likeness:** i.e., in the same form as the king

45. **perjure ... papers:** i.e., perjurer wearing a paper on his back or his head describing his offense (Longaville may come in with a poem stuck in his cap.)

50–52. **Thou makest ... Tyburn:** Berowne here suggests images in which Longaville completes a familiar threesome. **triumviry:** triumvirate **corner-cap:** three-cornered cap (This cap, worn by clergy and academics, could also have four corners.) **society:** fellowship **shape ... Tyburn:** Tyburn, a place of execution in London, had a triangular-shaped gallows. (See page 116.)

52. **hangs up:** hangs; **simplicity:** foolishness

53. **stubborn:** stiff; **move:** stir emotion

55. **numbers:** verses

56. **guards:** ornaments, trimmings

57. **shop:** perhaps a reference to the ornamental codpiece worn on men's **hose** (See note to 3.1.194.)

60. **whom:** i.e., which

62. **broke:** i.e., broken

63. **forswore:** renounced

Enter Longaville, ⌜with papers.⌝ The King steps aside.

What, Longaville, and reading! Listen, ear.
BEROWNE, ⌜*aside*⌝
Now, in thy likeness, one more fool appear!
LONGAVILLE   Ay me! I am forsworn.
BEROWNE, ⌜*aside*⌝
Why, he comes in like a perjure, wearing papers!   45
⌜KING, *aside*⌝
In love, I hope! Sweet fellowship in shame.
BEROWNE, ⌜*aside*⌝
One drunkard loves another of the name.
LONGAVILLE
Am I the first that have been perjured so?
BEROWNE, ⌜*aside*⌝
I could put thee in comfort: not by two that I know.
Thou makest the triumviry, the corner-cap of   50
    society,
The shape of love's Tyburn, that hangs up simplicity.
LONGAVILLE
I fear these stubborn lines lack power to move.
⌜*Reads.*⌝ *O sweet Maria, empress of my love*—
These numbers will I tear and write in prose.   55
                    ⌜*He tears the paper.*⌝
BEROWNE, ⌜*aside*⌝
O, rhymes are guards on wanton Cupid's hose.
Disfigure not his shop!
LONGAVILLE, ⌜*taking another paper*⌝ This same shall go.
    (*He reads the sonnet.*)
    Did not the heavenly rhetoric of thine eye,
       'Gainst whom the world cannot hold argument,   60
    Persuade my heart to this false perjury?
       Vows for thee broke deserve not punishment.
    A woman I forswore, but I will prove,
       Thou being a goddess, I forswore not thee.
    My vow was earthly, thou a heavenly love.   65

66. **grace:** favor, goodwill

67. **Vows . . . is:** Proverbial: "Words are but wind."

70. **Exhal'st:** draw up

72–73. **fool . . . paradise:** perhaps wordplay by Shakespeare, at Longaville's expense, on the proverb "To bring one into a fool's paradise" **To:** i.e., as to

74. **liver:** The liver was thought to be the seat of violent passion. **vein:** style

75. **green goose:** i.e., a young girl (See note to 1.1.99.)

76–77. **much out . . . way:** perhaps, far gone

79. **All . . . play:** **All hid** is the cry of children playing the game (**infant play**) of hide-and-seek.

80. **Like . . . sky:** See note to 4.3.19 SD.

81. **o'ereye:** watch

82. **More . . . mill:** proverbial

83. **woodcocks:** birds easily snared and therefore thought to be foolish

85. **coxcomb:** fool (literally, a fool's cap)

87. **corporal:** (1) perhaps a reference to Dumaine as a corporal in Cupid's army (as Berowne uses the term at 3.1.197); (2) perhaps a pun on "corporeal" and a reference to how Katherine is just flesh and blood

88. **Her . . . quoted:** The amber of her hair makes amber itself seem ugly. **quoted:** regarded as

89. **raven:** black-plumed fowl (punning on the word **foul**, line 88)

Thy grace being gained cures all disgrace in me.
Vows are but breath, and breath a vapor is.
  Then thou, fair sun, which on my earth dost
    shine,
Exhal'st this vapor-vow; in thee it is.   70
  If broken, then, it is no fault of mine.
  If by me broke, what fool is not so wise
To lose an oath to win a paradise?

BEROWNE, ⌜*aside*⌝
  This is the liver vein, which makes flesh a deity,
  A green goose a goddess. Pure, pure ⟨idolatry.⟩   75
  God amend us, God amend. We are much out o' th'
    way.

LONGAVILLE
  By whom shall I send this?—Company? Stay.
                            ⌜*He steps aside.*⌝

Enter Dumaine, ⌜*with a paper.*⌝

BEROWNE, ⌜*aside*⌝
  All hid, all hid—an old infant play.
  Like a demigod here sit I in the sky,   80
  And wretched fools' secrets heedfully o'ereye.
  More sacks to the mill. O heavens, I have my wish.
  Dumaine transformed! Four woodcocks in a dish.

DUMAINE O most divine Kate!

BEROWNE, ⌜*aside*⌝ O most profane coxcomb!   85

DUMAINE
  By heaven, the wonder in a mortal eye!

BEROWNE, ⌜*aside*⌝
  By earth, she is not, corporal. There you lie.

DUMAINE
  Her amber hairs for foul hath amber quoted.

BEROWNE, ⌜*aside*⌝
  An amber-colored raven was well noted.

DUMAINE
  As upright as the cedar.   90

91. Stoop: perhaps, "bend down," or "come back to earth"

92. with child: pregnant (i.e., swollen, humped)

99. a fever: i.e., like a fever

101. incision: i.e., letting blood, which was then a medicinal remedy for a fever

102. saucers: i.e., saucerfuls (To advertise their services, barber-surgeons displayed saucers of blood taken from patients.); **misprision:** mistaking one word for another

104. vary wit: alter intelligence

107. passing: surpassingly

108. wanton: (1) lewd; (2) playful

110. can: did (an archaic verb)

111. That: so that

Luna, or Phoebe, the moon goddess. (4.2.46)
From Johann Engel, *Astrolabium* [1488].

BEROWNE, ⌜*aside*⌝   Stoop, I say.
  Her shoulder is with child.
DUMAINE   As fair as day.
BEROWNE, ⌜*aside*⌝
  Ay, as some days, but then no sun must shine.
DUMAINE
  O, that I had my wish!   95
LONGAVILLE, ⌜*aside*⌝   And I had mine!
KING, ⌜*aside*⌝
  And mine too, good Lord!
BEROWNE, ⌜*aside*⌝
  Amen, so I had mine. Is not that a good word?
DUMAINE
  I would forget her, but a fever she
  Reigns in my blood, and will remembered be.   100
BEROWNE, ⌜*aside*⌝
  A fever in your blood? Why, then incision
  Would let her out in saucers! Sweet misprision.
DUMAINE
  Once more I'll read the ode that I have writ.
BEROWNE, ⌜*aside*⌝
  Once more I'll mark how love can vary wit.
DUMAINE *reads his sonnet.*
          On a day—alack the day!—   105
          Love, whose month is ever May,
          Spied a blossom passing fair,
          Playing in the wanton air.
          Through the velvet leaves the wind,
          All unseen, can passage find;   110
          That the lover, sick to death,
          ⌜*Wished*⌝ *himself the heaven's breath.*
          "Air," quoth he, "thy cheeks may blow.
          Air, would I might triumph so!"
          But, alack, my hand is sworn   115
          Ne'er to pluck thee from thy ⌜*thorn.*⌝

117. **unmeet:** unfitting, inappropriate

122. **Juno:** wife of **Jove** and queen of the Roman gods; **an Ethiope:** i.e., dark-skinned (See longer note on **fair** [4.3.273], page 237.)

123. **himself for:** i.e., that he was

126. **fasting pain:** i.e., suffering caused by not eating (Loss of appetite conventionally accompanies unrequited love.)

128. **Ill:** evil; **example:** justify by precedent

129. **perjured note:** stigma or reproach of perjury (See the note to 4.3.45 above.)

131. **charity:** i.e., Christian, selfless love

132. **That:** i.e., you who; **society:** fellowship

140. **wreathèd arms:** See 3.1.18–19 and notes.

142. **closely:** secretly

144. **fashion:** behavior, demeanor

145. **reek:** rise, emanate

"Love's Tyburn." (4.3.52, 5.2.12)
From Georgius Camerarius, *Emblemata amatoria* . . . (1627).

> *Vow, alack, for youth unmeet,*
> *Youth so apt to pluck a sweet.*
> *Do not call it sin in me*
> *That I am forsworn for thee—* 120
> *Thou for whom Jove would swear*
> *Juno but an Ethiope were,*
> *And deny himself for Jove,*
> *Turning mortal for thy love.*

This will I send, and something else more plain 125
That shall express my true love's fasting pain.
O, would the King, Berowne, and Longaville
Were lovers too! Ill to example ill
Would from my forehead wipe a perjured note,
For none offend where all alike do dote. 130

LONGAVILLE, ⌜*coming forward*⌝
Dumaine, thy love is far from charity,
That in love's grief desir'st society.
You may look pale, but I should blush, I know,
To be o'er-heard and taken napping so.

KING, ⌜*coming forward*⌝
⌜*To Longaville.*⌝ Come, sir, you blush! As his, your 135
      case is such.
You chide at him, offending twice as much.
You do not love Maria? Longaville
Did never sonnet for her sake compile,
Nor never lay his wreathèd arms athwart 140
His loving bosom to keep down his heart?
I have been closely shrouded in this bush
And marked you both, and for you both did blush.
I heard your guilty rhymes, observed your fashion,
Saw sighs reek from you, noted well your passion. 145
"Ay, me!" says one. "O Jove!" the other cries.
One, her hairs were gold, crystal the other's eyes.
⌜*To Longaville.*⌝ You would for paradise break faith
      and troth,

152. **when that;** i.e., when

157. **by:** i.e., of, concerning

158. **Now . . . hypocrisy:** i.e., now I will assume the role of the satirist (Often the title pages of printed books of satires depicted the satirist as a satyr with a whip.)

162. **coaches:** See 4.3.32.

165. **like of sonneting:** derive pleasure from writing poetry

167. **o'ershot:** i.e., outshot, defeated

168–70. **You . . . three:** An allusion to Matthew 7.3–5: " . . . first cast out the beam out of thine own eye, and then shalt thou see clearly to cast out the mote out of thy brother's eye." (See the similar passage at Luke 6.41–42.)

172. **teen:** grief, suffering

175. **gig:** top (See illustration, page 152.)

176. **profound:** having great insight or knowledge; **Solomon:** biblical king famous for his wisdom; **tune:** sing; **jig:** a lively mocking song; or a song-and-dance act

177. **Nestor:** wise old Greek councillor during the Trojan War; **pushpin:** a children's game

178. **critic:** carping, censorious; **Timon:** famous misanthrope of classical times; **idle toys:** foolish trifles

184. **betrayed:** exposed

⌐*To Dumaine.*¬ And Jove, for your love, would   150
    infringe an oath.
What will Berowne say when that he shall hear
Faith infringed, which such zeal did swear?
How will he scorn, how will he spend his wit!
How will he triumph, leap, and laugh at it!   155
For all the wealth that ever I did see,
I would not have him know so much by me.
BEROWNE, ⌐*coming forward*¬
Now step I forth to whip hypocrisy.
Ah, good my liege, I pray thee pardon me.
Good heart, what grace hast thou thus to reprove   160
These worms for loving, that art most in love?
Your eyes do make no ⌐coaches;¬ in your tears
There is no certain princess that appears.
You'll not be perjured, 'tis a hateful thing!
Tush, none but minstrels like of sonneting!   165
But are you not ashamed? Nay, are you not,
All three of you, to be thus much o'ershot?
⌐*To Longaville.*¬ You found his mote, the King your
    mote did see,
But I a beam do find in each of three.   170
O, what a scene of fool'ry have I seen,
Of sighs, of groans, of sorrow, and of teen!
O me, with what strict patience have I sat,
To see a king transformèd to a gnat!
To see great Hercules whipping a gig,   175
And profound Solomon to tune a jig,
And Nestor play at pushpin with the boys,
And critic Timon laugh at idle toys.
Where lies thy grief, O tell me, good Dumaine?
And gentle Longaville, where lies thy pain?   180
And where my liege's? All about the breast!
A caudle, ho!
KING   Too bitter is thy jest.
Are we betrayed thus to thy overview?

191. **Joan:** See note to 3.1.215.
192. **pruning me:** primping and preening myself
194. **state:** stature, figure
196. **Soft:** i.e., wait a minute
197. **A true:** i.e., an honest
198. **post from:** i.e., hasten away (literally, to travel by post-horses, the fastest mode of travel then)
200. **present:** (1) gift; (2) document
202. **makes treason:** i.e., is treason doing
204. **mar:** Proverbial: "To make or mar."
207. **person:** i.e., parson

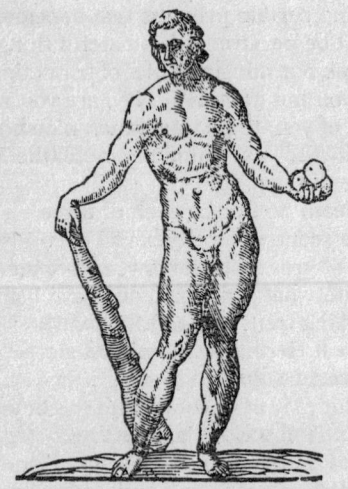

Hercules. (1.2.66)
From Vincenzo Cartari, *Le vere e noue imagini* . . . (1615).

BEROWNE
Not you ⌐to⌐ me, but I betrayed ⌐by⌐ you.   185
I, that am honest, I, that hold it sin
To break the vow I am engagèd in.
I am betrayed by keeping company
With men like ⌐you,⌐ men of inconstancy.
When shall you see me write a thing in rhyme?   190
Or groan for Joan? or spend a minute's time
In pruning me? When shall you hear that I
Will praise a hand, a foot, a face, an eye,
A gait, a state, a brow, a breast, a waist,
A leg, a limb—   195

Enter Jaquenetta, ⌐with a paper,⌐ and Clown ⌐Costard.⌐
                              ⌐Berowne begins to exit.⌐

KING   Soft, whither away so fast?
A true man, or a thief, that gallops so?
BEROWNE
I post from love. Good lover, let me go.
JAQUENETTA
God bless the King.
KING   What present hast thou there?   200
COSTARD
Some certain treason.
KING   What makes treason here?
COSTARD
Nay, it makes nothing, sir.
KING   If it mar nothing neither,
The treason and you go in peace away together.   205
JAQUENETTA
I beseech your Grace, let this letter be read.
Our person misdoubts it. 'Twas treason, he said.
KING Berowne, read it over.
                         ⌐Berowne⌐ *reads the letter.*
⌐To Jaquenetta.⌐   Where hadst thou it?

210, 212. **Of:** i.e., from

214. **toy:** trifle

218. **whoreson:** vile; **loggerhead:** blockhead

223. **mess:** a group of four eating together and helped from the same dishes

225. **pickpurses:** pickpockets or thieves (who, if caught, were hanged)

230. **turtles:** i.e., turtledoves, or lovers

231. **sirs:** a term of address for both men and women

232. **true:** loyal

234. **true:** steadfast in adherence to a promise or an oath

The magnificent Armada. (1.1.174, 196)
From John Pine, *The tapestry hangings of the House of Lords . . .* (1739).

JAQUENETTA   Of Costard.   210
KING, ⌜*to Costard*⌝ Where hadst thou it?
COSTARD   Of Dun Adramadio, Dun Adramadio.
                         ⌜*Berowne tears the paper.*⌝
KING, ⌜*to Berowne*⌝
   How now, what is in you? Why dost thou tear it?
BEROWNE
   A toy, my liege, a toy. Your Grace needs not fear it.
LONGAVILLE
   It did move him to passion, and therefore let's hear   215
      it.
DUMAINE, ⌜*picking up the papers*⌝
   It is Berowne's writing, and here is his name.
BEROWNE, ⌜*to Costard*⌝
   Ah, you whoreson loggerhead, you were born to do
      me shame.—
   Guilty, my lord, guilty. I confess, I confess.   220
KING   What?
BEROWNE
   That you three fools lacked me fool to make up
      the mess.
   He, he, and you—and you, my liege—and I
   Are pickpurses in love, and we deserve to die.   225
   O, dismiss this audience, and I shall tell you more.
DUMAINE
   Now the number is even.
BEROWNE   True, true, we are four.
   ⌜*Pointing to Jaquenetta and Costard.*⌝ Will these
      turtles be gone?   230
KING   Hence, sirs. Away.
COSTARD
   Walk aside the true folk, and let the traitors stay.
                         ⌜*Jaquenetta and Costard exit.*⌝
BEROWNE
   Sweet lords, sweet lovers, O, let us embrace.
   As true we are as flesh and blood can be.

235. **his:** its

237. **cross:** oppose

238. **of all hands:** in any case

239. **rent:** i.e., torn up

240–48. **Did . . . majesty?:** These lines develop the familiar poetic comparison between the beautiful beloved and the sun.

240. **Who:** i.e., what man is there who

242. **rude and savage:** uncivilized; **man of Ind:** See Jeremiah 13.33: "May a man of Ind change his skin . . .?" **Ind:** India

244. **vassal:** servile

246. **peremptory:** resolute; **eagle-sighted:** The eagle was reputed to be uniquely able to stare at the sun without being blinded.

251. **scarce . . . light:** i.e., hardly visible as a light

253. **but:** i.e., except

254. **Of . . . sovereignty:** i.e., the best selection from all complexions

256. **worthies:** i.e., things of value; **make one dignity:** combine to make a unique excellence

257. **wants:** is lacking; **want:** desire

258. **flourish:** showy ornamentation; **gentle:** noble

259. **painted:** artificial

260. **To . . . belongs:** Proverbial: "He praises who wishes to sell." **of sale:** for sale

261. **passes:** surpasses; **Then . . . blot:** i.e., therefore any praise, falling short, becomes a blemish (a **blot**)

262. **fivescore:** one hundred

264. **varnish:** disguise; adorn; **as if:** i.e., as if it were

The sea will ebb and flow, heaven show his face;   23
  Young blood doth not obey an old decree.
We cannot cross the cause why we were born;
Therefore of all hands must we be forsworn.

KING
What, did these rent lines show some love of thine?

BEROWNE
Did they, quoth you? Who sees the heavenly   24
  Rosaline
That, like a rude and savage man of Ind
  At the first op'ning of the gorgeous East,
Bows not his vassal head and, strucken blind,
  Kisses the base ground with obedient breast?   2
What peremptory eagle-sighted eye
  Dares look upon the heaven of her brow
That is not blinded by her majesty?

KING
  What zeal, what fury, hath inspired thee now?
My love, her mistress, is a gracious moon,   2
  She an attending star scarce seen a light.

BEROWNE
My eyes are then no eyes, nor I Berowne.
  O, but for my love, day would turn to night!
Of all complexions the culled sovereignty
  Do meet as at a fair in her fair cheek.   2
Where several worthies make one dignity,
  Where nothing wants that want itself doth seek.
Lend me the flourish of all gentle tongues—
  Fie, painted rhetoric! O, she needs it not!
To things of sale a seller's praise belongs.   2
  She passes praise. Then praise too short doth blot.
A withered hermit, fivescore winters worn,
  Might shake off fifty, looking in her eye.
Beauty doth varnish age, as if newborn,

265. **gives the:** i.e., gives to the

270. **book:** i.e., Bible

272. **If . . . look:** i.e., if beauty does not learn from Rosaline's eye how beauty should look

273. **fair:** beautiful, though Berowne is also playing on **fair** as "fair-haired" and "fair-skinned" (See longer note, page 237.) **full:** entirely

274–75. **Black is . . . the school of night:** i.e., black is . . . where night has learned blackness (See longer note, page 237.)

276. **beauty's crest:** (1) i.e., blackness (which Berowne has said is the symbol or crest of beauty); or (2) i.e., brightness, the symbol of true beauty (If the first meaning is accepted, the statement is sarcastic.)

277. **soonest:** most successfully; **resembling:** i.e., when they resemble (Compare 2 Corinthians 11.14: "Satan is himself transformed into an angel of light.")

279. **painting . . . hair:** i.e., cosmetics and wigs

282. **favor turns:** appearance changes

283. **native blood:** i.e., a naturally rosy complexion; **counted:** regarded as

284. **red:** i.e., rosiness

288. **crack:** boast

290. **in:** i.e., into the

And gives the crutch the cradle's infancy.　265
O, 'tis the sun that maketh all things shine!

KING
By heaven, thy love is black as ebony.

BEROWNE
Is ebony like her? O word divine!
A wife of such wood were felicity.
O, who can give an oath? Where is a book,　270
That I may swear beauty doth beauty lack
If that she learn not of her eye to look?
No face is fair that is not full so black.

KING
O, paradox! Black is the badge of hell,
The hue of dungeons and the school of night,　275
And beauty's crest becomes the heavens well.

BEROWNE
Devils soonest tempt, resembling spirits of light.
O, if in black my lady's brows be decked,
It mourns that painting ⌜and⌝ usurping hair
Should ravish doters with a false aspect:　280
And therefore is she born to make black fair.
Her favor turns the fashion of the days,
For native blood is counted painting now.
And therefore red, that would avoid dispraise,
Paints itself black to imitate her brow.　285

DUMAINE
To look like her are chimney-sweepers black.

LONGAVILLE
And since her time are colliers counted bright.

KING
And Ethiopes of their sweet complexion crack.

DUMAINE
Dark needs no candles now, for dark is light.

BEROWNE
Your mistresses dare never come in rain,　290
For fear their colors should be washed away.

293. **a fairer . . . today:** i.e., an unwashed face fairer (than hers)

299. **tread:** a path

300. **goes:** walks

303. **so:** as

306. **marry:** a mild oath

308. **quillets:** quibbles, subtle distinctions

311. **men-at-arms:** At this point the Quarto prints 28 lines that, in this edition, are printed (with explanatory notes) in an appendix on page 224. The lines are widely recognized as an incomplete first draft of this speech by Berowne. (See the headnote to the Appendix, page 223.)

"Earthly godfathers of heaven's lights." (1.1.90)
From Jakob Rüff, *De conceptu et generatione hominis . . .* (1580).

KING
　'Twere good yours did, for, sir, to tell you plain,
　　I'll find a fairer face not washed today.
BEROWNE
　I'll prove her fair, or talk till doomsday here.
KING
　No devil will fright thee then so much as she.　　295
DUMAINE
　I never knew man hold vile stuff so dear.
LONGAVILLE, ⌈*showing his shoe*⌉
　　Look, here's thy love; my foot and her face see.
BEROWNE
　O, if the streets were pavèd with thine eyes.
　　Her feet were much too dainty for such tread.
DUMAINE
　O vile! Then as she goes, what upward lies　　300
　　The street should see as she walked overhead.
KING
　But what of this? Are we not all in love?
BEROWNE
　Nothing so sure, and thereby all forsworn.
KING
　Then leave this chat, and, good Berowne, now prove
　　Our loving lawful, and our faith not torn.　　305
DUMAINE
　Ay, marry, there, some flattery for this evil.
LONGAVILLE
　　O, some authority how to proceed,
　Some tricks, some quillets, how to cheat the devil.
DUMAINE
　Some salve for perjury.
BEROWNE　　　　　　　　　O, 'tis more than need.　　310
　Have at you, then, affection's men-at-arms!
　O, we have made a vow to study, lords,
　And in that vow we have forsworn our books.

316. **numbers:** verses (as in the poems the lovers have written)

318. **Other . . . brain:** i.e., other branches of learning (in contrast to the art of love) are sluggish and remain fixed in the brain

320. **of their:** i.e., from their practicers'

323. **motion . . . elements:** activity of all the components of the body

324. **power:** faculty

326. **Above . . . offices:** i.e., above and beyond their customary functions

328. **will . . . blind:** i.e., exceed those of the eagle (See note to 4.3.246.)

330. **When . . . stopped:** i.e., when even the wary thief cannot hear

331. **feeling:** i.e., sense of touch; **soft and sensible:** i.e., sensitive

332. **cockled snails:** snails with shells (See picture on page 132.)

333. **Bacchus:** Roman god of wine

334–35. **Hercules . . . Hesperides:** One of Hercules' twelve labors was stealing the dragon-guarded golden apples from the garden of Hesperus, called by Shakespeare and many other writers the **Hesperides.**

336. **Sphinx:** a mythological monster (with a lion's body and a woman's head) that posed a riddle that only Oedipus could solve

337. **Apollo's lute:** the stringed instrument of the classical god of music (See page 134.)

338. **voice:** i.e., voices

341. **tempered:** mixed

345. **right:** true; **Promethean fire:** See longer note, page 238.

(continued)

For when would you, my liege, or you, or you,
In leaden contemplation have found out   315
Such fiery numbers as the prompting eyes
Of beauty's tutors have enriched you with?
Other slow arts entirely keep the brain
And therefore, finding barren practicers,
Scarce show a harvest of their heavy toil.   320
But love, first learnèd in a lady's eyes,
Lives not alone immurèd in the brain,
But with the motion of all elements
Courses as swift as thought in every power,
And gives to every power a double power,   325
Above their functions and their offices.
It adds a precious seeing to the eye.
A lover's eyes will gaze an eagle blind.
A lover's ear will hear the lowest sound,
When the suspicious head of theft is stopped.   330
Love's feeling is more soft and sensible
Than are the tender horns of cockled snails.
Love's tongue proves dainty Bacchus gross in taste.
For valor, is not love a Hercules,
Still climbing trees in the Hesperides?   335
Subtle as Sphinx, as sweet and musical
As bright Apollo's lute strung with his hair.
And when love speaks, the voice of all the gods
Make heaven drowsy with the harmony.
Never durst poet touch a pen to write   340
Until his ink were tempered with love's sighs.
O, then his lines would ravish savage ears
And plant in tyrants mild humility.
From women's eyes this doctrine I derive.
They sparkle still the right Promethean fire.   345
They are the books, the arts, the academes
That show, contain, and nourish all the world.
Else none at all in ought proves excellent.

346. **academes:** academies

348. **Else:** i.e., without them; **in ought:** i.e., at anything

358. **charity . . . law:** Compare Romans 13.8: "He that loveth another [i.e., that has **charity**] hath fulfilled the law."

360. **Saint Cupid:** a battle cry (The English battle cry was "Saint George.")

361. **Advance your standards:** lift up your banners

362–63. **be first advised . . . them:** i.e., first be careful that the sun is in their eyes (with a pun on getting [fathering] sons on them)

364. **these glozes:** i.e., this specious talk, the flattery Berowne was asked to provide (line 306)

369. **attach:** seize (the legal sense of **attach**)

371. **strange:** unusual, surprising

373. **masques:** disguisings, impromptu masquerades, in which the performers wear masks and fancy clothes (See page 158.)

376. **betime:** come to pass; **fitted:** i.e., fashioned to our use

A snail. (4.3.332)
From Thomas Trevelyon's pictorial commonplace book (1608).

Then fools you were these women to forswear,
Or, keeping what is sworn, you will prove fools. 350
For wisdom's sake, a word that all men love,
Or for love's sake, a word that loves all men,
Or for men's sake, the ⌜authors⌝ of these women,
Or women's sake, by whom we men are men,
⌜Let⌝ us once lose our oaths to find ourselves, 355
Or else we lose ourselves to keep our oaths.
It is religion to be thus forsworn,
For charity itself fulfills the law,
And who can sever love from charity?

KING
Saint Cupid, then, and, soldiers, to the field! 360

BEROWNE
Advance your standards, and upon them, lords.
Pell-mell, down with them. But be first advised
In conflict that you get the sun of them.

LONGAVILLE
Now to plain dealing. Lay these glozes by.
Shall we resolve to woo these girls of France? 365

KING
And win them, too. Therefore let us devise
Some entertainment for them in their tents.

BEROWNE
First, from the park let us conduct them thither.
Then homeward every man attach the hand
Of his fair mistress. In the afternoon 370
We will with some strange pastime solace them,
Such as the shortness of the time can shape;
For revels, dances, masques, and merry hours
Forerun fair love, strewing her way with flowers.

KING
Away, away! No time shall be omitted 375
That will betime and may by us be fitted.

377. **Allons:** let us go (French); **Sowed . . . corn:** i.e., the farmer who sowed weeds reaped no wheat
378. **in equal measure:** even-handedly
379. **Light:** (1) frivolous; (2) unchaste
380. **copper:** i.e., coin of little value

Apollo with his "lute." (4.3.337)
From Giulio Cesare Capaccio, *Gli apologi* . . . (1619).

BEROWNE
⌐*Allons! Allons!*⌐ Sowed cockle reaped no corn,
    And justice always whirls in equal measure.
Light wenches may prove plagues to men forsworn;
    If so, our copper buys no better treasure.   380
                        ⌐*They exit.*⌐

LOVE'S LABOR'S LOST

ACT 5

5.1 Armado, ordered by the King to provide some entertainment for the Princess and her ladies, consults Holofernes, who suggests that a pageant of the Nine Worthies be presented.

---

1. **Satis quid sufficit:** a misquotation of the Latin proverb "Satis est quod sufficit," which means "Enough is sufficient" (See longer note to 4.2.3–4.)

2. **reasons:** discussions

4. **affection:** affectation

5. **impudency:** insolent disrespect; **opinion:** conceit, arrogance

6–7. **this quondam day:** i.e., the other day

10. **Novi . . . te:** I know the man as well as I know you (See longer note, page 238.); **humor:** disposition

11. **filed:** smooth, polished

13. **thrasonical:** bragging (after the name Thraso, the braggart soldier in the Roman dramatist Terence's play *Eunuchus*)

14. **picked:** refined, finical

15. **peregrinate:** outlandish, conspicuously foreign

16 SD. **Draw:** i.e., he draws; **table book:** pocket notebook

17–18. **He draweth . . . argument:** i.e., he (Armado) employs a finer style of expression than is appropriate for his subject matter **staple:** fiber that is spun into thread **argument:** subject matter

19. **fanatical:** extravagant; **phantasimes:** See note to 4.1.108. **insociable:** unsociable

20. **point-devise:** extremely precise; **companions:** fellows (a term of contempt); **rackers:** torturers

21. **fine:** i.e., mincingly

⟨ACT⟩ ⌐5¬

⌐Scene 1¬
Enter ⌐Holofernes¬ the Pedant, ⌐Nathaniel¬ the Curate,
and Dull ⌐the Constable.¬

HOLOFERNES *Satis quid sufficit.*

NATHANIEL   I praise God for you, sir. Your reasons at
dinner have been sharp and sententious, pleasant
without scurrility, witty without affection, auda-
cious without impudency, learned without opinion,   5
and strange without heresy. I did converse this
quondam day with a companion of the King's, who
is intituled, nominated, or called Don Adriano de
Armado.

HOLOFERNES *Novi ⌐hominem¬ tanquam te.* His humor   10
is lofty, his discourse peremptory, his tongue filed,
his eye ambitious, his gait majestical, and his general behavior vain, ridiculous, and thrasonical. He is
too picked, too spruce, too affected, too odd, as it
were, too peregrinate, as I may call it.   15

NATHANIEL   A most singular and choice epithet.

Draw out his table book.

HOLOFERNES He draweth out the thread of his verbosi-
ty finer than the staple of his argument. I abhor
such fanatical phantasimes, such insociable and
point-devise companions, such rackers of orthog-   20
raphy, as to speak "dout," fine, when he should
say "doubt"; "det" when he should pronounce

139

23. **clepeth:** calls (an archaic word in Shakespeare's time)

23–24. **calf . . . half:** Holofernes demands that the *l* be pronounced.

24. **vocatur:** is said (Latin)

26–27. **It . . . insanie:** (See longer note, page 238.)

27. **Ne . . . domine:** Do you understand, sir?

29. **Laus . . . intelligo:** Praise be to God, I understand well. (See longer note, page 238.)

30. **bene:** the Latin word for "well"; **Priscian:** a sixth-century Latin grammarian ("To break Priscian's head" was a proverbial way to say "To speak poor Latin.")

32. **Videsne quis venit:** Do you see who is coming? (Latin)

33. **Video, et gaudeo:** I see and I rejoice.

34. **Chirrah:** perhaps Armado's attempt at the Greek salutation *chaere* ("hail"), included in elementary school texts as a greeting

35. **Quare:** why

41. **almsbasket:** basket of food scraps for the poor

42–43. **thou . . . honorificabilitudinitatibus:** i.e., you are shorter than this word, which was often called the longest word in the world (meaning, roughly, "loaded with honors")

44. **flapdragon:** raisin in a dish of burning brandy

45. **peal:** i.e., peal of bells

46–47. **lettered:** learned, educated

48. **the hornbook:** i.e., the alphabet (which, for schoolboys, was printed on a leaf of paper mounted on a small board and covered with translucent horn) See page 180.

50. **pueritia:** child (literally, childhood)

53. **Quis:** who, or what

"debt"—*d, e, b, t,* not *d, e, t.* He clepeth a calf
"cauf," half "hauf," neighbor *vocatur* "nebor";
neigh abbreviated *ne.* This is abhominable—which   25
he would call "abominable." It insinuateth me of
⌈insanie.⌉ *Ne intelligis, domine?* To make frantic,
lunatic.

NATHANIEL   *Laus Deo,* ⌈*bone*⌉ *intelligo.*

HOLOFERNES   ⌈*Bone? Bone*⌉ for ⌈*bene?*⌉ Priscian a little   30
scratched; 'twill serve.

Enter ⌈*Armado the*⌉ *Braggart, Boy,* ⌈*and Costard.*⌉

NATHANIEL   *Videsne quis venit?*

HOLOFERNES   *Video, et gaudeo.*

ARMADO   *Chirrah.*

HOLOFERNES   *Quare* "chirrah," not "sirrah"?   35

ARMADO   Men of peace, well encountered.

HOLOFERNES   Most military sir, salutation.

BOY, ⌈*aside to Costard*⌉ They have been at a great feast
of languages and stolen the scraps.

COSTARD, ⌈*aside to Boy*⌉ O, they have lived long on the   40
almsbasket of words. I marvel thy master hath not
eaten thee for a word, for thou art not so long by the
head as *honorificabilitudinitatibus.* Thou art easier
swallowed than a flapdragon.

BOY, ⌈*aside to Costard*⌉ Peace, the peal begins.   45

ARMADO, ⌈*to Holofernes*⌉ Monsieur, are you not lettered?

BOY   Yes, yes, he teaches boys the hornbook.—What is
a, b spelled backward, with the horn on his head?

HOLOFERNES   *Ba, pueritia,* with a horn added.   50

BOY   *Ba,* most silly sheep, with a horn.—You hear his
learning.

HOLOFERNES   *Quis, quis,* thou consonant?

BOY   The last of the five vowels, if you repeat them; or
the fifth, if I.   55

HOLOFERNES   I will repeat them: *a, e, i*—

57. **u:** (1) you; (2) ewe

58. **salt:** salty (with a pun on **salt** as stingingly witty)

59. **touch:** hit (in fencing); **venue:** fencing thrust

63. **wit-old:** with a pun on "wittol," a cuckold who knows his wife is unfaithful (See note to 4.1.130.)

64. **figure:** (1) figure of speech; (2) emblem

67. **gig:** top (See page 152.)

69. **unum cita:** cite one (i.e., supply me with an example of your infamy); **of:** i.e., made of

74. **halfpenny:** i.e., tiny

78. **ad dunghill:** See longer note, page 238.

81. **Arts-man:** scholar, i.e., someone schooled in the liberal arts; **preambulate:** walk ahead; **singuled:** Armado's word for "singled out," "separated"

83. **charge-house:** boarding school (See longer note, page 239.)

84. **mons:** Latin for "mountain"

86. **sans question:** without question (French)

88. **congratulate:** salute

91–92. **generous:** noble, highborn

92. **liable:** suitable; **measurable:** proportionate

BOY   The sheep. The other two concludes it: *o, u.*

ARMADO   Now by the salt ⟨wave⟩ of the Mediterrane-
um, a sweet touch, a quick venue of wit! Snip, snap,
quick and home. It rejoiceth my intellect. True   60
wit.

BOY   Offered by a child to an old man—which is
wit-old.

HOLOFERNES   What is the figure? What is the figure?

BOY   Horns.   65

HOLOFERNES   Thou disputes like an infant. Go whip thy
gig.

BOY   Lend me your horn to make one, and I will whip
about your infamy—*unum cita*—a gig of a cuckold's horn.   70

COSTARD   An I had but one penny in the world, thou
shouldst have it to buy gingerbread! Hold, there is
the very remuneration I had of thy master, thou
halfpenny purse of wit, thou pigeon egg of discretion. ⌜*He gives him money.*⌝ O, an the heavens were   75
so pleased that thou wert but my bastard, what a
joyful father wouldest thou make me! Go to, thou
hast it *ad dunghill*, at the fingers' ends, as they say.

HOLOFERNES   Oh, I smell false Latin! *Dunghill* for *unguem.*   80

ARMADO   Arts-man, preambulate. We will be singuled
from the barbarous. Do you not educate youth at
the charge-house on the top of the mountain?

HOLOFERNES   Or *mons*, the hill.

ARMADO   At your sweet pleasure, for the mountain.   85

HOLOFERNES   I do, *sans question.*

ARMADO   Sir, it is the King's most sweet pleasure and
affection to congratulate the Princess at her pavilion in the posteriors of this day, which the rude
multitude call the afternoon.   90

HOLOFERNES   "The posterior of the day," most generous sir, is liable, congruent, and measurable for

97. **inward:** secret, private

98. **remember thy courtesy:** This phrase could mean either "remove your hat" or "put your hat back on."

104. **excrement:** hair (with probable wordplay, at Armado's expense, on bodily excretions)

111. **chuck:** a term of endearment

111–12. **ostentation:** spectacular show

112. **antic:** grotesque pageant

117–18. **Nine Worthies:** See longer note, page 239.

119. **entertainment:** spending

121. **illustrate:** illustrious

125. **present:** represent

126–27. **Joshua . . . Judas Maccabaeus:** See longer note, page 240.

128. **pass:** possibly, surpass

128–29. **Pompey the Great:** the elder Pompey, a great Roman military leader (See page 190.)

Iosue

Joshua.
Tipped into *Chronologie et sommaire des souuerains . . .* (1622).

"the afternoon"; the word is well culled, chose, sweet, and apt, I do assure you, sir, I do assure.

ARMADO Sir, the King is a noble gentleman, and my 95 familiar, I do assure you, very good friend. For what is inward between us, let it pass. I do beseech thee, remember thy courtesy; I beseech thee apparel thy head. And among other important and most serious designs, and of great import indeed, too— 100 but let that pass; for I must tell thee, it will please his Grace, by the world, sometimes to lean upon my poor shoulder and with his royal finger thus dally with my excrement, with my mustachio—but, sweetheart, let that pass. By the world, I recount no 105 fable! Some certain special honors it pleaseth his Greatness to impart to Armado, a soldier, a man of travel, that hath seen the world—but let that pass. The very all of all is—but sweetheart, I do implore secrecy—that the King would have me present the 110 Princess, sweet chuck, with some delightful ostentation, or show, or pageant, or antic, or firework. Now, understanding that the curate and your sweet self are good at such eruptions and sudden breaking out of mirth, as it were, I have acquainted you 115 withal to the end to crave your assistance.

HOLOFERNES Sir, you shall present before her the Nine Worthies.—Sir ⌈Nathaniel,⌉ as concerning some entertainment of time, some show in the posterior of this day, to be ⌈rendered⌉ by our ⌈assistance,⌉ the 120 King's command, and this most gallant, illustrate, and learned gentleman, before the Princess—I say, none so fit as to present the Nine Worthies.

NATHANIEL Where will you find men worthy enough to present them? 125

HOLOFERNES Joshua, yourself; myself; and this gallant gentleman, Judas Maccabaeus. This swain, because of his great limb or joint, shall pass Pompey the Great; the page, Hercules—

132. **his club:** See illustration, page 120.

133. **have audience:** i.e., be given a hearing

134. **enter:** i.e., entrance

135. **strangling a snake:** Hercules, still in the cradle, strangled two snakes sent to destroy him. (See page 214.) **apology:** speech of explanation

146. **fadge not:** i.e., does not turn out well; **an antic:** See note to 5.1.112.

148. **Via:** come on

151. **Allons:** let's go (French)

152. **make one:** join

153. **tabor:** small drum (See page 154.)

154. **hay:** a country dance having a serpentine or winding movement, like a reel

5.2 Boyet reports to the Princess that the King and his lords, disguised as Russians, will visit the ladies. The Princess tells her ladies that she and they will cover their faces with masks and exchange the gifts sent to them. Each will wear another's gift. The King and the lords will then mistake the ladies for each other and each lord will vow his love to the wrong lady. Later, when the lords return in their proper dress, the ladies will be able to mock them for their mistakes. All occurs as the Princess plans. (Scene heading continues on page 188.)

———————

2. **fairings:** gifts (originally gifts purchased at fairs)

ARMADO Pardon, sir—error. He is not quantity 130
enough for that Worthy's thumb; he is not so big as
the end of his club!

HOLOFERNES Shall I have audience? He shall present
Hercules in minority. His enter and exit shall be
strangling a snake; and I will have an apology for 135
that purpose.

BOY An excellent device. So, if any of the audience
hiss, you may cry "Well done, Hercules, now thou
crushest the snake." That is the way to make an
offense gracious, though few have the grace to do it. 140

ARMADO For the rest of the Worthies?

HOLOFERNES I will play three myself.

BOY Thrice-worthy gentleman!

ARMADO, ⌜to Holofernes⌝ Shall I tell you a thing?

HOLOFERNES We attend. 145

ARMADO We will have, if this fadge not, an antic. I
beseech you, follow.

HOLOFERNES *Via*, goodman Dull. Thou hast spoken no
word all this while.

DULL Nor understood none neither, sir. 150

HOLOFERNES ⌜*Allons!*⌝ We will employ thee.

DULL I'll make one in a dance, or so; or I will play on
the tabor to the Worthies and let them dance the
hay.

HOLOFERNES Most dull, honest Dull. To our sport! 155
Away.

They exit.

⌜Scene 2⌝
Enter the Ladies (⌜the Princess, Rosaline,
Katherine, and Maria.⌝)

PRINCESS
Sweethearts, we shall be rich ere we depart,
If fairings come thus plentifully in.

3. **A lady:** i.e., the figure of a lady, perhaps in a pendant

6. **love in rhyme:** i.e., love poetry

8. **margent:** margin

9. **That:** i.e., so that; **fain:** obliged; **seal . . . name:** i.e., place his wax seal on top of the word "Cupid" in his poem

10. **wax:** i.e., grow (with a pun on "wax" as sealing wax)

11. **five . . . boy:** i.e., a boy since the beginning of the world (as it was then calculated)

12. **shrewd:** mischievous, malicious; **gallows:** i.e., one deserving death on the gallows

15. **heavy:** grieved, despondent

16. **light:** cheerful, merry

20. **dark:** mysterious; **mouse:** a term of endearment; **light:** frivolous

22. **light condition:** unchaste nature

24. **taking it in snuff:** i.e., taking offense, getting angry (Literally, **snuff** is charred, foul-smelling candle wick. Katherine's figure of speech puns on **light** as candle.)

A lady walled about with diamonds!
Look you what I have from the loving king.
⌜*She shows a jewel.*⌝

ROSALINE
Madam, came nothing else along with that?   5
PRINCESS
Nothing but this? Yes, as much love in rhyme
As would be crammed up in a sheet of paper
Writ o' both sides the leaf, margent and all,
That he was fain to seal on Cupid's name.
ROSALINE
That was the way to make his godhead wax,   10
For he hath been five thousand year a boy.
KATHERINE
Ay, and a shrewd unhappy gallows, too.
ROSALINE
You'll ne'er be friends with him. He killed your
    sister.
KATHERINE
He made her melancholy, sad, and heavy,   15
And so she died. Had she been light like you,
Of such a merry, nimble, stirring spirit,
She might ha' been ⟨a⟩ grandam ere she died.
And so may you, for a light heart lives long.
ROSALINE
What's your dark meaning, mouse, of this light   20
    word?
KATHERINE
A light condition in a beauty dark.
ROSALINE
We need more light to find your meaning out.
KATHERINE
You'll mar the light by taking it in snuff;
Therefore I'll darkly end the argument.   25

26. **Look what:** whatever; **still:** always

28. **weigh not:** i.e., do not weigh as much as

30. **past care ... cure:** Proverbial: "What cannot be helped is not to be worried about."

31. **bandied, set:** terms in tennis

32. **favor:** token of affection (In line 36 Rosaline puns on **favor** in the sense of "face" or of "appearance.")

34. **would:** wish

38. **numbers true:** meter regular; **numb'ring:** reckoning, i.e., evaluation

39. **on the ground:** i.e., on earth

40. **fairs:** beauties

41. **drawn my picture:** i.e., painted me in words

43. **Much ... praise:** i.e., I look like the letters (with my dark hair), but not like the flattering description

45. **text B:** The elaborate **B** in text-hand (a large, formal style of handwriting) is **fair** (i.e., beautiful) but dark with **ink.** (See longer note on **fair** [4.3.273], page 237.)

46. **Ware:** i.e., beware; **pencils:** finely pointed brushes (used by artists to paint portraits just as the ladies here are painting verbal portraits of each other); **Let ... debtor:** i.e., I'll pay you back for your remark

47. **red ... golden:** referring to Katherine's rosy complexion and blond hair **red dominical:** a (usually large) red letter (See longer note, page 240.)

48. **O's:** perhaps, the circular scars left by smallpox

49. **pox of:** curse on; **beshrew:** curse; **shrows:** i.e., shrews

ROSALINE
Look what you do, you do it still i' th' dark.
KATHERINE
So do not you, for you are a light wench.
ROSALINE
Indeed, I weigh not you, and therefore light.
KATHERINE
You weigh me not? O, that's you care not for me.
ROSALINE
Great reason: for past care is still past cure. 30
PRINCESS
Well bandied both; a set of wit well played.
But, Rosaline, you have a favor too.
Who sent it? And what is it?
ROSALINE   I would you knew.
An if my face were but as fair as yours, 35
My favor were as great. Be witness this.
                              ⌜*She shows a gift.*⌝
Nay, I have verses too, I thank Berowne;
The numbers true; and were the numb'ring too,
I were the fairest goddess on the ground.
I am compared to twenty thousand fairs. 40
O, he hath drawn my picture in his letter.
PRINCESS   Anything like?
ROSALINE
Much in the letters, nothing in the praise.
PRINCESS
Beauteous as ink: a good conclusion.
KATHERINE
Fair as a text B in a copybook. 45
ROSALINE
Ware pencils, ho! Let me not die your debtor,
My red dominical, my golden letter.
O, that your face were not so full of O's!
PRINCESS
A pox of that jest! And I beshrew all shrows.

56. **translation:** expression of something in another medium or form

57. **compiled:** (1) arranged; (2) heaped together; **simplicity:** foolishness

62. **Ay . . . part:** Maria may here wrap the chain of pearls around her hands.   **would:** wish

66. **in by th' week:** ensnared, caught; deeply in love

68. **wait the season:** i.e., await the time appointed (by me); **observe the times:** i.e., keep to the times that are favorable and convenient (to me)

69. **bootless rhymes:** i.e., unavailing poetic complaints

70. **hests:** behests, commands

72. **pair-taunt-like:** i.e., as if I held the winning hand in the card game called "post and pair"; **o'ersway his state:** overmaster his greatness or power

74. **catched:** captured; captivated

75. **wit:** intelligence

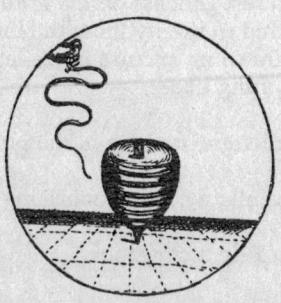

A top, or gig. (4.3.175, 5.1.67)
From Giovanni Ferro, *Teatro d'imprese* . . . (1623).

But, Katherine, what was sent to you 50
From fair Dumaine?
KATHERINE
Madam, this glove. ⌈*She shows the glove.*⌉
PRINCESS Did he not send you twain?
KATHERINE Yes, madam, and moreover,
Some thousand verses of a faithful lover, 55
A huge translation of hypocrisy,
Vilely compiled, profound simplicity.
⟨MARIA⟩
This, and these ⟨pearls,⟩ to me sent Longaville.
⌈*She shows a paper and pearls.*⌉
The letter is too long by half a mile.
PRINCESS
I think no less. Dost thou not wish in heart 60
The chain were longer and the letter short?
⟨MARIA⟩
Ay, or I would these hands might never part.
PRINCESS
We are wise girls to mock our lovers so.
ROSALINE
They are worse fools to purchase mocking so.
That same Berowne I'll torture ere I go. 65
O, that I knew he were but in by th' week,
How I would make him fawn, and beg, and seek,
And wait the season, and observe the times,
And spend his prodigal wits in bootless rhymes,
And shape his service wholly to my ⌈hests,⌉ 70
And make him proud to make me proud that jests!
So ⌈pair-taunt-like⌉ would I o'ersway his state,
That he should be my fool, and I his fate.
PRINCESS
None are so surely caught, when they are catched,
As wit turned fool. Folly in wisdom hatched 75
Hath wisdom's warrant and the help of school,
And wit's own grace to grace a learnèd fool.

78. **blood:** passion

79. **gravity's revolt:** i.e., the change of dignity or solemn conduct

80. **note:** stigma, reproach

88. **Encounters:** battles, skirmishes

90. **surprised:** with wordplay on the military sense of "suddenly captured"

93. **Saint Denis:** patron saint of France

94. **breath:** i.e., words

98. **might:** i.e., did; **addressed:** making their way

101. **overhear:** i.e., hear over again now

102. **by and by:** soon

104. **embassage:** message

Playing the tabor and pipe. (5.1.153)
From William Kemp, *Kempes nine daies wonder . . .* (1884).

ROSALINE
The blood of youth burns not with such excess
As gravity's revolt to ⌜wantonness.⌝
MARIA
Folly in fools bears not so strong a note   80
As fool'ry in the wise, when wit doth dote,
Since all the power thereof it doth apply
To prove, by wit, worth in simplicity.

Enter Boyet.

PRINCESS
Here comes Boyet, and mirth is in his face.
BOYET
O, I am ⟨stabbed⟩ with laughter. Where's her Grace?   85
PRINCESS
Thy news, Boyet?
BOYET   Prepare, madam, prepare.
Arm, wenches, arm. Encounters mounted are
Against your peace. Love doth approach, disguised,
Armèd in arguments. You'll be surprised.   90
Muster your wits, stand in your own defense,
Or hide your heads like cowards, and fly hence.
PRINCESS
Saint Denis to Saint Cupid! What are they
That charge their breath against us? Say, scout, say.
BOYET
Under the cool shade of a sycamore,   95
I thought to close mine eyes some half an hour.
When, lo, to interrupt my purposed rest,
Toward that shade I might behold addressed
The King and his companions. Warily
I stole into a neighbor thicket by,   100
And overheard what you shall overhear:
That, by and by, disguised, ⟨they⟩ will be here.
Their herald is a pretty knavish page
That well by heart hath conned his embassage.

105. **Action:** gesture

107. **ever and anon:** i.e., over and over again; **made a doubt:** expressed their fear

108. **put him out:** i.e., cause him to forget his part

116. **rubbed his elbow:** a gesture of satisfaction; **fleered:** grinned, sneered

118. **his finger . . . thumb:** perhaps, snapping his fingers

121. **turned . . . toe:** i.e., did a pirouette

123–25. **With such . . . tears:** an elaborate way of saying they laughed until they cried **spleen:** i.e., excess of laughter (The **spleen** was thought to be the seat of laughter and of other strong emotions.)

130. **love-feat:** i.e., exploit inspired by love (often emended to "love suit")

131. **several:** particular; **mistress:** sweetheart; **which:** i.e., whom

133. **tasked:** put into difficulty

135. **have the grace:** i.e., be given the privilege

136. **suit:** (1) courtship; (2) petition

A Russian ambassador. (5.2.128)
From Cesare Vecellio, *Habiti antichi et moderni . . .* (1598).

Action and accent did they teach him there: 105
"Thus must thou speak," and "thus thy body bear."
And ever and anon they made a doubt
Presence majestical would put him out;
"For," quoth the King, "an angel shalt thou see;
Yet fear not thou, but speak audaciously." 110
The boy replied "An angel is not evil.
I should have feared her had she been a devil."
With that, all laughed and clapped him on the
shoulder,
Making the bold wag by their praises bolder. 115
One rubbed his elbow thus, and fleered, and swore
A better speech was never spoke before.
Another with his finger and his thumb,
Cried *"Via!* We will do 't, come what will come."
The third he capered and cried "All goes well!" 120
The fourth turned on the toe, and down he fell.
With that, they all did tumble on the ground
With such a zealous laughter so profound
That in this spleen ridiculous appears,
To check their folly, passion's solemn tears. 125

PRINCESS
But what, but what? Come they to visit us?

BOYET
They do, they do; and are appareled thus,
Like Muscovites, or Russians, as I guess.
Their purpose is to parley, to court, and dance,
And every one his love-feat will advance 130
Unto his several mistress—which they'll know
By favors several which they did bestow.

PRINCESS
And will they so? The gallants shall be tasked,
For, ladies, we will every one be masked,
And not a man of them shall have the grace, 135
Despite of suit, to see a lady's face.
Hold, Rosaline, this favor thou shalt wear,

139. **Hold:** i.e., here

142. **removes:** i.e., shifting of favors from one lady to another

143. **most in sight:** i.e., where they are most visible

145. **cross:** thwart

147. **mock for mock:** Proverbial: "He who mocks shall be mocked."

148. **counsels:** secrets, confidences

149. **withal:** i.e., for it

154. **their penned speech:** i.e., the speech written for the boy Mote

159. **out:** i.e., forced out of his part

"We will every one be masked." (4.3.373, 5.2.134)
From Giacomo Franco, *Habiti d'huomeni et donne venetiane* . . . [1609?].

And then the King will court thee for his dear.
Hold, take thou this, my sweet, and give me thine
So shall Berowne take me for Rosaline. 140
⌜*Princess and Rosaline exchange favors.*⌝
And change you favors too. So shall your loves
Woo contrary, deceived by these removes.
⌜*Katherine and Maria exchange favors.*⌝

ROSALINE
Come on, then, wear the favors most in sight.
KATHERINE, ⌜*to Princess*⌝
But in this changing, what is your intent?
PRINCESS
The effect of my intent is to cross theirs. 145
They do it but in mockery merriment,
And mock for mock is only my intent.
Their several counsels they unbosom shall
To loves mistook, and so be mocked withal
Upon the next occasion that we meet, 150
With visages displayed, to talk and greet.
ROSALINE
But shall we dance, if they desire us to 't?
PRINCESS
No, to the death we will not move a foot,
Nor to their penned speech render we no grace,
But while 'tis spoke each turn away ⌜her⌝ face. 155
BOYET
Why, that contempt will kill the speaker's heart,
And quite divorce his memory from his part.
PRINCESS
Therefore I do it, and I make no doubt
The rest will ⌜ne'er⌝ come in if he be out.
There's no such sport as sport by sport o'erthrown, 160
To make theirs ours and ours none but our own.
So shall we stay, mocking intended game,
And they, well mocked, depart away with shame.
Sound trumpet, ⌜*within.*⌝

164 SD. **Blackamoors:** Africans with dark skin (probably Navarre's attendants so disguised)

166. **taffeta:** probably a reference to the ladies' taffeta masks

167. **parcel:** small party or company

180. **brings:** i.e., puts

181. **perfectness:** i.e., word-perfectness

182. **What would these strangers:** i.e., what do these foreigners want?

A "blackamoor." (5.2.164 SD)
From Cesare Vecellio, *Degli habiti antichi et moderni . . .* (1590).

BOYET
　The trumpet sounds. Be masked; the maskers come.
　　　　　　　　　　　⌜*The Ladies mask.*⌝

Enter Blackamoors with music, the Boy with a speech,
⌜*the King, Berowne,*⌝ *and the rest of the Lords disguised.*

BOY
　All hail, the richest beauties on the earth!　　　　165
⌜BOYET⌝
　Beauties no richer than rich taffeta.
BOY
　A holy parcel of the fairest dames
　　　　　　　　(The Ladies turn their backs to him.)
　That ever turned their—backs—to mortal views.
BEROWNE　*Their eyes, villain, their eyes!*
BOY
　That ⟨ever⟩ turned their eyes to mortal views.　　170
　Out—
BOYET　True; out indeed.
BOY
　Out of your favors, heavenly spirits, vouchsafe
　Not to behold—
BEROWNE　*Once to behold, rogue!*　　　　175
BOY
　Once to behold with your sun-beamèd eyes—
　With your sun-beamèd eyes—
BOYET
　They will not answer to that epithet.
　You were best call it "daughter-beamèd eyes."
BOY
　They do not mark me, and that brings me out.　　180
BEROWNE
　Is this your perfectness? Begone, you rogue!
　　　　　　　　　　　⌜*Boy exits.*⌝
ROSALINE, ⌜*speaking as the Princess*⌝
　What would these ⟨strangers?⟩ Know their minds,
　　Boyet.

185. **plain:** readily understood
189. **gentle:** courteous
194. **measured:** traveled
195. **tread a measure:** i.e., join in a stately dance
200. **told:** said; counted

Morocco, the dancing horse. (1.2.53)
From Robert Chambers, *The book of days* . . . [1869].

If they do speak our language, 'tis our will
That some plain man recount their purposes. 185
Know what they would.
BOYET   What would you with the
⌈Princess?⌉
BEROWNE
Nothing but peace and gentle visitation.
ROSALINE   What would they, say they? 190
BOYET
Nothing but peace and gentle visitation.
ROSALINE
Why, that they have, and bid them so be gone.
BOYET
She says you have it, and you may be gone.
KING
Say to her we have measured many miles
To tread a measure with her on this grass. 195
BOYET
They say that they have measured many a mile
To tread a measure with you on this grass.
ROSALINE
It is not so. Ask them how many inches
Is in one mile. If they have measured many,
The measure then of one is eas'ly told. 200
BOYET
If to come hither you have measured miles,
And many miles, the Princess bids you tell
How many inches doth fill up one mile.
BEROWNE
Tell her we measure them by weary steps.
BOYET
She hears herself. 205
ROSALINE   How many weary steps
Of many weary miles you have o'ergone
Are numbered in the travel of one mile?

211. **still:** always

214. **clouded:** i.e., masked

218. **eyne:** eyes

220. **moonshine:** something insubstantial and unreal

221. **measure:** dance; **change:** i.e., round (with a probable pun on the changes of the moon, picked up by Rosaline in line 224)

222. **strange:** (1) foreign; (2) unaccountable, surprising

227. **moon, man:** a reference to "the man in the moon"

232. **nice:** coy

BEROWNE
　We number nothing that we spend for you.
　Our duty is so rich, so infinite,　　　　　　　　　　210
　That we may do it still without account.
　Vouchsafe to show the sunshine of your face
　That we, like savages, may worship it.
ROSALINE
　My face is but a moon, and clouded too.
KING
　Blessèd are clouds, to do as such clouds do!　　　215
　Vouchsafe, bright moon, and these thy stars, to
　　　shine,
　Those clouds removed, upon our watery eyne.
ROSALINE
　O vain petitioner, beg a greater matter!
　Thou now requests but moonshine in the water.　　220
KING
　Then in our measure do but vouchsafe one change.
　Thou bidd'st me beg; this begging is not strange.
ROSALINE
　Play music, then. Nay, you must do it soon.
　　　　　　　　　　　　　⌈*Music begins.*⌉
　Not yet? No dance! Thus change I like the moon.
KING
　Will you not dance? How come you thus estranged?　225
ROSALINE
　You took the moon at full, but now she's changed.
KING
　Yet still she is the moon, and I the man.
　The music plays. Vouchsafe some motion to it.
ROSALINE
　Our ears vouchsafe it.
KING　　　　　　　　　　But your legs should do it.　230
ROSALINE
　Since you are strangers and come here by chance,
　We'll not be nice. Take hands. We will not dance.
　　　　　　　　　　　⌈*She offers her hand.*⌉

236. More measure: a greater amount; **this measure:** this dance

238. Prize you yourselves: i.e., set your own value (with a pun on **price**)

242. Twice . . . you: This line has defied explanation.

243. deny: refuse

248. two treys: two threes (in a roll of the dice); **nice:** precise

249. Metheglin: spiced fermented honey and water; **wort:** unfermented beer; **malmsey:** sweet wine

252. cog: cheat (at dice)

255. grievest: injure; **gall:** sore or wound (The Princess puns on **gall** as [1] bile, and also [2] bitterness.)

A pedant. (3.1.187)
From *Pedantius* (1631).

KING
Why take we hands then?

ROSALINE   Only to part friends.—
Curtsy, sweethearts—and so the measure ends.   235

KING
More measure of this measure! Be not nice.

ROSALINE
We can afford no more at such a price.

KING
Prize you yourselves. What buys your company?

ROSALINE
Your absence only.

KING   That can never be.   240

ROSALINE
Then cannot we be bought. And so adieu—
Twice to your visor, and half once to you.

KING
If you deny to dance, let's hold more chat.

ROSALINE
In private, then.

KING   I am best pleased with that.   245
                        ⌜*They move aside.*⌝

BEROWNE, ⌜*to the Princess*⌝
White-handed mistress, one sweet word with thee.

PRINCESS, ⌜*speaking as Rosaline*⌝
Honey, and milk, and sugar—there is three.

BEROWNE
Nay then, two treys, an if you grow so nice,
Metheglin, wort, and malmsey. Well run, dice!
There's half a dozen sweets.   250

PRINCESS   Seventh sweet, adieu.
Since you can cog, I'll play no more with you.

BEROWNE
One word in secret.

PRINCESS   Let it not be sweet.

BEROWNE
Thou grievest my gall.   255

257. **meet:** appropriate

258. **change:** exchange

265. **was . . . tongue:** This comment on Longaville's silence includes a reference to the **tongue** of the **vizard**, or mask, which was a projection (on the inside of the mask) held in the mouth to secure the mask against the face.

268. **You . . . tongue:** a suggestion that Katherine is duplicitous, or that she is so talkative that she has one tongue to spare

269. **would afford:** i.e., wish to give

270. **Veal:** i.e., well (as it would be pronounced by a **Dutchman**) See longer note, page 241.

273. **part:** share, divide

274. **half:** i.e., better half, or spouse

275. **an ox:** literally, a castrated bull; figuratively, a fool

277. **give horns:** i.e., make your husband a cuckold (See page 90.)

"Jove's lightning." (4.2.139)
From Vincenzo Cartari, *Le vere e noue imagini* . . . (1615).

PRINCESS ⸀⸀⸀ Gall! Bitter.
BEROWNE ⸀⸀⸀ Therefore meet.
⌐*They move aside.*¬

DUMAINE, ⌐*to Maria*¬
Will you vouchsafe with me to change a word?
MARIA, ⌐*speaking as Katherine*¬
Name it.
DUMAINE Fair lady— 260
MARIA ⸀⸀⸀ Say you so? Fair lord!
Take that for your "fair lady."
DUMAINE ⸀⸀⸀ Please it you
As much in private, and I'll bid adieu.
⌐*They move aside.*¬
⌐KATHERINE, *speaking as Maria*¬
What, was your vizard made without a tongue? 265
LONGAVILLE
I know the reason, lady, why you ask.
⌐KATHERINE¬
O, for your reason! Quickly, sir, I long.
LONGAVILLE
You have a double tongue within your mask,
And would afford my speechless vizard half.
⌐KATHERINE¬
Veal, quoth the Dutchman. Is not veal a calf? 270
LONGAVILLE
A calf, fair lady?
⌐KATHERINE¬ No, a fair Lord Calf.
LONGAVILLE
Let's part the word.
⌐KATHERINE¬ No, I'll not be your half.
Take all and wean it. It may prove an ox. 275
LONGAVILLE
Look how you butt yourself in these sharp mocks.
Will you give horns, chaste lady? Do not so.
⌐KATHERINE¬
Then die a calf before your horns do grow.

284. **Above ... sense:** i.e., beyond the power of the senses; **sensible:** (1) intelligent; (2) acutely felt, markedly painful

285. **conference:** conversation; **conceits:** figures of speech

290. **dry-beaten:** thrashed (literally, with the flat of a sword so as not to draw blood); **scoff:** mockery

291. **simple:** foolish

296. **Well-liking:** healthy, plump

297. **O ... flout:** This line can be read as mockery of Rosaline's **poverty in wit** or of the king's.

The pomewater tree. (4.2.4)
From John Gerard, *The herball or generall historie of plantes* ... (1597).

LONGAVILLE
  One word in private with you ere I die.
⌜KATHERINE⌝
  Bleat softly, then. The butcher hears you cry.   280
                      ⌜*They move aside.*⌝

BOYET
  The tongues of mocking wenches are as keen
    As is the razor's edge invisible,
  Cutting a smaller hair than may be seen;
    Above the sense of sense, so sensible
  Seemeth their conference. Their conceits have   285
      wings
  Fleeter than arrows, bullets, wind, thought, swifter
      things.
ROSALINE
  Not one word more, my maids. Break off, break off!
      ⌜*The Ladies move away from the Lords.*⌝
BEROWNE
  By heaven, all dry-beaten with pure scoff!   290
KING
  Farewell, mad wenches. You have simple wits.
        ⌜*King, Lords, and Blackamoors*⌝ *exit.*
             ⌜*The Ladies unmask.*⌝
PRINCESS
  Twenty adieus, my frozen Muskovits.—
  Are these the breed of wits so wondered at?
BOYET
  Tapers they are, with your sweet breaths puffed
    out.   295
ROSALINE
  Well-liking wits they have; gross, gross; fat, fat.
PRINCESS
  O poverty in wit, kingly-poor flout!
  Will they not, think you, hang themselves tonight?
  Or ever but in vizards show their faces?
  This pert Berowne was out of count'nance quite.   300

301. **cases:** (1) states; (2) masks

302. **weeping ripe for:** i.e., ready to weep if he did not get

305. **No point:** certainly not (French *non point*), with wordplay on the sword's (blunt) **point; straight:** straightway, immediately

307. **came o'er:** took possession of

308. **trow you:** do you know

312. **better wits:** i.e., more intelligent men; **worn . . . statute-caps:** i.e., been mere commoners (who, by statute, had to wear simple woollen caps)

319. **In . . . shapes:** i.e., without their disguises

320. **digest:** swallow; endure

324. **change:** exchange; **repair:** come back

325. **Blow:** bloom

"Piercing a hogshead." (4.2.105)
From Guillaume de La Perrière, *La morosophie* . . . (1553).

ROSALINE
    They were all in lamentable cases.
  The King was weeping ripe for a good word.
PRINCESS
    Berowne did swear himself out of all suit.
MARIA
  Dumaine was at my service, and his sword.
    "No point," quoth I. My servant straight was   305
      mute.
KATHERINE
  Lord Longaville said I came o'er his heart.
    And trow you what he called me?
PRINCESS   Qualm, perhaps.
KATHERINE   Yes, in good faith.   310
PRINCESS   Go, sickness as thou art!
ROSALINE
    Well, better wits have worn plain statute-caps.
  But will you hear? The King is my love sworn.
PRINCESS
    And quick Berowne hath plighted faith to me.
KATHERINE
  And Longaville was for my service born.   315
MARIA
    Dumaine is mine as sure as bark on tree.
BOYET
  Madam, and pretty mistresses, give ear.
  Immediately they will again be here
  In their own shapes, for it can never be
  They will digest this harsh indignity.   320
PRINCESS
  Will they return?
BOYET   They will, they will, God knows,
  And leap for joy, though they are lame with blows.
  Therefore change favors, and when they repair,
  Blow like sweet roses in this summer air.   325

328. damask . . . commixture: deep pink, the mixture of "red and white" (See 1.2.90–107.)

329. vailing clouds: i.e., lowering clouds and becoming visible; **blown:** in bloom

330. Avaunt, perplexity: i.e., away, riddler

333. as . . . disguised: i.e., as much when they are themselves as when they wore disguises

335. shapeless: unshapely, ugly

338. carriage: behavior, deportment

341. runs: i.e., run

343. Please . . . Majesty: i.e., is it your majesty's pleasure to

The Damosell.

A damsel. (1.1.290)
From [Richard Day,] *A booke of christian prayers . . .* (1578).

PRINCESS
How "blow"? How "blow"? Speak to be understood.
BOYET
Fair ladies masked are roses in their bud.
Dismasked, their damask sweet commixture shown,
Are angels vailing clouds, or roses blown.
PRINCESS
Avaunt, perplexity!—What shall we do   330
If they return in their own shapes to woo?
ROSALINE
Good madam, if by me you'll be advised,
Let's mock them still, as well known as disguised.
Let us complain to them what fools were here,
Disguised like Muscovites in shapeless gear,   335
And wonder what they were, and to what end
Their shallow shows and prologue vilely penned,
And their rough carriage so ridiculous,
Should be presented at our tent to us.
BOYET
Ladies, withdraw. The gallants are at hand.   340
PRINCESS
Whip to our tents, as roes runs o'er land.
⌜*The Princess and the Ladies*⌝ *exit.*

Enter the King and the rest, ⌜*as themselves.*⌝

KING, ⌜*to Boyet*⌝
Fair sir, God save you. Where's the Princess?
BOYET
Gone to her tent. Please it your Majesty
Command me any service to her thither?
KING
That she vouchsafe me audience for one word.   345
BOYET
I will, and so will she, I know, my lord.   *He exits.*
BEROWNE
This fellow pecks up wit as pigeons peas,

348. **utters:** (1) says; (2) offers for sale

350. **wakes:** parish festivals; **wassails:** riotous festivities, revels

351. **by gross:** wholesale

352. **grace it:** adorn or embellish it

353. **pins . . . sleeve:** i.e., makes the ladies absolutely dependent upon him

354. **had:** would have

355. **carve:** This word describes some kind of courtly behavior that scholars cannot identify.

357. **ape of form:** slavish observer of etiquette; **Nice:** fastidious (See page 178.)

358. **tables:** backgammon

359. **honorable:** courteous (rather than swearing at them)

359–60. **sing . . . meanly:** i.e., sing a middle part (tenor or alto) moderately well

360. **ushering:** performing the tasks of a gentleman usher

361. **Mend . . . can:** i.e., just let anyone try to better him **Mend:** improve

364. **whale's bone:** ivory from the walrus (**Whale's** is pronounced with two syllables.)

365. **consciences:** i.e., conscientious people

369. **Behavior:** good manners, elegant deportment

370. **madman:** wildly foolish person

373. **all hail:** i.e., a hailstorm

And utters it again when God doth please.
He is wit's peddler, and retails his wares
At wakes and wassails, meetings, markets, fairs.   350
And we that sell by gross, the Lord doth know,
Have not the grace to grace it with such show.
This gallant pins the wenches on his sleeve.
Had he been Adam, he had tempted Eve.
He can carve too, and lisp. Why, this is he   355
That kissed his hand away in courtesy.
This is the ape of form, Monsieur the Nice,
That, when he plays at tables, chides the dice
In honorable terms. Nay, he can sing
A mean most meanly; and in ushering   360
Mend him who can. The ladies call him sweet.
The stairs, as he treads on them, kiss his feet.
This is the flower that smiles on everyone
To show his teeth as white as whale's bone;
And consciences that will not die in debt   365
Pay him the due of "honey-tongued Boyet."

KING
A blister on his sweet tongue, with my heart,
That put Armado's page out of his part!

Enter the Ladies, ⌈with Boyet.⌉

BEROWNE
See where it comes! Behavior, what wert thou
Till this madman showed thee? And what art thou   370
    now?
KING, ⌈*to Princess*⌉
All hail, sweet madam, and fair time of day.
PRINCESS
    "Fair" in "all hail" is foul, as I conceive.
KING
Construe my speeches better, if you may.
PRINCESS
    Then wish me better. I will give you leave.   375

379. **Nor . . . nor:** Neither . . . nor

381. **virtue:** power (In line 382 **virtue** has the meaning "goodness.")

382. **nickname:** misname

383. **virtue's . . . breaks:** i.e., it was never the function of virtue to break

388–89. **a breaking . . . Of:** i.e., a reason for breaking

390. **desolation:** solitariness, loneliness

394. **A mess of:** i.e., four (See note to 4.3.223.)

397. **courtship:** courtliness of manners; **state:** pomp

399. **to . . . days:** i.e., in the custom of our time

400. **undeserving:** i.e., undeserved

402. **habit:** clothing

"Monsieur the Nice." (5.2.357)
From Cesare Vecellio, *Habiti antichi et moderni . . .* (1598).

KING
  We came to visit you, and purpose now
    To lead you to our court. Vouchsafe it, then.
PRINCESS
  This field shall hold me, and so hold your vow.
    Nor God nor I delights in perjured men.
KING
  Rebuke me not for that which you provoke.   380
    The virtue of your eye must break my oath.
PRINCESS
  You nickname virtue; "vice" you should have spoke,
    For virtue's office never breaks men's troth.
  Now by my maiden honor, yet as pure
    As the unsullied lily, I protest,   385
  A world of torments though I should endure,
    I would not yield to be your house's guest,
  So much I hate a breaking cause to be
  Of heavenly oaths vowed with integrity.
KING
  O, you have lived in desolation here,   390
    Unseen, unvisited, much to our shame.
PRINCESS
  Not so, my lord. It is not so, I swear.
    We have had pastimes here and pleasant game.
  A mess of Russians left us but of late.
KING
  How, madam? Russians?   395
PRINCESS   Ay, in truth, my lord.
  Trim gallants, full of courtship and of state.
ROSALINE
  Madam, speak true.—It is not so, my lord.
  My lady, to the manner of the days,
  In courtesy gives undeserving praise.   400
  We four indeed confronted were with four
  In Russian habit. Here they stayed an hour
  And talked apace; and in that hour, my lord,

404. **happy:** felicitous

406. **fain:** gladly

407. **dry:** This wordplay on **thirsty** (line 406) puns on **dry** as (1) caustically witty and (2) dried up, or stale

409. **heaven's fiery eye:** i.e., the sun

411. **to . . . store:** i.e., compared to your huge supply (in this case, of intelligence and wealth)

415. **But that:** i.e., except for the fact that

420. **vizards:** masks

422–23. **that vizard . . . face:** Proverbial: "A well-favored visor will hide an ill-favored face." **case:** mask

425. **to a jest:** i.e., into a joke

426. **Amazed:** astounded, dumbfounded

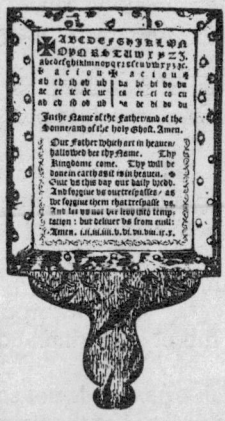

A hornbook. (5.1.48)
From Andrew White Tuer, *History of the horn-book . . .* (1896).

They did not bless us with one happy word.
I dare not call them fools; but this I think: 405
When they are thirsty, fools would fain have drink.

BEROWNE
This jest is dry to me. Gentle sweet,
Your wits makes wise things foolish. When we greet,
With eyes' best seeing, heaven's fiery eye,
By light we lose light. Your capacity 410
Is of that nature that to your huge store
Wise things seem foolish and rich things but poor.

ROSALINE
This proves you wise and rich, for in my eye—

BEROWNE
I am a fool, and full of poverty.

ROSALINE
But that you take what doth to you belong, 415
It were a fault to snatch words from my tongue.

BEROWNE
O, I am yours, and all that I possess!

ROSALINE
All the fool mine?

BEROWNE　　　　　　I cannot give you less.

ROSALINE
Which of the vizards was it that you wore? 420

BEROWNE
Where? When? What vizard? Why demand you this?

ROSALINE
There; then; that vizard; that superfluous case
That hid the worse and showed the better face.

KING, ⌐*aside to Dumaine*⌐
We were descried. They'll mock us now downright.

DUMAINE, ⌐*aside to King*⌐
Let us confess and turn it to a jest. 425

PRINCESS, ⌐*to King*⌐
Amazed, my lord? Why looks your Highness sad?

431. **face of brass:** i.e., face utterly insensible of shame

433. **confound:** destroy

435. **conceit:** understanding, mental capacity

436. **wish:** entreat

437. **wait:** i.e., will I wait, or attend, on you

440. **friend:** lover

441. **blind harper's song:** perhaps, ballad (A **harper,** or harpist, was proverbially blind.)

442–50. **Taffeta . . . noes:** In this elaborate series of figures of speech in which language is compared to cloth, ornate language is like the costly fabrics worn by the nobility, and straightforward speech is like plain, sturdy fabric.

443. **Three-piled hyperboles:** i.e., exaggerations that are like high-quality velvet, whose pile is three times normal thickness

444. **Figures:** i.e., figures of speech

445. **blown . . . ostentation:** i.e., puffed me up, as if they had laid their eggs in me

450. **russet:** coarse homespun cloth worn by peasants; **kersey:** plain (literally, coarse) cloth

451. **law:** exclamation of admiration (vulgar, like the rest of the language in this line)

452. **sans:** without (French)

453. **Sans "sans":** i.e., without the affectation of **"sans"**

454–55. **trick / Of:** i.e., habit from

455. **rage:** madness

456. **Soft:** i.e., wait a minute

457. **Lord . . . us:** words written on the door of a house containing someone stricken with the bubonic plague

459. **of:** from

ROSALINE
  Help, hold his brows! He'll swoon!—Why look you
    pale?
  Seasick, I think, coming from Muscovy.
BEROWNE
  Thus pour the stars down plagues for perjury.   430
    Can any face of brass hold longer out?
  Here stand I, lady. Dart thy skill at me.
    Bruise me with scorn, confound me with a flout.
  Thrust thy sharp wit quite through my ignorance.
    Cut me to pieces with thy keen conceit,   435
  And I will wish thee nevermore to dance,
    Nor nevermore in Russian habit wait.
  O, never will I trust to speeches penned,
    Nor to the motion of a schoolboy's tongue,
  Nor never come in vizard to my friend,   440
    Nor woo in rhyme like a blind harper's song.
  Taffeta phrases, silken terms precise,
    Three-piled hyperboles, spruce ⌐affection,⌐
  Figures pedantical—these summer flies
    Have blown me full of maggot ostentation.   445
  I do forswear them, and I here protest
    By this white glove—how white the hand, God
      knows!—
  Henceforth my wooing mind shall be expressed
    In russet yeas and honest kersey noes.   450
  And to begin: Wench, so God help me, law,
  My love to thee is sound, sans crack or flaw.
ROSALINE
  Sans "sans," I pray you.
BEROWNE   Yet I have a trick
  Of the old rage. Bear with me, I am sick;   455
  I'll leave it by degrees. Soft, let us see:
  Write "Lord have mercy on us" on those three.
  They are infected; in their hearts it lies.
  They have the plague, and caught it of your eyes.

460. **visited:** afflicted; **free:** i.e., free of infection

461. **Lord's tokens:** (1) plague spots; (2) love tokens (See longer note, page 241.)

462. **free:** (1) fancy-free; (2) generous

463. **Our ... forfeit:** i.e., we have forfeited our status as honorable men (with wordplay on the forfeiting of **states** [estates] through lawsuits); **undo:** release or **free** (with wordplay on **undo** as ruin or destroy)

465. **sue:** (1) bring the lawsuit; (2) woo

466. **have to do with:** have further dealings with (This phrase can also mean "have intercourse with.")

474. **were ... advised:** i.e., did you consider what you did

479. **challenge:** lay claim to

482. **Your ... forswear:** i.e., having already broken your oath, you attach no importance to false swearing

"Like osiers bowed." (4.2.129–30)
From Henry Peacham, *Minerua Britanna* . . . (1612).

These lords are visited. You are not free,   460
For the Lord's tokens on you do I see.
PRINCESS
No, they are free that gave these tokens to us.
BEROWNE
Our states are forfeit. Seek not to undo us.
ROSALINE
It is not so, for how can this be true,
That you stand forfeit, being those that sue?   465
BEROWNE
Peace, for I will not have to do with you.
ROSALINE
Nor shall not, if I do as I intend.
BEROWNE, ⌜*to King, Longaville, and Dumaine*⌝
Speak for yourselves. My wit is at an end.
KING, ⌜*to Princess*⌝
Teach us, sweet madam, for our rude transgression
Some fair excuse.   470
PRINCESS   The fairest is confession.
Were not you here but even now, disguised?
KING
Madam, I was.
PRINCESS   And were you well advised?
KING
I was, fair madam.   475
PRINCESS   When you then were here,
What did you whisper in your lady's ear?
KING
That more than all the world I did respect her.
PRINCESS
When she shall challenge this, you will reject her.
KING
Upon mine honor, no.   480
PRINCESS   Peace, peace, forbear!
Your oath once broke, you force not to forswear.
KING
Despise me when I break this oath of mine.

503. **Neither of either:** i.e., neither the one nor the other; **remit:** resign, surrender; **both twain:** i.e., both of them

504. **on:** i.e., in; **a consent:** an agreement

505. **Knowing:** i.e., since they knew

506. **dash:** spoil, ruin; **comedy:** i.e., interlude or biblical play

507. **carry-tale:** tattletale; **please-man:** i.e., one who will do anything to please

508. **zany:** assistant to a clown or mountebank, who mimics his master's skills in ridiculously awkward ways

509. **mumble-news:** tale-bearer; **trencher-knight:** dependent, parasite

510. **Dick:** knave, fellow

A "nightwatch constable." (3.1.186)
From [Thomas Dekker,] *The belman of London* . . . (1616).

PRINCESS
   I will, and therefore keep it.—Rosaline,
   What did the Russian whisper in your ear?   485
ROSALINE
   Madam, he swore that he did hold me dear
   As precious eyesight, and did value me
   Above this world, adding thereto moreover
   That he would wed me or else die my lover.
PRINCESS
   God give thee joy of him! The noble lord   490
   Most honorably doth uphold his word.
KING
   What mean you, madam? By my life, my troth,
   I never swore this lady such an oath.
ROSALINE
   By heaven, you did! And to confirm it plain,
   You gave me this. ⌐*She shows a token.*¬ But take it,   495
      sir, again.
KING
   My faith and this the Princess I did give.
   I knew her by this jewel on her sleeve.
PRINCESS
   Pardon me, sir. This jewel did she wear.
                          ⌐*She points to Rosaline.*¬
   And Lord Berowne, I thank him, is my dear.   500
   ⌐*To Berowne.*¬ What, will you have me, or your pearl
      again?   ⌐*She shows the token.*¬
BEROWNE
   Neither of either. I remit both twain.
   I see the trick on 't. Here was a consent,
   Knowing aforehand of our merriment,   505
   To dash it like a Christmas comedy.
   Some carry-tale, some please-man, some slight
      ⟨zany,⟩
   Some mumble-news, some trencher-knight, some
      Dick,   510

511. **smiles . . . years:** i.e., smiles his face into wrinkles

512. **my lady:** i.e., the lady whom he serves

515. **she:** i.e., the lady each of us meant to woo

518. **Much . . . 'tis:** i.e., some such events as these are surely what happened

520. **know . . . squier:** i.e., know how to assess accurately the lady you serve (proverbial: "have the length of her foot") **by th' squier:** i.e., according to the carpenter's set square, precisely

521. **laugh upon:** i.e., smile or look pleasantly on; **apple:** pupil

522. **stand . . . fire:** i.e., use your body to screen hers from the fire's heat

523. **Holding a trencher:** i.e., presenting a wooden platter (as if he were an attentive waiter)

525. **smock:** i.e., woman's undergarment, a shift or chemise

529. **brave:** splendid; **manage, career:** short gallop at full speed

530. **tilting:** charging on horseback with a lance; **straight:** straightway, immediately

5.2 (continued)   Costard introduces the pageant of the Nine Worthies. The pageant is interrupted by Costard's announcement that Jaquenetta is pregnant and that Armado is the father. Armado challenges Costard to a duel. (Scene heading continues on page 206.)

532. **would:** wish to

533. **Worthies:** See longer note to 5.1.117–18.

(continued)

That smiles his cheek in years and knows the trick
To make my lady laugh when she's disposed,
Told our intents before; which once disclosed,
The ladies did change favors; and then we,
Following the signs, wooed but the sign of she.   515
Now, to our perjury to add more terror,
We are again forsworn in will and error.
Much upon this 'tis. ⌜*To Boyet.*⌝ And might not you
Forestall our sport, to make us thus untrue?
Do not you know my lady's foot by th' squier?   520
   And laugh upon the apple of her eye?
And stand between her back, sir, and the fire,
   Holding a trencher, jesting merrily?
You put our page out. Go, you are allowed.
Die when you will, a smock shall be your shroud.   525
You leer upon me, do you? There's an eye
Wounds like a leaden sword.

BOYET   Full merrily
Hath this brave ⌜manage,⌝ this career been run.

BEROWNE
Lo, he is tilting straight! Peace, I have done.   530

                   Enter Clown ⌜Costard.⌝

Welcome, pure wit. Thou part'st a fair fray.

COSTARD   O Lord, sir, they would know
Whether the three Worthies shall come in or no.

BEROWNE
What, are there but three?

COSTARD   No, sir; but it is vara fine,   535
For every one pursents three.

BEROWNE   And three times thrice
      is nine.

COSTARD
Not so, sir, under correction, sir, I hope it is not so.

535. **vara:** very (dialect pronunciation)

536. **pursents:** presents (dialect)

539. **under:** i.e., subject to

540. **You . . . us:** i.e., we are not fools (Proverbial: "Let him be begged for a fool.")

544. **whereuntil:** i.e., to how much

546. **By Jove:** a mild conventional oath

547. **you should get:** i.e., if you had to earn

548. **reckoning:** counting, calculating

552. **parfect:** dialect for "perfect" (or, perhaps a mistake for "perform")

553. **Pompion:** i.e., Pompey (literally, pumpkin)

557. **degree:** rank

563. **some policy:** i.e., a wise move

564. **show:** entertainment

564–65. **the King's . . . company:** i.e., the Muscovites' masque

Pompey the Great. (5.1.128–29)
From [Guillaume Rouillé,] . . . *Prima pars promptuarii* . . . (1553).

You cannot beg us, sir, I can assure you, sir; we 540
  know what we know.

I hope, sir, three times thrice, sir—

BEROWNE   Is not nine?

COSTARD   Under correction, sir, we know whereuntil it
  doth amount. 545

BEROWNE

By Jove, I always took three threes for nine.

COSTARD   O Lord, sir, it were pity you should get your
  living by reckoning, sir.

BEROWNE   How much is it?

COSTARD   O Lord, sir, the parties themselves, the ac- 550
  tors, sir, will show whereuntil it doth amount. For
  mine own part, I am, as ⟨they⟩ say, but to parfect one
  man in one poor man—Pompion the Great, sir.

BEROWNE   Art thou one of the Worthies?

COSTARD   It pleased them to think me worthy of Pom- 555
  pey the Great. For mine own part, I know not the
  degree of the Worthy, but I am to stand for him.

BEROWNE   Go bid them prepare.

COSTARD

We will turn it finely off, sir. We will take some
  care.   *He exits.* 560

KING

Berowne, they will shame us. Let them not
  approach.

BEROWNE

We are shame-proof, my lord; and 'tis some policy
To have one show worse than the King's and his
  company. 565

KING   I say they shall not come.

PRINCESS

Nay, my good lord, let me o'errule you now.
That sport best pleases that doth ⟨least⟩ know how,

569. **content:** satisfy

569–70. **the contents . . . presents:** i.e., the subject matter is destroyed by its overenthusiastic presentation

571. **confounded:** destroyed; **most . . . mirth:** i.e., the best entertainment

572. **great . . . birth:** i.e., ambitious undertakings die in the struggle to be born **laboring:** literally, suffering the pains of childbirth

573. **A right:** an accurate; **our sport:** i.e., the Muscovites' masque

574. **Anointed:** i.e., your highness (When crowned, a king is anointed with balm.)

579. **God his:** i.e., God's

580. **That . . . one:** i.e., it does not matter

583. **fortuna de la guerra:** the fortune of war

584–85. **couplement:** couple

586. **like:** i.e., likely

587. **presence:** company

589. **pedant:** schoolmaster

592. **habits:** clothes (i.e., costumes)

596–97. **hedge-priest:** i.e., the curate (literally, an illiterate or uneducated priest of inferior status)

597. **fool:** i.e., Costard the Clown

598. **Abate . . . novum:** i.e., bar a throw of the dice, or pure chance (See longer note, page 241.)

599. **in his vein:** i.e., with his peculiarity

Where zeal strives to content, and the contents
Dies in the zeal of that which it presents. 570
Their form confounded makes most form in mirth,
When great things laboring perish in their birth.
BEROWNE
A right description of our sport, my lord.

Enter Braggart ⌐Armado.⌐

ARMADO, ⌐*to King*⌐ Anointed, I implore so much expense of thy royal sweet breath as will utter a brace 575
of words. ⌐*Armado and King step aside, and
Armado gives King a paper.*⌐
PRINCESS Doth this man serve God?
BEROWNE Why ask you?
PRINCESS
He speaks not like a man of God his making.
ARMADO, ⌐*to King*⌐ That is all one, my fair sweet honey 580
monarch, for, I protest, the schoolmaster is exceeding fantastical, too, too vain, too, too vain. But
we will put it, as they say, to *fortuna de la guerra.*—I
wish you the peace of mind, most royal couplement! *He exits.* 585
KING, ⌐*reading the paper*⌐ Here is like to be a good
presence of Worthies. He presents Hector of Troy,
the swain Pompey the Great, the parish curate
Alexander, Armado's page Hercules, the pedant
Judas Maccabaeus. 590
And if these four Worthies in their first show thrive,
These four will change habits and present the other
five.
BEROWNE There is five in the first show.
KING You are deceived. 'Tis not so. 595
BEROWNE The pedant, the braggart, the hedge-
priest, the fool, and the boy.
Abate throw at novum, and the whole world again
Cannot pick out five such, take each one in his vein.

600. **amain:** at full speed

604. **With leopard's . . . knee:** an allusion to Pompey's insignia, a heraldic leopard (which may here be displayed on the knee of the costume or on a shield that Costard is carrying awkwardly)

611. **targe:** a light shield, or buckler

618. **had done:** i.e., will have finished

621. **perfect:** i.e., word perfect

622. **My hat . . . halfpenny:** i.e., I'll wager anything that (Noblemen's hats in the period were large, made of rich fabric, and ornately decorated.)

623 SD. **for:** i.e., as

Alexander the Great. (5.2.623 SD)
From Valentin Thilo, *Icones heroum . . .* (1589).

KING
  The ship is under sail, and here she comes amain.   600

  Enter ⌜Costard as⌝ Pompey.

COSTARD
  I Pompey am—
BEROWNE   You lie; you are not he.
COSTARD
  I Pompey am—
BOYET   With leopard's head on knee.
BEROWNE
  Well said, old mocker. I must needs be friends with   605
    thee.
COSTARD
  I Pompey am, Pompey, surnamed the Big—
DUMAINE "The Great."
COSTARD It is "Great," sir.—*Pompey, surnamed the
    Great,*   610
  *That oft in field, with targe and shield, did make my
    foe to sweat.*
  *And traveling along this coast, I here am come by
    chance,*
  *And lay my arms before the legs of this sweet lass of   615
    France.*
    (*⌜He places his weapons at the feet of the Princess.⌝*)
  If your Ladyship would say "Thanks, Pompey," I
  had done.
⌜PRINCESS⌝ Great thanks, great Pompey.
COSTARD 'Tis not so much worth, but I hope I was   620
    perfect. I made a little fault in "Great."
BEROWNE My hat to a halfpenny, Pompey proves the
    best Worthy.   ⌜*Costard stands aside.*⌝

  Enter Curate ⌜Nathaniel⌝ for Alexander.

NATHANIEL
  *When in the world I lived, I was the world's
    commander.*   625

628. **scutcheon:** coat of arms on a shield

630. **right:** straight (According to the historian Plutarch, Alexander held his head awry; hence his nose would have been at an angle.)

631–32. **Your ... knight:** Alexander was reported to have had a sweet-smelling breath and skin. Here Berowne suggests that it is Boyet's **tender-smelling** (sensitive) **nose** that has detected Nathaniel as an impostor.

644. **painted cloth:** wall hanging, onto which the scene was painted (The Nine Worthies were often depicted in tapestries and painted wall hangings.); **Your lion:** i.e., Alexander's coat of arms

644–45. **that ... close-stool:** See longer note, page 241. **polax:** poleax, a medieval battle-ax **close-stool:** chamber pot enclosed in a box or stool

645. **Ajax:** a Greek warrior who fought in the Trojan War (with wordplay on "a jakes" or privy)

649. **dashed:** discouraged

652. **a little o'erparted:** i.e., having a part to play that was a bit too difficult for him

653. **sort:** way

   By east, west, north, and south, I spread my
     conquering might.
   My scutcheon plain declares that I am Alisander—
BOYET
   Your nose says no, you are not, for it stands too
     right.   630
BEROWNE, ⌈*to Boyet*⌉
   Your nose smells "no" in ⟨this⟩, most tender-
     smelling knight.
PRINCESS
   The conqueror is dismayed.—Proceed, good
     Alexander.
NATHANIEL
   When in the world I lived, I was the world's   635
     commander—
BOYET
   Most true; 'tis right. You were so, Alisander.
BEROWNE, ⌈*to Costard*⌉ Pompey the Great—
COSTARD   Your servant, and Costard.
BEROWNE   Take away the conqueror. Take away Alisan- 640
     der.
COSTARD, ⌈*to Nathaniel*⌉ O sir, you have overthrown
     Alisander the Conqueror. You will be scraped out of
     the painted cloth for this. Your lion, that holds his
     polax sitting on a close-stool, will be given to Ajax. 645
     He will be the ninth Worthy. A conqueror, and
     afeard to speak? Run away for shame, Alisander.
                      Nathaniel exits.
     There, an 't shall please you, a foolish mild man, an
     honest man, look you, and soon dashed. He is a
     marvelous good neighbor, faith, and a very good 650
     bowler. But, for Alisander—alas, you see how 'tis—
     a little o'erparted. But there are Worthies a-coming
     will speak their mind in some other sort.

   Enter Pedant ⌈*Holofernes*⌉ *for Judas, and the Boy*
                for Hercules.

656. **Cerberus:** the mythological three-headed dog who guards the gates of Hades; **canus:** an error for *canis*, or dog (See longer note to 4.2.3–4, page 234.)

658. **manus:** hands

659. **Quoniam:** since; **seemeth in minority:** i.e., appears as a child, as underage

660. **Ergo:** therefore; **apology:** speech of explanation

661. **state:** dignity

663–64. **Judas . . . Iscariot:** Judas Iscariot was the apostle in the New Testament who betrayed Jesus; thus the name **Judas** became synonymous with treachery.

665. **yclept:** called

666. **clipped:** (1) wordplay on **yclept;** (2) abbreviated; (3) embraced (hence the word **kissing** in line 667)

667. **kissing:** To identify Jesus to his enemies, Judas kissed him.

674–75. **Judas . . . elder:** "Then Judas . . . repented, . . . and went and hanged himself" (Matthew 27.3–5). That he hanged himself on an **elder** tree was a common medieval tradition.

679. **cittern-head:** grotesquely carved head of a cithern, an early kind of guitar

680. **bodkin:** woman's hairpin, sometimes with an ornate head in the shape of a bird or insect

681. **death's face:** death's-head, or skull

682. **of:** i.e., on

682–83. **scarce seen:** i.e., nearly obliterated

684. **pommel:** knob at the end of a sword handle; **falchion:** curved sword

PRINCESS, ⌜*to Costard*⌝ Stand aside, good Pompey.

HOLOFERNES
  Great Hercules is presented by this imp,   655
    Whose club killed Cerberus, that three-headed canus,
  And when he was a babe, a child, a shrimp,
    Thus did he strangle serpents in his manus.
  Quoniam *he seemeth in minority,*
  Ergo *I come with this apology.*   660
    ⌜*To Boy.*⌝ Keep some state in thy exit, and vanish.
                        Boy ⌜*steps aside.*⌝

HOLOFERNES
  Judas I am—

DUMAINE A Judas!

HOLOFERNES Not Iscariot, sir.
  Judas I am, yclept Maccabaeus.   665

DUMAINE Judas Maccabaeus clipped is plain Judas.

BEROWNE A kissing traitor.—How art thou proved
  Judas?

HOLOFERNES
  Judas I am—

DUMAINE The more shame for you, Judas.   670

HOLOFERNES What mean you, sir?

BOYET To make Judas hang himself.

HOLOFERNES Begin, sir, you are my elder.

BEROWNE **Well** followed. Judas was hanged on an
  elder.   675

HOLOFERNES I will not be put out of countenance.

BEROWNE Because thou hast no face.

HOLOFERNES What is this? ⌜*He points to his own face.*⌝

BOYET A cittern-head.

DUMAINE The head of a bodkin.   680

BEROWNE A death's face in a ring.

LONGAVILLE The face of an old Roman coin, scarce
  seen.

BOYET The pommel of Caesar's falchion.

685. **flask:** a gunpowder flask of horn or bone

686. **St. George's half-cheek:** the profile of England's patron saint

687. **brooch of lead:** worn by members of guilds on their caps to indicate their trades

688. **tooth-drawer:** puller of teeth

689–90. **put . . . countenance:** encouraged you

693. **outfaced:** disconcerted, shamed

694–95. **lion . . . ass:** These lines may play on Aesop's fable of the ass who attempted to disguise himself in a lion's skin.

703. **baited:** attacked

704. **Achilles:** Hector's chief opponent in the Trojan War

706. **come . . . me:** redound against me

707. **merry:** facetious, amused

708. **Troyan:** (1) inhabitant of Troy; (2) ordinary fellow

710. **clean-timbered:** well-built

712. **calf:** (1) lower leg; (2) dolt; (3) meek fellow

Iudas Macabee

Judas Maccabaeus.
Tipped into *Chronologie et sommaire des souuerains . . .* (1622).

DUMAINE   The carved-bone face on a flask.   685
BEROWNE   Saint George's half-cheek in a brooch.
DUMAINE   Ay, and in a brooch of lead.
BEROWNE   Ay, and worn in the cap of a tooth-drawer.
    And now forward, for we have put thee in counte-
    nance.   690
HOLOFERNES   You have put me out of countenance.
BEROWNE   False. We have given thee faces.
HOLOFERNES   But you have outfaced them all.
BEROWNE
   An thou wert a lion, we would do so.
BOYET
   Therefore, as he is an ass, let him go.—   695
   And so adieu, sweet Jude. Nay, why dost thou stay?
DUMAINE   For the latter end of his name.
BEROWNE
   For the "ass" to the "Jude"? Give it him.—Jud-as,
   away!
HOLOFERNES
   This is not generous, not gentle, not humble.   700
BOYET
   A light for Monsieur Judas! It grows dark; he may
     stumble.   ⌐*Holofernes exits.*¬
PRINCESS
   Alas, poor Maccabaeus, how hath he been baited!

     Enter Braggart ⌐*Armado as Hector.*¬

BEROWNE   Hide thy head, Achilles. Here comes Hector
    in arms.   705
DUMAINE   Though my mocks come home by me, I will
    now be merry.
KING   Hector was but a Troyan in respect of this.
BOYET   But is this Hector?
KING   I think Hector was not so clean-timbered.   710
LONGAVILLE   His leg is too big for Hector's.
DUMAINE   More calf, certain.

713. **endued:** endowed; **small:** the leg below the calf

716. **armipotent:** powerful in arms

718. **gilt nutmeg:** nutmeg glazed with egg yolk, used to flavor drinks

721. **cloven:** Dumaine perhaps plays on **lemon** as "leman" (i.e., sweetheart), and refers obscenely to women's genitals.

724. **Ilion:** Troy

725. **so breathed:** i.e., with such good wind, or so fit

730. **rein:** check, halt

731. **give . . . rein:** i.e., let it run

735. **chucks:** a term of endearment

737. **device:** dramatic representation

737–38. **bestow . . . hearing:** i.e., listen to me (literally, grant me the power to hear)

738 SD. **Berowne steps forth:** See longer note, page 241.

742. **yard:** three feet (with the slang sense of "penis")

Hector.
From [Guillaume Rouillé,] . . . *Prima pars promptuarii* . . . (1553).

202

BOYET No, he is best endued in the small.

BEROWNE This cannot be Hector.

DUMAINE He's a god or a painter, for he makes faces. 715

ARMADO
The armipotent Mars, of lances the almighty,
    Gave Hector a gift—

DUMAINE A ⟨gilt⟩ nutmeg.

BEROWNE A lemon.

LONGAVILLE Stuck with cloves. 720

DUMAINE No, cloven.

ARMADO Peace!
The armipotent Mars, of lances the almighty,
    Gave Hector a gift, the heir of Ilion,
A man so breathed, that certain he would fight, yea, 725
    From morn till night, out of his pavilion.
I am that flower—

DUMAINE That mint.

LONGAVILLE That columbine.

ARMADO Sweet Lord Longaville, rein thy tongue. 730

LONGAVILLE I must rather give it the rein, for it runs
    against Hector.

DUMAINE Ay, and Hector's a greyhound.

ARMADO The sweet warman is dead and rotten. Sweet
    chucks, beat not the bones of the buried. When he 735
    breathed, he was a man. But I will forward with my
    device. ⌜*To Princess.*⌝ Sweet royalty, bestow on me
    the sense of hearing.

                                        Berowne steps forth.

PRINCESS
    Speak, brave Hector. We are much delighted.

ARMADO I do adore thy sweet Grace's slipper. 740

BOYET Loves her by the foot.

DUMAINE He may not by the yard.

ARMADO
    This Hector far surmounted Hannibal.
    The party is gone—

749. **quick:** quick with child, pregnant

750. **brags . . . yours:** Armado's role is that of the Braggart.

751. **infamonize:** Armado's version of "infamize," or defame

753. **whipped:** Whipping was the punishment for fornication.

754. **quick:** pregnant (with wordplay on **quick** as "alive")

755. **dead by him:** a reference to Armado's threat at line 752

761. **moved:** aroused, ready to act; **Ates:** Ate was the Greek goddess of bloodshed and strife.

765. **sup:** feed

769. **bepray:** perhaps, pray or beseech (This word is not recorded elsewhere.)

770. **my arms:** i.e., the weapons I used in playing Pompey

772 SD. **doublet:** close-fitting jacket

774–75. **take . . . lower:** (1) help you open your doublet; (2) humiliate you (proverbial: "take you down a buttonhole" or "take you down a peg or two")

775. **uncasing:** undressing

COSTARD Fellow Hector, she is gone; she is two 745
    months on her way.

ARMADO What meanest thou?

COSTARD Faith, unless you play the honest Troyan, the
    poor wench is cast away. She's quick; the child
    brags in her belly already. 'Tis yours. 750

ARMADO Dost thou infamonize me among potentates?
    Thou shalt die!

COSTARD Then shall Hector be whipped for Jaque-
    netta, that is quick by him, and hanged for Pompey,
    that is dead by him. 755

DUMAINE Most rare Pompey!

BOYET Renowned Pompey!

BEROWNE Greater than "Great"! Great, great, great
    Pompey. Pompey the Huge!

DUMAINE Hector trembles. 760

BEROWNE Pompey is moved. More Ates, more Ates!
    Stir them ⌈on,⌉ stir them on.

DUMAINE Hector will challenge him.

BEROWNE Ay, if he have no more man's blood in his
    belly than will sup a flea. 765

ARMADO, ⌈*to Costard*⌉ By the North Pole, I do challenge
    thee!

COSTARD I will not fight with a pole like a northern
    man! I'll slash. I'll do it by the sword.—I bepray
    you, let me borrow my arms again. 770

DUMAINE Room for the incensed Worthies!

COSTARD I'll do it in my shirt. ⌈*He removes his doublet.*⌉

DUMAINE Most resolute Pompey!

BOY, ⌈*to Armado*⌉ Master, let me take you a buttonhole
    lower. Do you not see Pompey is uncasing for the 775
    combat? What mean you? You will lose your reputa-
    tion.

ARMADO Gentlemen and soldiers, pardon me. I will
    not combat in my shirt.

780. **deny it:** refuse to

782. **bloods:** i.e., people of noble stock

785. **woolward for penance:** i.e., I wear no shirt under my woolen outer garment as an act of penance

786. **want:** lack

788. **dishclout:** dishcloth

789. **favor:** love token

5.2 (continued)   A messenger from the French court arrives to announce the death of the Princess's father. The King and his lords try once again to prevail upon the Princess and her ladies to accept their love, but the women insist that the King and lords spend the following year—the Princess's year of mourning for her father—undergoing specific penances. At the end of the year the men may, if they wish, renew their proposals of marriage.

798–800. **I have . . . discretion:** Proverbial: "One may see day at a little hole," meaning "I am no fool." **discretion:** ability to discern what is right as regards one's own conduct

DUMAINE You may not deny it. Pompey hath made the 780
    challenge.
ARMADO Sweet bloods, I both may and will.
BEROWNE What reason have you for 't?
ARMADO The naked truth of it is, I have no shirt. I go
    woolward for penance. 785
BOYET True, and it was enjoined him in Rome for want
    of linen; since when, I'll be sworn, he wore none
    but a dishclout of Jaquenetta's, and that he wears
    next his heart for a favor.

Enter a Messenger, Monsieur Marcade.

MARCADE, ⌜*to Princess*⌝ God save you, madam. 790
PRINCESS Welcome, Marcade,
  But that thou interruptest our merriment.
MARCADE
  I am sorry, madam, for the news I bring
  Is heavy in my tongue. The King your father—
PRINCESS
  Dead, for my life. 795
MARCADE   Even so. My tale is told.
BEROWNE
  Worthies, away! The scene begins to cloud.
ARMADO For mine own part, I breathe free breath. I
    have seen the day of wrong through the little hole
    of discretion, and I will right myself like a soldier. 800
                          Worthies exit.
KING, ⌜*to Princess*⌝ How fares your Majesty?
PRINCESS
  Boyet, prepare. I will away tonight.
KING
  Madam, not so. I do beseech you stay.
PRINCESS, ⌜*to Boyet*⌝
  Prepare, I say.—I thank you, gracious lords,
  For all your fair endeavors, and entreat, 805
  Out of a new-sad soul, that you vouchsafe

808. **liberal:** unrestrained, imprudent, indecorous

810. **converse of breath:** i.e., conversation; **gentleness:** courtesy, affability

811. **guilty of:** to be blamed for, responsible for

813. **so:** therefore

814. **my great . . . obtained:** This line is the only indication in the play of the Princess's success in her embassy.

815–18. **The extreme . . . arbitrate:** i.e., the pressure of time forces decisions that could not be made through extensive discussion **extreme:** last, latest **extremely:** stringently, strictly **at . . . loose:** at the very last moment (literally, at the moment that an arrow is discharged from a bow) **process:** discussion

821. **convince:** demonstrate, prove

822. **on foot:** in active existence

825. **wholesome-profitable:** i.e., wholesomely profitable

827. **double:** i.e., doubled (by my inability to understand you)

829. **badges:** signs (i.e., the following words)

832. **humors:** likings, inclinations

833. **to . . . intents:** i.e., to the opposite of what we intended

835. **unbefitting strains:** unbecoming compulsions

836. **wanton:** playful

838. **habits:** appearances

In your rich wisdom to excuse or hide
The liberal opposition of our spirits,
If overboldly we have borne ourselves
In the converse of breath; your gentleness   810
Was guilty of it. Farewell, worthy lord.
A heavy heart bears not a humble tongue.
Excuse me so, coming too short of thanks
For my great suit so easily obtained.

KING
The extreme parts of time extremely forms   815
All causes to the purpose of his speed,
And often at his very loose decides
That which long process could not arbitrate.
And though the mourning brow of progeny
Forbid the smiling courtesy of love   820
The holy suit which fain it would convince,
Yet since love's argument was first on foot,
Let not the cloud of sorrow jostle it
From what it purposed, since to wail friends lost
Is not by much so wholesome-profitable   825
As to rejoice at friends but newly found.

PRINCESS
I understand you not. My griefs are double.

BEROWNE
Honest plain words best pierce the ear of grief,
And by these badges understand the King:
For your fair sakes have we neglected time,   830
Played foul play with our oaths. Your beauty, ladies,
Hath much deformed us, fashioning our humors
Even to the opposèd end of our intents.
And what in us hath seemed ridiculous—
As love is full of unbefitting strains,   835
All wanton as a child, skipping and vain,
Formed by the eye and therefore, like the eye,
Full of ⌜strange⌝ shapes, of habits, and of forms,
Varying in subjects as the eye doth roll

841–45. **Which parti-coated . . . make:** i.e., if, in your eyes, our love seems unbecoming, it was your eyes that tempted us to commit the faults that those eyes now look into **parti-coated:** in a parti-colored coat such as was worn by a professional jester **loose:** wanton, unrestrained **Have misbecomed:** was inappropriate to **gravities:** dignities **Suggested:** tempted

848. **By being once false:** i.e., by breaking our oath to see no women

850. **falsehood:** i.e., oath-breaking, forswearing

851. **grace:** virtue

854. **rated:** assessed

855. **At:** i.e., as of no more value than; **courtship:** courtliness

856. **bombast:** high-sounding language about trivial subjects (literally, stuffing or padding in clothes)

857. **devout:** solemn, reverential; **respects:** consideration

859. **a merriment:** i.e., a piece of fooling, mere fun

862. **quote:** regard

866. **world-without-end:** eternal

868. **dear:** (1) dire; (2) endearing

To every varied object in his glance; 840
Which parti-coated presence of loose love
Put on by us, if, in your heavenly eyes,
Have misbecomed our oaths and gravities,
Those heavenly eyes, that look into these faults,
Suggested us to make. Therefore, ladies, 845
Our love being yours, the error that love makes
Is likewise yours. We to ourselves prove false
By being once false forever to be true
To those that make us both—fair ladies, you.
And even that falsehood, in itself a sin, 850
Thus purifies itself and turns to grace.

PRINCESS
We have received your letters full of love;
Your favors, ⟨the⟩ ambassadors of love;
And in our maiden council rated them
At courtship, pleasant jest, and courtesy, 855
As bombast and as lining to the time.
But more devout than this ⌜in⌝ our respects
Have we not been, and therefore met your loves
In their own fashion, like a merriment.

DUMAINE
Our letters, madam, showed much more than jest. 860

LONGAVILLE
So did our looks.

ROSALINE   We did not quote them so.

KING
Now, at the latest minute of the hour,
Grant us your loves.

PRINCESS   A time, methinks, too short 865
To make a world-without-end bargain in.
No, no, my lord, your Grace is perjured much,
Full of dear guiltiness, and therefore this:
If for my love—as there is no such cause—
You will do aught, this shall you do for me: 870
Your oath I will not trust, but go with speed

872. **forlorn:** deserted; **naked:** unfurnished

874. **celestial signs:** i.e., signs of the zodiac, which, taken together, signify a year's time

875. **brought . . . reckoning:** i.e., completed the year

878. **weeds:** clothes

880. **last love:** persist as love

882. **challenge:** lay claim to; **by these deserts:** i.e., according to what you deserve

884–87. **And till . . . death:** i.e., I will observe the (customary) one-year period of mourning

889. **entitled in:** i.e., with any rightful claim to

891. **flatter up:** indulge unduly, pamper

893. **Hence hermit:** i.e., I go hence a hermit; **breast:** See longer note, page 242.

900. **mark:** pay attention to; **smooth-faced:** beardless

Henry IIII, King of France and Navarre.
From Jean de Serres, *A generall historie of France* . . . (1611).

To some forlorn and naked hermitage,
Remote from all the pleasures of the world.
There stay until the twelve celestial signs
Have brought about the annual reckoning.   875
If this austere insociable life
Change not your offer made in heat of blood;
If frosts and fasts, hard lodging, and thin weeds
Nip not the gaudy blossoms of your love,
But that it bear this trial, and last love;   880
Then, at the expiration of the year,
Come challenge me, challenge me by these deserts,
⌜*She takes his hand.*⌝
And by this virgin palm now kissing thine,
I will be thine. And till that ⟨instant⟩ shut
My woeful self up in a mourning house,   885
Raining the tears of lamentation
For the remembrance of my father's death.
If this thou do deny, let our hands part,
Neither entitled in the other's heart.

KING
If this, or more than this, I would deny,   890
    To flatter up these powers of mine with rest,
The sudden hand of death close up mine eye!
    Hence hermit, then. My heart is in thy breast.
⌜*They step aside.*⌝

DUMAINE, ⌜*to Katherine*⌝
But what to me, my love? But what to me?
A wife?   895

KATHERINE   A beard, fair health, and honesty.
With threefold love I wish you all these three.

DUMAINE
O, shall I say "I thank you, gentle wife"?

KATHERINE
Not so, my lord. A twelvemonth and a day
I'll mark no words that smooth-faced wooers say.   900

907. **change:** exchange; **friend:** lover

908. **stay:** wait

909. **liker:** more like

910. **Studies my lady?:** i.e., are you deep in contemplation?

912. **attends:** awaits

917. **comparisons:** satirical or scoffing similes

918. **all estates:** all kinds of people; **execute:** inflict (as if the **flouts** were capital punishments)

920. **wormwood:** i.e., bitterness (literally, a woody herb that yields a bitter oil)

924. **still:** constantly

927. **the painèd impotent:** i.e., those helpless with suffering

"Hercules in minority . . . strangling a snake."
(5.1.134–35)
From *Le dodichi fatiche d'Hercole . . .* [c. 1600].

Come when the King doth to my lady come;
Then, if I have much love, I'll give you some.
DUMAINE
I'll serve thee true and faithfully till then.
KATHERINE
Yet swear not, lest you be forsworn again.
⌜*They step aside.*⌝
LONGAVILLE
What says Maria? 905
MARIA   At the twelvemonth's end
I'll change my black gown for a faithful friend.
LONGAVILLE
I'll stay with patience, but the time is long.
MARIA
The liker you; few taller are so young.
⌜*They step aside.*⌝
BEROWNE, ⌜*to Rosaline*⌝
Studies my lady? Mistress, look on me. 910
Behold the window of my heart, mine eye,
What humble suit attends thy answer there.
Impose some service on me for thy love.
ROSALINE
Oft have I heard of you, my Lord Berowne,
Before I saw you; and the world's large tongue 915
Proclaims you for a man replete with mocks,
Full of comparisons and wounding flouts,
Which you on all estates will execute
That lie within the mercy of your wit.
To weed this wormwood from your fruitful brain, 920
And therewithal to win me, if you please,
Without the which I am not to be won,
You shall this twelvemonth term from day to day
Visit the speechless sick, and still converse
With groaning wretches; and your task shall be, 925
With all the fierce endeavor of your wit,
To enforce the painèd impotent to smile.

930. **agony:** death throes

931. **gibing:** jeering, scoffing

932. **influence:** power; **begot of:** derived from; **grace:** goodwill, favorable regard

937. **Deafed:** deafened; **dear:** grievous, dire

939. **withal:** as well

946. **bring:** accompany, conduct

948. **Jack hath not Jill:** in contrast to the proverb: "Jack shall have Jill"; **courtesy:** benevolence, kindness

949. **made . . . comedy:** i.e., given our play a happy ending

950. **wants:** lacks

Lawn bowling. (4.1.163)
From *Le centre de l'amour* . . . [1650?].

BEROWNE
 To move wild laughter in the throat of death?
 It cannot be, it is impossible.
 Mirth cannot move a soul in agony.   930
ROSALINE
 Why, that's the way to choke a gibing spirit,
 Whose influence is begot of that loose grace
 Which shallow laughing hearers give to fools.
 A jest's prosperity lies in the ear
 Of him that hears it, never in the tongue 935
 Of him that makes it. Then if sickly ears,
 Deafed with the clamors of their own dear groans,
 Will hear your idle scorns, continue then,
 And I will have you and that fault withal.
 But if they will not, throw away that spirit, 940
 And I shall find you empty of that fault,
 Right joyful of your reformation.
BEROWNE
 A twelvemonth? Well, befall what will befall,
 I'll jest a twelvemonth in an hospital.
PRINCESS, ⌈*to King*⌉
 Ay, sweet my lord, and so I take my leave. 945
KING
 No, madam, we will bring you on your way.
BEROWNE
 Our wooing doth not end like an old play.
 Jack hath not Jill. These ladies' courtesy
 Might well have made our sport a comedy.
KING
 Come, sir, it wants a twelvemonth and a day, 950
 And then 'twill end.
BEROWNE   That's too long for a play.

    Enter Braggart ⌈*Armado.*⌉

ARMADO Sweet Majesty, vouchsafe me—

957. **votary:** one who has sworn a vow

961. **followed in:** i.e., come at

968 SP. The early printed texts give no indication which characters take the parts of **Spring** and **Winter.**

969. **lady-smocks:** cuckoo flowers, mayflowers

970. **cuckoo-buds:** an unknown kind of flower

972–73. **cuckoo . . . men:** Because the **cuckoo** does not build nests but leaves its eggs for other birds to hatch and feed, its song of "cuckoo" is linked to "cuckold," a man whose wife is unfaithful. The cuckoo's song was considered a mocking cry directed to **married men.**

979. **turtles:** turtledoves; **tread:** copulate; **daws:** jackdaws, small crowlike birds

The crabapple tree. (4.2.6)
From John Gerard, *The herball or generall historie of plantes . . .* (1597).

PRINCESS
  Was not that Hector?
DUMAINE   The worthy knight of Troy.   955
ARMADO   I will kiss thy royal finger, and take leave. I
    am a votary; I have vowed to Jaquenetta to hold the
    plow for her sweet love three year. But, most
    esteemed Greatness, will you hear the dialogue that
    the two learned men have compiled in praise of the   960
    owl and the cuckoo? It should have followed in the
    end of our show.
KING   Call them forth quickly. We will do so.
ARMADO   Holla! Approach.

                      Enter all.

  This side is *Hiems,* Winter; this *Ver,* the Spring; the   965
  one maintained by the owl, th' other by the cuckoo.
  Ver, begin.
                      The Song.

⌈SPRING⌉
        When daisies pied and violets blue,
            And lady-smocks all silver-white,
        And cuckoo-buds of yellow hue   970
            Do paint the meadows with delight,
        The cuckoo then on every tree
        Mocks married men; for thus sings he:
                              "Cuckoo!

        Cuckoo, cuckoo!" O word of fear,   975
        Unpleasing to a married ear.

        When shepherds pipe on oaten straws,
            And merry larks are plowmen's clocks;
        When turtles tread, and rooks and daws,
            And maidens bleach their summer smocks;   980
        The cuckoo then on every tree
        Mocks married men, for thus sings he:
                              "Cuckoo!

987. **blows his nail:** i.e., blows on his hands to warm them

990. **ways:** roads

993. **keel the pot:** i.e., cool the contents of the pot by stirring, skimming, or pouring in something cold

994. **all aloud:** i.e., very loud

995. **saw:** speech (i.e., sermon)

998. **crabs:** crabapples; **bowl:** i.e., of spiced and sugared ale

1002. **Mercury:** in mythology, the messenger of the gods

1003. **Apollo:** in mythology, the god of light, reason, and art; **You, we:** The division between **you** and **we** is at the reader's or director's discretion. Perhaps the division is between the Princess's party and the King's, or between the nobles and the commoners, or between the players and the audience.

"Greasy Joan." (5.2.993)
From Jacob Cats, *Alle de wercken* . . . (1712).

    Cuckoo, cuckoo!" O word of fear,
    Unpleasing to a married ear.   985

WINTER
    When icicles hang by the wall,
      And Dick the shepherd blows his nail,
    And Tom bears logs into the hall,
      And milk comes frozen home in pail;
    When blood is nipped, and ways be ⟨foul,⟩   990
    Then nightly sings the staring owl
    "Tu-whit to-who." A merry note,
    While greasy Joan doth keel the pot.

    When all aloud the wind doth blow,
      And coughing drowns the parson's saw,   995
    And birds sit brooding in the snow,
      And Marian's nose looks red and raw;
    When roasted crabs hiss in the bowl,
    Then nightly sings the staring owl
    "Tu-whit to-who." A merry note,   1000
    While greasy Joan doth keel the pot.

⟨ARMADO⟩ The words of Mercury are harsh after the
    songs of Apollo. ⟨You that way; we this way.⟩
                           ⟨They all exit.⟩

Appendix

On the following pages (224–25) are, first, twenty-eight lines that are part of a speech by Berowne, printed after our 4.3.311 in the First Quarto and, second, six lines of dialogue printed in the Quarto after our 5.2.894.

It has long been recognized by editors and critics that Berowne's speech in 4.3 is printed in the Quarto as one very long speech that incorporates in it both an incomplete first draft and a complete second draft. However, previous editors have judged that lines 1–5, as printed on page 224, should be considered the introduction to the second draft of the speech. For an explanation of why we differ from previous editors on this matter, see the longer note to 4.3.311+ Appendix, page 242.

Like the speech by Berowne, lines 5.2.894+ are generally accepted by editors as being a first-draft version of lines that appear elsewhere in a slightly different, more finished form. See lines 910–27 for the second version of the lines printed on page 225. See also the longer notes to 5.2.894+ Appendix, page 243, for a discussion of the implications of these first and second versions of speeches in this play.

4.3.311+

Consider what you first did swear unto:
To fast, to study, and to see no woman—
Flat treason 'gainst the kingly state of youth.
Say, can you fast? Your stomachs are too young,
And abstinence engenders maladies. 5
And where that you have vowed to study, lords,
In that each of you have forsworn his book,
Can you still dream and pore and thereon look?
For when would you, my lord, or you, or you,
Have found the ground of study's excellence 10
Without the beauty of a woman's face?
From women's eyes this doctrine I derive;
They are the ground, the books, the academes
From whence doth spring the true Promethean fire.
Why, universal plodding poisons up 15
The nimble spirits in the arteries,
As motion and long-during action tires
The sinewy vigor of the traveler.
Now, for not looking on a woman's face,
You have in that forsworn the use of eyes, 20
And study too, the causer of your vow.
For where is any author in the world
Teaches such beauty as a woman's eye?
Learning is but an adjunct to ourself,
And where we are, our learning likewise is. 25
Then when ourselves we see in ladies' eyes,
With ourselves,
Do we not likewise see our learning there?

5.2.894+

BEROWNE
And what to me, my love? And what to me?
ROSALINE
You must be purgèd to your sins are racked.
You are attaint with faults and perjury.
Therefore if you my favor mean to get,
A twelvemonth shall you spend and never rest,   5
But seek the weary beds of people sick.

Explanatory Notes

4.3.311+

6. where that: whereas
7. have: i.e., has
12. this doctrine: See longer note, page 242.
13. academes: academies
14. Promethean: See longer note to 4.3.345, page 238.
15–20. Why . . . eyes: See longer note, page 243.
17. long-during: long-continuing

5.2.894+

2. You . . . racked: See longer note, page 244.   **to:** i.e., till   **racked:** i.e., tortured
3. attaint with: attainted with, convicted of

Longer Notes

1.1.0 SD. Navarre, Berowne, Longaville, Dumaine: While the incidents in *Love's Labor's Lost* are apparently fictional, these four characters are named after men who were very prominent in French political life of the 1590s, the decade in which the play was probably written. The play's king shares the name Navarre with Henry of Navarre (1553–1610), who became King Henry IV of France in 1589 after the assassination of Henry III. (The play's king is sometimes called Ferdinand in stage directions and speech headings. This name may also point to the historical kingdom of Navarre, one of whose sixteenth-century rulers was Ferdinand the Catholic. See longer note to 1.1.12, **Navarre,** page 228.)

The historical Henry of Navarre was, for a good part of his life, the champion of the French Protestants, or Huguenots, in their long and bloody religious war with the Catholic League (1562–93). Queen Elizabeth I of England, also a Protestant monarch, provided troops and money to support Henry of Navarre in his wars. She is known to have been bitterly disappointed when Henry, by then King of France as Henry IV, finally ended the religious wars in 1593 by converting to Catholicism. (He had once before converted to Catholicism for reasons of state and had later renounced the conversion.) It should be noted that only by converting could he enter Paris and finally be crowned king; his declaration that "Paris is well worth a mass" indicates that his conversion was merely nominal. Nevertheless, the emphasis in *Love's Labor's Lost* on the male characters' oath-breaking may well glance satirically at Henry of Navarre's official conversions and renunciations.

Navarre's male companions in the play are an odd
assortment when viewed from an historical perspective.
Berowne, an Anglicization of the baron de Biron's
name, may refer to the elder baron de Biron, who fought
against Navarre until Navarre became king of France,
after which Biron supported him, dying in his service in 1592 at the age of sixty-eight. Or **Berowne** may
refer to the younger duc de Biron, who also served
Henry as marshal of France. **Longaville** seems to refer
to the duc de Longueville, a Catholic noble loyal to
Navarre. While Berowne and Longaville are characters
based on followers of Navarre, **Dumaine** hardly belongs in Navarre's company, since Dumaine's name
alludes to the duc de Mayenne, who warred against
Navarre before—and after—the king's conversion.
Mayenne was ridiculed by Navarre as *"le gros duc"* (the
fat duke).

Modern editors and readers can only speculate about
what pleasures may have arisen for London theater
audiences of the 1590s from the resemblances and
disparities between Shakespeare's characters in *Love's
Labor's Lost* and the historical figures whose names
these characters appear to share.

1.1.12 **Navarre:** Now a province in northern Spain,
Navarre was an independent kingdom until the nineteenth century, though annexed to Spain in 1512. (See
map, page xii.)

1.1.174. **Armado:** This name, a spelling of the word
"armada," was probably a mocking allusion to the
great Spanish armada that sailed against England in
1588 only to be utterly destroyed, mainly by bad weather, to the great joy of the English. (See illustration, page
122.)

1.2.0 SD. **Mote:** The name of Armado's page, which we spell "Mote," is spelled "Moth" in the First Quarto. Apparently "moth" and "mote" were pronounced the same way in Elizabethan English, and editors have been uneasy about the better way to spell the name for modern readers. Both moths and motes are tiny; hence, either name would be appropriate for this character, who is described by other characters as being very small. Our decision to spell his name "Mote" is based on a First Quarto spelling at 4.3.168–69, where Berowne refers to the motes in the eyes of his friends. In this allusion to Matthew 7.3–5 ("Hypocrite, first cast out the beam out of thine own eye, and then shalt thou see clearly to cast out the mote out of thy brother's eye"), the First Quarto spells "mote" as "moth" ("You found his Moth, the King your Moth did see:/ But I a Beame do finde in each of three"). All editors modernize the spelling of "moth" to "mote" at 4.3.168–69, since the meaning clearly calls for the word we now spell as "mote" (which was also spelled "mote" in sixteenth-century English Bibles). Since, in this allusion to Matthew, the First Quarto spells the word "mote" as "moth," in our judgment we are also to read the First Quarto's spelling of the character's name ("Moth") as "Mote." In speech prefixes and stage directions, we do not, however, change the quarto's "Boy" to the character's proper name ("Mote"), as most editions do. We consider the quarto's "Boy" a helpful reminder (especially to directors and actors) that this character is, in fact, a boy.

1.2.106–7. **the reason of white and red:** Editors have usually interpreted this phrase as an allusion to cosmetics—ceruse (called "Spanish white") and rouge (French for "red"). There is, however, no need to invoke cosmetics, because the phrase may mean no more than "the inferences (regarding fear or blameworthiness) usually drawn from women's rosy or pale complexions."

2.1.41 SP. **Maria:** The 1598 quarto of *Love's Labor's Lost* gives the speech beginning "I know him, madam" to "1. *Lady*," the speech at line 54 to "*Lad.*," the speech beginning at line 57 to "2 *Lad.*," and the speech beginning at line 65 to "3. *Lad.*". (The Folio gives the speech at line 65 to "*Rossa.*") Editors since 1709 have noted the Princess's speech at 78–80,

> God bless my ladies, are they all in love,
> That every one her own hath garnishèd
> With such bedecking ornaments of praise?

and have therefore matched up the speeches of each of the three ladies with the lord who is praised. Since Maria is later paired with Longaville, she is given the speech of "First Lady"; Katherine is later paired with Dumaine, and is thus given the speech of "Second Lady"; "Third Lady" praises Berowne (and is called "*Rossa.*" in the Folio), and thus is assumed to be Rosaline. Editors and directors generally follow these designations.

A different set of choices faces editors and directors with speech prefixes beginning at line 117. There, in the Quarto, the woman sparring with Berowne (lines 116–31) is "*Kather[ine]*"; a few lines later, at lines 185–99, Berowne spars with "*Ros[aline]*." Editors and directors here choose either to follow the Quarto and have Berowne (for whatever reason) pursue two of the ladies in rapid succession, or else assume that the name "*Kather[ine]*" in lines 116–31 is an error, and give the lines to Rosaline, as does the Folio. Our decision to give both sets of dialogue to Rosaline is finally based on the difficulties created for audiences and readers if Berowne, having expressed his interest in one anonymous lady with whom he once danced in Brabant, almost immediately addresses a different lady with the words "Lady, I will commend you to my own heart," claiming that he is in love with her. As editors, we are aware of the serious arguments that have been put forward about Shakespeare's intentions here, and of the arguments about the kinds of revisions and errors that could have left the text with this double courtship. We, too, feel that an error may have been made, and feel as well that it is not possible to trace the source of error. Our decision is to correct in the direction of understandable exposition, though we see the attractions of leaving the double courtship in place. Since our changes away from the quarto text are marked with brackets, readers and directors can see the quarto readings in the textual notes and reverse our decision should they like.

What we judge to be confusion of "Rosaline" and "Katherine" spills over into the dialogue near the end of the scene when, beginning at line 200, each lord enters to ask the name of the lady in whom he is interested. When Dumaine asks the name of his lady, he is told that "*Rosalin[e]*" is her name; and when Berowne asks "What's her name in the cap?" he is told that her name is "*Katherin[e]*." Since, for the remainder of the play, Dumaine is clearly linked to Katherine and Berowne to Rosaline, this interchanging of the ladies' names seems to almost all editors and directors to introduce only confusion; thus almost all editions change the names. This editorial decision, with which we agree, is supported by the fact that when Berowne next enters (3.1.150) he addresses Costard with the words "there is a gentle lady. / When tongues speak sweetly, then they name her

name, / And Rosaline they call her. Ask for her, / And to
her white hand see thou do commend / This sealed-up
counsel" (3.1.173–78.).

3.1.151–84. My . . . And: Most of Berowne's speeches
in this scene, but not elsewhere, begin in the First
Quarto with *O*. Line 151, "My good knave Costard," for
instance, in the First Quarto reads "O my good knave
Costard . . . "; line 155 reads "O what is a remuneration," etc. While it is just possible that the *O*'s in
Berowne's speeches indicate the sighs and groans to
which he later says that he, as a lover, is susceptible, it is
not characteristic of this play or other Shakespeare plays
to employ quite so mechanical a device as to begin a
whole series of speeches with the same word. We
therefore judge the mechanical repetition of *O* to be an
error, which we have emended.

In an attempt to explain how this apparent error
entered the First Quarto, some editors have speculated
that, in the manuscript printer's copy for the First
Quarto, Berowne's speech prefixes were abbreviated to
"Bero," and the typesetter here misread the abbrevia-
tion as "Ber O." (The same editors have charged the
typesetter with the identical error in just one other place
[2.1.220].) Such speculation not only makes a claim to
achieve the impossible—namely, the reconstruction of
the details of a lost document—but also fails to explain
why the phenomenon is so highly localized.

3.1.190. Signior Junior: Cupid is represented as a boy
(junior), but he is the oldest, or most senior, of the gods
because, in classical mythology, it is love (or Cupid) who,
at creation, brought order and harmony out of chaos.

4.1.73–74. pernicious: Some editors print "penurious" for **pernicious,** on the grounds that neither the

beggar maid nor Jaquenetta is **pernicious.** While we agree with this assessment of the beggar maid and Jaquenetta, we have difficulty with the emendation on two grounds. First, we find the expression "penurious . . . beggar," which is produced by the emendation, redundant and therefore little less problematic than the reading that the emendation seeks to correct. Second, and more fundamentally, we doubt the relevance to Armado's speeches of conventional editorial principles regarding emendation. According to such principles, editors are obliged to emend words that are at odds with their contexts, as "pernicious" is at odds with what we are told about the beggar maid and Jaquenetta. However, Armado's letter is funny chiefly because its language and sentiments are so inappropriate for a love letter; in other words, its humor turns on the words being at odds with the context. Thus conventional principles of emendation seem to have little application here.

4.1.77, 78 **came, see, overcame:** The First Quarto's **see** is emended to **saw** (the reading of the Second Folio of 1632) by most editors in the belief that **see** is a printing-house error. We follow the First Quarto because, for several reasons, **see** is unlikely to be an error introduced during the printing of the First Quarto. Relevant considerations are, first, that "came, see, overcame" appears twice in the speech; and, second, that the Quarto was printed in William White's printing house, about which we know a great deal. Introduction of such an error would have been uncharacteristic of the workmen who set type and read proof in White's printing house where the First Quarto was manufactured in 1598. (1) "White's compositors erroneously altered the tenses of strong verbs only three times in the

three reprints of plays they set in 1599 and 1600, and
they never did so in successive lines [as here, where **see**
appears in successive lines], twice on the same page, or
for verbs in a series" ("Variants in the First Quarto of
Love's Labor's Lost," *Shakespeare Studies* 12 [1979] :
42). (2) We can have some confidence that White's
proofreader would have corrected the tense of **see** if it
were in need of correction because he corrected the
tenses of two other verbs on this page, changing "sets"
to **set** (line 73) and "is was" to **was** (line 75). While
mistranslation of familiar Latin is not a characteristic
error of Armado, there may be a joke here in the
awkward translation of **veni, vidi, vici** as **came,
see, overcame.** We thus let the First Quarto reading
stand.

4.2.3–4. sanguis, in blood: Sometimes, as here,
Holofernes's Latin grammar is not strictly correct,
and if these lines were delivered onstage in the form
in which they are printed, Holofernes may have
been laughed at by those in the audience who had
attended a Latin grammar school. Strictly translated,
sanguis means "blood," not **in blood,** which in
Latin would be *in sanguine.* In the same way, **caelo**
(line 5) may be in the wrong grammatical case; **caelo**
(or *Celo,* as it is spelled in the First Quarto) is in the
ablative, not the genitive (*caeli*) required to indicate
possession (of . . . the sky) or the nominative (*caelum*),
the case in which nouns are usually cited. Later in the
scene (lines 97–98), Holofernes's quotation of a Latin
proverb also contains an error, **Vir sapis** for *Vir sapit.* In
these cases where the errors may have been included for
comic effect, we have not regularized the mistaken
words.

We acknowledge, however, that these errors and others like them may have been made by the typesetters of the First Quarto, who certainly made many typographical errors in the play's English. A typesetter seems responsible, for example, for the reduction to utter nonsense of the pseudo-Italian proverb beginning "Venetia, Venetia" (lines 116–17). It is hard to imagine how those lines as printed *("vemchie, vencha, que non te unde, que non te perreche")* would ever have been entertaining as comic errors.

4.2.13. intimation: It is possible, though by no means certain, that Holofernes, as a Latin pedant, is using **intimation** (and other English words derived from Latin) in particular senses that are exclusive to Latin. In that case, **intimation** could mean "intrusion," **insinuation** could mean "insertion," **explication** could mean "unfolding," and **replication** could mean "folding back." Since it is not clear whether these Latin meanings are in force in this speech, in our facing-page notes we also provide the more common sixteenth-century meanings of these words (if the meanings have changed since then). If Holofernes is using English words in the sense of their Latin roots, this would be only one of the verbal extravagances to which he is addicted. Even though his choice of words can generally be explained to some extent in our facing-page notes, his language is highly unusual for its time.

4.2.82 SP. HOLOFERNES: This is the first of many speech prefixes in this scene that, in the early printings of the play, confuse Nathaniel and Holofernes. Seven of Holofernes's speeches in this scene are prefixed *"Nath."* in the First Quarto (which is followed by the Folio), and three of Nathaniel's speeches are prefixed *"Holo."* Further, at 4.2.161 the confusion is present within the dialogue as well, as Holofernes is made to address Nathaniel as "Sir Holofernes," an error that is repeated at 5.1.118. Most explanations of these confusions attribute the errors to Shakespeare, either imagining him as muddled about the names of the characters or as writing in haste while away from his desk. An alternative explanation would focus on the way play manuscripts were copied by authors and scribes (who usually added speech prefixes after they had copied a whole page of speeches) and on the way scribal copies could sometimes have been misread in printing houses.

4.2.112–13. **Facile . . . Ruminat:** In their proper form as *"Fauste, precor gelida quando pecus omne sub umbra / Ruminat"* ("Faustus, since your whole flock is ruminating in the cool shade, I pray—"), these lines begin the first poem in the *Eclogues* (1498) of Johannes Baptista Spagnolo of Mantua (known as Mantuan). Mantuan wrote his *Eclogues*, or pastoral poems, in imitation of Virgil's, and some of Mantuan's admirers in the sixteenth century thought him Virgil's equal. The lines were extremely well known, and so it is unlikely that anyone with any education, including Shakespeare, would misquote them as badly as they are printed in the First Quarto of *Love's Labor's Lost*. Either the typesetter, or possibly a scribe who copied the play before it was printed, has corrupted them, or Shakespeare has created a comic version of them for Holofernes to speak. We prefer the second hypothesis because, unlike the pseudo-Italian in lines 116–17 below, **Facile . . . Ruminat** does make some comic sense.

4.2.126–43. **If . . . tongue:** Berowne's poem and those later read by Longaville and Dumaine were printed with some verbal differences in *The Passionate Pilgrim*

(1599), a collection of poems by several authors, but all attributed to Shakespeare.

4.2.144. apostrophus: In a line of verse, an apostrophe marks a contraction or elision (i.e., omission of a syllable) made in order to keep the rhythm regular. Berowne's sonnet has only one contraction and no elisions.

4.3.273. fair: Berowne's line "No face is fair that is not full so black" introduces a paradox built on the double meaning of **fair** as (1) beautiful and (2) blond, fairhaired. By Elizabethan standards of beauty, only fair hair and fair skin are beautiful; hence there is usually no tension between these meanings of **fair**. Berowne, however, in responding to the King's "thy love is black as ebony" (line 267), does not deny Rosaline's "blackness." He had himself, at 3.1.207, described Rosaline as having "two pitch-balls stuck in her face for eyes." He instead responds by claiming that only black is beautiful, a claim that carries with it the paradox that, therefore, only black-haired or black-skinned women are fairhaired and fair-skinned.

4.3.274–75. Black is . . . the school of night. In 1903 it was pointed out that the phrase "school of night" is similar to the title of Chapman's *The Shadow of Night*. When Chapman first published this poem, he prefaced it with a letter to the minor poet Matthew Roydon, whose patron was Sir Walter Raleigh. On the basis of this letter to Roydon, it was argued that Chapman wished to associate his poem *The Shadow of Night* with Sir Walter Raleigh's circle of intellectual friends who were once branded the "Schoole of Atheism." Thus began the construction of "school of night" in *Love's Labor's Lost* as an allusion to Raleigh, Marlowe, and their circle. No one has yet found evidence that the words "school of night" were used in Shakespeare's day to refer to Raleigh's circle, and few scholars today see any connection between the play and this circle.

4.3.345. Promethean fire: In classical mythology Prometheus stole fire from the gods and gave it to humankind. Some versions of the myth represent Prometheus as the creator of humankind, and the fire he stole as the spark of life itself.

5.1.10. Novi hominem tanquam te: The First Quarto reading *"hominum"* for *hominem* is very likely a scribe's or typesetter's error rather than a joke, because the error would be hard for an audience to hear.

5.1.26–27. It insinuateth me of insanie: This nonsense is perhaps an English version of the Latin sentence *"insinuat in me insaniam,"* which means "he puts me into a state of frenzy" or "he makes me frantic," as Holofernes himself goes on to say in lines 27–28, "To make frantic, lunatic."

5.1.29. Laus . . . intelligo: Although in the First Quarto this line is printed in correct Latin (*"Laus deo, bene intelligo"*), Holofernes's correction of Nathaniel in line 30 has convinced editors, including ourselves, that Nathaniel must have made a mistake and used *bone* for the Latin adverb *bene* ("well").

5.1.78. ad dunghill: As Holofernes points out, this is a mistake for *ad unguem,* a Latin proverb meaning "down to the fingernails," or exact in every detail.

Costard's "at the fingers' ends" may be a further mistake, since the phrase "at *one's* fingers' ends" means "ready at hand."

5.1.83. charge-house: It has been argued that "the charge-house on the top of the mountain" alludes to a passage familiar to Latin grammar-school students in Erasmus's *Familiaria Colloquia,* a standard schoolboy text. There, Erasmus includes a dialogue about "the college of the mountain with the sharp crest," from which the speaker says he has returned not with a load of learning but with lice. This dialogue seems to be an attack on Erasmus's own boyhood school, the College de Mont Aigu in Paris, where he had been a very unhappy schoolboy.

5.1.117–18. Nine Worthies: Ordinarily, the Nine Worthies, featured in masques and pageants since the Middle Ages, consisted of three Jews, three pagans, and three Christians. The three Jews were usually **Joshua,** David, and **Judas Maccabaeus.** Joshua's story is narrated in the biblical Book of Joshua, David's in 1 and 2 Samuel, and Judas Maccabaeus's in 1 and 2 Maccabees. The three pagans were usually the legendary **Hector,** who was the eldest son of King Priam of Troy and leader of the Trojan army during the Greek siege in the Trojan War; Alexander the Great, the Macedonian conqueror of Asia in the fourth century B.C., and Julius Caesar, a Roman military leader and politician in the first century B.C., about whose assassination Shakespeare wrote his *Julius Caesar.* The three Christians were usually the legendary English king Arthur (stories of whom may be ultimately based on a historical general who fought the invading Germanic tribes in the sixth century A.D.); Charlemagne, also called Charles the Great, who was crowned emperor of the West in Rome in 800 A.D.; and Godfrey of Bouillon, duke of Lorraine and a Crusader, who became the first Latin ruler of Jerusalem at the end of the eleventh century A.D. The list was not stable, however. Guy of Warwick (legendary English giant-killer) was often substituted for Godfrey. The Nine Worthies in this play do not conform to the ordinary pattern; David, Caesar, Arthur, Charlemagne, and Godfrey are not mentioned or depicted in the play, while **Hercules** and **Pompey** are added to the usual list.

5.1.126–27. Joshua . . . Judas Maccabaeus: Editors have puzzled over both the failure of Holofernes to assign himself a role and the discrepancy between the roles assigned here and those actually represented by himself and his colleagues in 5.2. There Nathaniel plays Alexander the Conqueror; Holofernes himself, rather than "this gallant gentleman" (Armado?), plays Judas Maccabaeus; and no one appears as Joshua. Since it is not unusual in Shakespeare's plays to find such discrepancies between stated plans and final outcomes, we have not followed those editors who alter the text in this scene to make it conform to the text in 5.2.

5.2.47. red dominical: A letter, selected from among the first seven letters of the alphabet, assigned to the Sundays of a particular year. The first day of the year is assigned the letter *A;* the second is assigned the letter *B,* etc. After seven days, the letters repeat. The dominical letter for a given year—the letter assigned to the first Sunday, and all succeeding Sundays in that year— depends on the day of the week that January 1 falls on. If the year begins on a Friday, the dominical letter for that year is *C.* Dominical letters were printed in red; hence

Rosaline's term "red dominical"—and hence the common phrase "red-letter day."

5.2.270. **Veal:** Editors have suggested a variety of puns and other wordplay in Katherine's response to Longaville. There is perhaps a pun on "veil," or "mask," her name for what Longaville called his "speechless vizard." It is also possible that **veal** is "ville," the last syllable of the name Longaville, the first syllable of which is Katherine's last word in her previous speech (line 267). **Veal** is also a name for **calf,** a word that meant (1) dolt or (2) meek fellow, and was also (3) a term of endearment.

5.2.461. **Lord's tokens:** This pun plays on "Lord's tokens" as plague spots (so called because of the belief that plague was God's punishment for sin), and on "lords' tokens" as the tokens of affection given to the ladies by the king and the lords.

5.2.598. **Abate throw at novum.** *Novum* or *novem quinque* was a game of dice in which the winning throws seem to have been nine and five, two of the numbers under discussion here. Unfortunately, little more is known about *novem quinque,* but editors agree that Berowne's comment is somehow tied to his claim that five players will be performing nine roles.

5.2.644–45. **that holds his polax sitting on a close-stool:** The Middle Ages, in transforming figures of classical history into images of medieval knights, gave Alexander a coat of arms that consisted of a lion on a throne holding a battle-ax. Costard makes the throne into a close-stool, or enclosed chamber pot.

5.2.738 SD. **Berowne steps forth:** The meaning of this stage direction remains a mystery after much editorial conjecture and debate. Many editions add a direction for Berowne to whisper to Costard, thus linking Berowne with Costard's accusation at 5.2.745–50.

5.2.893. **breast:** The First Quarto here prints six lines of an exchange between Berowne and Rosaline in which Rosaline imposes on Berowne the task of visiting the sick; she describes the same task in 923–27. Like other editors, we believe this first description to be an incomplete first draft of the later exchange. We therefore print the six lines in the Appendix, page 225.

Longer Notes to Appendix

4.3.311+ Appendix. The first five lines of this speech as printed in our appendix, the lines in which Berowne says he will discuss in order the three parts of the men's oath "To fast, to study, and to see no woman," seem to us to constitute an introduction to the first draft of the speech, subsequently abandoned. Neither the first draft nor the second version of the speech takes up these three issues in sequence, as promised in this (abandoned) introduction; instead, the issues of studying and eschewing women are discussed as a single, combined topic. The second draft, in our opinion, begins with "O, we have made a vow to study, lords" (4.3.312 in the body of our text)—though we fully appreciate that differences of opinion will likely persist about how Berowne's speech ought to be printed in editions.

4.3.311+, line 12. **this doctrine:** The doctrine that Berowne develops in the following lines is a Neoplatonic doctrine of love that has its origins in Plato's dialogue entitled *The Symposium*. There the character Socrates argues that the beginning of the path to true knowledge is the love of another person, whom one perceives to be beautiful. Socrates is speaking of what we now call homosexual love; Renaissance Neoplatonists adapted the doctrine to heterosexual love. This doctrine was available in Book Four of Sir Thomas Hoby's 1561 translation of Castiglione's *The Courtier*.

4.3.311+, lines 15–20. **Why . . . eyes:** This imagery describing the male body deprived of the presence of female beauty can be usefully compared with the following passage from Hoby's translation of *The Courtier* presenting the effect of woman's beauty on the male: "the influence of beauty when it is present giveth a wonderous delight to the lover, and, setting his heart on fire, quickeneth and melteth certain virtues in a trance and congealed in the soul, the which, nourished with the heat of love, flow about and go bubbling nigh the heart, and thrust out through the eyes those spirits which be most fine vapors made of the purest and clearest part of the blood, which receive the image of beauty and deck it with a thousand sundry furnitures."

5.2.894+ Appendix. Some editors have argued that the appearance in the *Love's Labor's Lost* Quarto of both unfinished first drafts and completed second drafts proves that Shakespeare also revised some of his plays after he had first written them. These editors imagine that the 1623 Folio version of *King Lear*, for example, is Shakespeare's revision of the 1608 quarto version of that play. To our minds, there is a world of difference between, on the one hand, attempting to write a speech or a bit of dialogue one way, abandoning that draft before completing it, and then beginning a second draft and bringing it to successful completion (as is the case in *Love's Labor's Lost*), and, on the other hand, writing one whole version of *King Lear* and then later revising that version to produce a second version (as some editors have imagined Shakespeare doing with *King Lear*). *Love's Labor's Lost* does not, as far as we can see, offer a ready answer to questions about the origins of differences between the printed texts of *King Lear*.

5.2.894+, line 2. **You must be purgèd to your sins are racked:** This difficult line has been emended in several ways by editors: (1) "You must be purgèd till your sins are racked," the emendation "till" making explicit in the text a meaning of the First Quarto's reading "to"; (2) "You must be purgèd too, your sins are rank," with the spelling variant "too" taken from the First Folio text of 1623, and with "rank" first printed in Rowe's edition of 1709.

Textual Notes

The reading of the present text appears to the left of the square bracket. Unless otherwise noted, the reading to the left of the bracket is from **Q**, the First Quarto text of 1598 (upon which this edition is based). The earliest sources of readings not in **Q** are indicated as follows: **F** is the First Folio of 1623; **Q2** is the Second Quarto of 1631; **F2** is the Second Folio of 1632; **F3** is the Third Folio of 1663–64; **F4** is the Fourth Folio of 1685; **Ed.** is an earlier editor of Shakespeare, beginning with Rowe in 1709. No sources are given for emendations of punctuation or for corrections of obvious typographical errors, like turned letters that produce no known word. **SD** means stage direction; **SP** means speech prefix; *uncorr.* means the first or uncorrected state of the First Quarto; *corr.* means the second or corrected state of the First Quarto; ~ stands in place of a word already quoted before the square bracket; ʌ indicates the omission of a punctuation mark.

1.1 0. SD *King*] Q (K.)   1 *and hereafter to* 1.1.304. SP KING] *Ferdinand* (or *Ferd., Fer.*) Q   5. buyʌ] ~: Q   10. desires,] ~. Q   16. me,] ~: Q   18. schedule] Q (sedule)   25. three] F; thee Q   30. delightsʌ] ~: Q   31. slaves.] ~ʌ Q   32. pomp] F; pome Q   34. over.] ~, Q   41. besides] Q (beside)   51. please.] ~, Q   58. common] Q (cammon)   64. feast] Ed.; fast Q, F   65. fineʌ] ~. Q   67. hard-a-keeping] Q (hard a keeping)   72. quite] Q (quit)   74. Why,] ~? Q   74. and] F; but Q   131. SP BEROWNE] Ed.; *omit* Q, F   131. gentility] Q (gentletie)   134. *public*] publibue Q   136. This] *Ber.* This Q, F   137. embassy] Q (Embassaie)   141. bedrid] Q (bedred)   145. overshot.] ~, Q   170. One] Q

(On) 171. enchanting] inchannting Q 173. umpire] Q (vmpier) 176. knight ₐ] ~: Q 184. SD *Enter a Constable with Costard with a letter.* Q 185 *and hereafter in this act except at* 1.1.271. SP DULL] Ed.; *Constab. (Const.)* Q, F 186. This,] ~ ₐ Q 194 *and hereafter except at* 4.3.212. SP COSTARD] Ed.; *Clowne* (or *Clow., Clo.*) Q, F 194. contempts] Contempls Q 205. merriness] Q (merrines) ⸜224. welkin's] welkis Q 224. vicegerent] Q (*Vizgerent*) 225. dominator] Q (*dominatur*) 227. Costard] Q *corr.* (*Costard*); Costart Q *uncorr.* 235. besieged] F; besedged Q 266. *as my*] Q *corr.; asmy* Q *uncorr.* 268. officer] Gfficer Q 271. SP DULL] Ed.; *Antho.* Q, F 271. an 't] ‾Q (ant) 281. worst] Q (wost) 294. varied] Q (varried) 299. SP COSTARD] *Col.* Q 313–14. prosperity] prosperie Q 314. Affliction] affliccio Q

1.2. 0 *and hereafter. Mote*] Q (*Moth*) 4. Why,] ~? Q 14. epitheton] Q (apethaton) 100. blushing] F2; blush-in Q 104. For] Eor Q 108, 110. ballad] Q (Ballet) 130. dey-woman] Q (Day womand) 134 *and hereafter in this scene.* SP JAQUENETTA] Ed.; *Maide* or *Ma.* Q, F 145. SP DULL] Ed.; *Clo.* Q, F 162. Master] Q (M.) 179. *duello*] F; *Duella* Q

2.1. 0. SD *other*] Ed.; *three* Q 2. Consider] Cosider Q 11. besides] Q (beside) 13. SP PRINCESS] Ed.; *Queene* Q 13. Lord] Q (L.) 32. Importunes] F; Importuous Q 34. humble-visaged] F; humble visage Q 36. SD *1 line earlier in* Q 36. SD *Boyet*] Q (*Boy.*) 39. SP A LORD] Ed.; *Lor.* Q, F 39. Lord Longaville] Ed.; *Longauill* Q, F 41. SP MARIA] Ed.; 1. *Lady* Q, F 41. madam.] ~ ₐ Q 42. Lord] Q (L.) 43. solemnizèd ₐ] ~. Q 45. parts] F; peerelsse Q 48, 49. gloss] Q (glose) 51. cut, ... wills ₐ] ~ ₐ ... ~, Q 54. SP MARIA] Ed.; *Lad.* Q; *Lad.* 1. F 57. SP KATHERINE] Ed.; 2 *Lad.* Q, F 62. Alanson's] Q (*Alansoes*) 65. SP ROSALINE] F (*Rossa.*); 3 *Lad.* Q 75. tales,] ~. Q 81. SP A LORD] Q (*Lord.*); *Ma.* F 90.

unpeopled] F; vnpeeled Q 91. Here] F; *Bo.* Heere
Q 92 *and hereafter to* 2.1.113. SP KING] Ed.; *Nauar,
Nau.* Q, F 102. it, will˄] ~˄~, Q 117–30. SP ROSA-
LINE] F; *Kather.* or *Kath.* Q 125. o'] Q (a) 132 *and
hereafter to* 2.1.172. SP KING] F; *Ferd.* Q 134. of an] F;
of, of an Q 144. friendship] faiendship Q 146. de-
mand] pemaund Q 148. On] Q (One) 166. special]
spciall Q 179. heart,] ~. Q 180. house.] ~, Q 184. SP
KING] F; *Na.* Q 186. own] F; none Q 193. SP
BEROWNE] *Bar.* Q 195. prick 't] Q (prickt) 201. Kath-
erine] Ed.; *Rosalin* Q 217. Rosaline] Ed.; *Katherin*
Q 220. You]F; O you Q 221. SD *Berowne*] Q (*Bero.*)
222. SP MARIA] Q (*Lady Maria*) 222. lord] Q (L.) 228.
SP KATHERINE] Q (*Lady Ka.*); *La. Ma.* F 231–36. SP
KATHERINE] Ed.; *La.* or *Lad.* Q, F 237. but, gentles,]
~˄~˄ Q 240. lies,] lyes˄ Q *corr.*; lyes? Q *uncorr.* 241.
wi' th'] Q (with) 268. SP MARIA] Ed.; *Lad.* Q; *Lad. Ro.*
F 269. SP KATHERINE] Ed.; *Lad. 2* Q; *La. Ma.* F 270.
SP ROSALINE] Ed.; *Lad. 3* Q; *Lad. 2.* F 273. SP MARIA]
Ed.; *Lad.* Q; *La. 1.* F 276. SP MARIA] Ed.; *Lad.* Q; *Lad. 2.*
F

3.1. 1–70. SP ARMADO] Ed.; *Brag.* or *Bra.* Q, F 14.
as] Ed.; *omit* Q, F 14, 15. sometimes] Q (sometime)
15. singing love,] ~ ~˄ Q 16. through the nose] F2;
through: nose Q, F 17. love;] ~˄ Q 19. thin-belly] F;
thinbellies Q 25. me?—] Ed.; men˄ Q 28. penny]
Ed.; penne Q 36. Negligent] Q (Necligent) 41. live;
and this] ~˄(~~) Q *corr.*; ~˄ (~) ~ Q *uncorr.* 59.
Thy] F; The Q 70. voluble] Q (volable) 73. SD *Boy*]
Page Q, F 74 *and hereafter in this scene except line* 113.
SP BOY] *Pag.* Q, F 78. the mail] Q (thee male) 78.
plain] pline Q 111. SP ARMADO] *Ar.* Q *corr.*; *Arm.* Q
uncorr. 111. argument] Q *corr.*; argumet Q *uncorr.*
131. liberty,] ~. Q 143. ounce] ouce Q 146. farthings
—*remuneration.*]~˄~, Q 146. *remuneration*] remura-
tion Q 147. One penny] Q (i.d.) 148–49. Why, . . .

it! *Remuneration.* Why,] ~? . . . ~ ₐ ~:~? Q   151. My] Ed.;
O my Q, F   155. What] F; O what Q   157. Why] Ed.; O,
why Q, F   159. Stay] Ed.; O stay Q, F   163. This] Ed.; O
this Q, F   165. Thou] Ed.; O thou Q, F   184. And] Ed.; O
and Q, F   185. beadle] Q (Bedell)   186. critic] Crietick
Q   190. Junior] Ed.; *Iunios* Q   200. clock] F2; Cloake Q,
F   206. whitely] Q (whitly)   214. sue] Q (shue)

4.1.   1 *and hereafter in this scene.* SP PRINCESS] F2;
Quee. Q, F   2. steep uprising] Q (steepe vp rising)   11.
SP PRINCESS] *Qnee.* Q   29. do 't] Q (doote)   34. praise,]
~ ₐ Q   52. mistress] Mistrs Q   53. o'] Q (a)   54. fit] Q
corr.; fir Q *uncorr.*   73. *set*] Q *corr.* (set); sets Q *uncorr.*
75. *was*] Q *corr.* (was); is was Q *uncorr.*   78. *overcame*]
couercame Q   83.   *King's*] Q2; King Q, F   89. *What*ₐ]
~, Q   92. *picture*] Q *corr.*; pictture Q *uncorr.*   95. *Adri-
ano*] Q (Adriana)   113. you:] ~, Q   140. France]
Frannce Q   141. touching] touchiug Q   144. touching]
Q (toching)   148. SD *placed as in* F, *2 lines earlier in*
Q   150. did] Q *corr.*; hid Q *uncorr.*   151. it] F4; *omit* Q,
F   156. o' the] Q *corr.* (a'the); a the Q *uncorr.*   157. he]
a' Q *corr.*; a Q *uncorr.*   157. ne'er] Q (neare)   160. pin]
F2; is in Q, F   172. o' th' one] Ed.; ath toothen Q; ath to
the F   176. o' t' other] Q (atother)   177. a] F2; *omit* Q,
F   177. SD *Shout*] F2; Shoot Q, F *1 line later in* Q *and* F,
after "Exeunt"   178. SD *He exits.*] this ed.; *Exeunt* Q, F

4.2.   1. reverend] Q (reuerent)   3. SP HOLOFERNES]
Ed.; *Ped.* Q, F   8. SP NATHANIEL] Q (*Curat Nath.*)   8.
Master] Q (M.)   8. epithets] Q (epythithes)   9. varied]
vatried Q   14–15.   explication; *facere*,] ~ ₐ ~: Q   32.
of] Ed.; *omit* Q, F   34. indiscreet] indistreell Q   43.
Dictynna . . . Dictynna] Ed.; *Dictisima . . . dictisima* Q,
F   56. pollution] Q (polusion)   57. besides] Q (beside)   58. 'twas] Q *corr.*; was Q *uncorr.*   61. ignorant,
call I] Ed.; ignorault cald Q; ignorant call'd F   61.
deer,ₐ] ~: Q   63. Master] Q (M.)   64. scurrility] Q
(squirilitie)   82. SP HOLOFERNES] Ed.; *Nath.* Q, F   86.

pia mater] Ed.; primater Q, F 88. in whom] F; whom Q 90. SP NATHANIEL] Ed.; *Holo.* Q, F 90. Lord] Q (L.) 95. SP HOLOFERNES] Ed.; *Nath.* Q, F 95. ingenious] Ed.; ingenous Q; ingennous F 100, 103, 108. Master] Q (M.) 101. SP HOLOFERNES] Ed.; *Nath.* Q, F 101. pierce one] Person Q, F 102. pierced] Q (perst) 103–4. likeliest] Q (liklest) 105, 112, 124, 156. SP HOLOFERNES] *Nath.* Q, F 105. piercing] Q (persing) 112. peccas] pecas Q 112. umbra.] *vmbra* ˄ Q 116–17. *Venetia . . . pretia*] Ed.; *vemchie, vencha, que non te vnde, que non te perreche* Q, F 123. SP NATHANIEL] Ed.; *Holo.* Q, F 124. stanza] stauze Q; stanze F 131. eyes,] ~. Q 142. wrong] Q *corr.*; woug Q *uncorr.* 144, 174, 178, 188. SP HOLOFERNES] Q (*Pedan., Ped.,* or *Peda.*) 144. apostrophus] apostraphas Q 145. canzonet. Here] Ed.; cangenet. *Nath.* Here Q, F 150. fancy, . . . invention?] ~? . . . ˄ Q 150. *Imitari*] imitarie Q, F 159. writing] Ed.; written Q, F 161. *Berowne.* Sir Nathaniel] Ed.; Berowne. *Ped.* Sir *Holofernes* Q, F (*Per.*) 168. forgive] forgine Q 169. SP JAQUENETTA] Ed.; *Mayd.* Q, F 172. SP NATHANIEL] Ed.; *Holo.* Q, F 182. *ben*] Ed.; *bien* Q, F

4.3. 8. o'] Q (a) 13, 14. melancholy] Q (mallicholie) 15. o'] Q (a') 26. *smote* ˄] Q (smot.) 36. *wilt*] F; will Q 40. paper] Q *corr.;* pa d er Q *uncorr.* 46. SP KING] Ed.; *Long.* Q, F 50. triumviry] Q (triumpherie) 59. heavenly] heanenly Q 70. *vaporvow*;] ~-~ ˄ Q 75. idolatry] F; ydotarie Q 76. o'] Q (a) 78. SD *1 line earlier in* Q 87. corporal] Q *corr.* (corporall); croporall Q *uncorr.* 88. hairs] Q (heires) 103. ode] Odo Q 109. *velvet* ˄] ~, Q 112. *Wished*] *Passionate Pilgrim,* F2; Wish Q, F 116. *thorn*] *England's Helicon,* Ed.; throne Q, F 125. plain ˄] ~. Q 162. coaches; . . . tears ˄] Ed.; couches ˄ . . . teares. Q 185. to] Ed.; by Q, F 185. by] Ed.; to Q, F 189. you] Ed.; *omit* Q, F 191. Joan] Q *corr.* (Ione); Loue Q *uncorr.*

192. me?] ~ ⌄ Q   195. SD *4 lines later in* Q, *3 in* F   208.
SD *Berowne*] Ed.; *He* Q, F   210. SP JAQUENETTA] *Iaqn.*
Q   242.   Ind⌄]   ~.   Q   246.   peremptory]   Q
(peromptorie)   254. culled] Q (culd)   279. and] F4;
omit Q, F   280. doters] Q (dooters)   300.   lies⌄] ~ ?
Q   303. Nothing] F2; O nothing Q, F   311. See Appendix, page 224.   Appendix 23. woman's] womas Q   317.
beauty's] beautis Q   318. brain⌄] ~: Q   329. sound,] ~.
Q   333. dainty⌄] ~, Q   336. Subtle] Subtir Q   353.
authors] Ed.; authour Q, F   355. Let] F2; Lets Q, F
361. standards] Q (standars)   377. *Allons! Allons!*] Ed.;
Alone alone Q, F   379. forsworn] forsorne Q

5.1.   0. ACT 5] Ed.; *Actus Quartus* F   1 *and hereafter.*
SP HOLOFERNES] Ed.; *Pedant* (or *Ped.* or *Peda.*) Q, F   2
and hereafter. SP NATHANIEL] Ed.; *Curat.* Q, F   10.
hominem] F3; *hominum* Q, F   20–21. orthography] Q
(ortagriphie)   27. insanie] Ed.; infamie Q, F   29. *bone*]
Ed.; *bene* Q, F   30. *Bone? Bone*] Ed.; *Bome boon* Q,
F   30. *bene*] Ed.; *boon* Q, F   33. *gaudeo*] Q (*gaudio*)   34
and hereafter. SP ARMADO] Ed.; *Brag.* Q, F   35. *Quare*] Q
(*Quari*)   41. master] Q (M.)   45 *and hereafter.* SP
BOY] Ed.; *Page* Q, F   50. SP HOLOFERNES] *Poda.* Q   58.
wave] F;   wane   Q   58–59.   Mediterraneum]   Q
(meditaranium)   76. wert] Q (wart)   78. *dunghill*] Q
(*dungil*)   79. *Dunghill*] Q (*dunghel*)   93. culled] Q
(culd)   99. important] Q (importunt); importunate F
102. sometimes] Q (sometime)   104. mustachio] Q
(mustachie)   108. travel] Q (trauayle)   110. secrecy] Q
(secretie)   118. Nathaniel] Ed.; *Holofernes* Q, F   120.
rendered] F; rended Q   120. assistance] Ed.; assistants
Q, F   151. *Allons*] Ed.; Alone Q, F

5.2.   1 *and hereafter.* SP PRINCESS] Ed.; *Queen* Q,
F   8. o'] Q (a)   13. ne'er] Q (neare)   18. ha'] Q (a)   18.
been a] F (bin a); bin Q   58, 62. SP MARIA] F (*Mar.*);
Marg. Q   58. pearls] F; Pearle Q   70. hests] Ed.; deuice
Q,F   72.   pair-taunt-like] Ed.; perttaunt like Q; per-

taunt like F   75. hatched.] ~: Q   79. wantonness] F2;
wantons be Q, F   85. stabbed] F; stable Q   89. peace.]
~ ^ Q   93. Saint Cupid] Q (S. *Cupid*)   95. sycamore]
Siccamone Q   99. companions.] ~ ^ Q   99. Warily] Q
(warely)   101. overheard] Q (ouer hard)   102. they] F;
thy Q   104. embassage.] ~ ^ Q   141. too] Q (two)   155.
her] F2; his Q, F   159. ne'er] F2; ere Q, F   163. SD
trumpet] Q (*Trom.*)   166. SP BOYET] Ed.; *Berow.* Q,
F   167. SD *1 line later in* Q, F   170. ever] F; euen
Q   182. strangers] F; stranges Q   188. Princess] F4;
Princes Q, F   208. travel] Q (trauaile)   224. yet?] ~ ^
Q   228. The music] Ed.; *Rosa.* The musique Q, F   229.
SP ROSALINE Our] Ed.; Our Q, F   236. measure!]
measue ^ Q   241. cannot] cennot Q   265–80. SP
KATHERINE] Ed.; *Maria* (*Mari.* or *Mar.*) Q, F   276. Look]
Q (Loke)   283. seen;] ~, Q   284. of sense, so sensi-
ble ^]~~ ^ ~~, Q   285. conference.] ~, Q   291. SD *exit*]
Q (*Exe*)   296. have;] ~ ^ Q   309. perhaps] perhapt
Q   329. vailing] varling Q; vailing F   333. still,] ~ ^
Q   356. his hand away] Ed.; his hand, a way Q; away his
hand F   360. ushering] Q (hushering)   363. flower] Q
(floure)   374. Construe] Q (Consture)   374. speeches]
spaches Q   385. unsullied] Q (vnsallied)   408. foolish.]
~ ^ Q   409. With] Wtih Q   413. eye—] ~. Q   427.
Help, . . . brows!] ~ ^ . . . ~, Q   432. I, lady.] ~, ~ ^
Q   443. affectation] Ed.; affection Q, F   451. begin:] ~ ^
Q   453. Sans ^ "sans,"] *Sans, sans,* Q   504. on 't] Q
(ant)   508. zany] F; saine Q   528. merrily] Q (merely)   529. manage] Ed.; nuage Q; manager F   552. they]
F; thy Q   560. SD *2 lines earlier in* Q, F   568. least] F;
best Q   583. *de la guerra*] Ed.; *delaguar* Q, F   604.
leopard's] Q (Libbards)   619. SP PRINCESS] F2; *Lady* Q;
La. F   631. this] F; his Q   640. conqueror] Conqueronr
Q   647. SD Q (*Exit Curat.*) *6 lines later in* Q, F   653. SD
1 line later in Q, F   661.SD *steps aside*] Ed.; *Exit* Q   667.
proved] Q (proud)   675. elder] Flder Q   693. outfaced]

Q (outfaste) 703. SD *Enter*] *Eeter* Q 718. gilt] F; gift Q 761. moved.] ~ ⌄ Q 761. Ates!] ~ ⌄ Q 762. on, stir] Ed.; or stir Q, F 783. for 't] Q (fort) 784. have] hane Q 792. interruptest] interrnpptest Q 838. strange] Ed.; straying Q, F 839. roll] Q (roule) 841. parti-coated] Q (partie coted) 853. the] F; *omit* Q 857. in] Ed.; *omit* Q, F 868. therefore] rherefore Q 884. in-stant] F; instance Q 889. entitled] inriled Q 893. hermit] Ed.; herrite Q; euer F 893. then.] ~ ⌄ Q 893. breast.] See Appendix, page 225. Appendix 2. to ⌄] ~, Q 895–96. A wife? | KATHERINE A beard. . . .]Ed.; *Kath.* A wife? a beard, . . . Q, F 900. smooth-faced] Q (smothfast) 918. estates] estetes Q 919. wit] wi Q 965. This] F; *Brag.* This Q 967. Ver] F; *B. Ver* Q 968. SP SPRING] Ed.; *omit* Q, F 969–70. Ed.; 969 *and* 970 *reversed in* Q *and* F. 990. foul] F; full Q 1002. SP ARMADO] F (*Brag.*); *omit* Q 1003. You . . . way.] F; *omit* Q

Love's Labor's Lost:
A Modern Perspective
William C. Carroll

Love's Labor's Lost begins with the young King of Navarre anticipating the "disgrace of death," when he and his courtiers will succumb to "cormorant devouring time" and become "heirs of all eternity" (1.1.3–7); the play ends with the stunningly dramatic entrance of Marcade, whose brief "tale" (5.2.796) announces the death of the old King of France, and with the futile efforts of the young courtiers to "make a world-without-end bargain" (5.2.866) with the ladies they have courted. Within this rather somber, even apocalyptic frame, however, *Love's Labor's Lost* is a witty, lively, romantic comedy that contains some of the most exuberant and fantastic language Shakespeare ever composed. Earlier critics tended to stress the verbal exuberance in their accounts of the play, linking its linguistic energies to the supposed "youth" of the author, who was likely around thirty—virtually middle-aged in the sixteenth century—when he wrote the play. The eighteenth century's general disapproval of linguistic exuberance, and especially of the pun, which is the linguistic DNA of *Love's Labor's Lost*, led to faint praise that dismissed the play as "early" and "immature." By contrast, modern criticism of *Love's Labor's Lost* has looked more closely at the play's framing conception, along with its complex representations of gender and court politics, and has attempted to relate both structural form and ideological content to the play's wit and romance. This wider view has led to several provocative modern reassessments of the play and its place in the Shakespeare canon.

To many modern readers, one of the play's most distinctive features is its extraordinary uses of language —not only in its subplots, where Holofernes and Armado are said to have been "at a great feast of languages and stolen the scraps" (5.1.38–39), but also in the court figures, whose language is by turns lyrical, witty, narcissistic, obtuse, and eloquent. This rich linguistic texture is the product of the play's historical moment: a time that looked back at the humanist tradition of eloquence and copiousness, now petrified in the ludicrous synonymic lists of the schoolmaster Holofernes, but also a time that expressed a new, contemporary confidence in the dynamic possibilities of language, marked by the coining of new words and a nearly uncontrollable fertility of invention. What once seemed Shakespeare's "immaturity" in this linguistic profusion is now seen as sophisticated experimentation, a self-consciousness about testing verbal limits and an enthusiastic foray into excess. One comic mark of this exhilaration may be seen in Costard's reaction to being given three farthings by Armado (which in Armado's elevated diction is termed a "remuneration" [3.1.138–39]), and a much more generous shilling by Berowne (which in Berowne's affected French diction is termed a "guerdon," misheard by Costard however as a "gardon" [3.1.178–80]). As happy as he is to receive the money, Costard is nearly as delighted with the remarkable sounds of these words, and he leaves the stage uttering the magical names "Gardon! Remuneration!" (3.1.183). This exchange is a kind of visual pun on the "coining" of new words.[1]

The play acknowledges Shakespeare's contemporary

precursors, especially Sir Philip Sidney and the playwright John Lyly, by allusion to and parody of their typical linguistic characteristics, but it also obviously seeks to go beyond them. The play acknowledges as well the classical tradition absorbed by all Elizabethan schoolboys—Ovid, Horace, Quintillian, Cicero—but they too are more honored in the breach than in the observance. "Ovidius Naso was the man" (4.2.148), Holofernes declares, but for the schoolmaster he is only an instrument, a useful aid—a "Naso," or nose —for help in "smelling out the odoriferous flowers of fancy." Finally, *Love's Labor's Lost*'s lyricism has also suggested its links to an early "lyrical group" among Shakespeare's plays—*Romeo and Juliet, A Midsummer Night's Dream,* and *Richard II*—as well as to his own sonnets, many of which were probably written at roughly the same time.[2] Indeed, one mark of the fine line Shakespeare treads between lyricism and excess, between poetic convention and open parody, is the fact that three of the lords' love sonnets, read aloud in 4.2 and 4.3 as examples of comic hypocrisy and poetic narcissism, were later reprinted "straight" in regular collections of love poems.[3]

Shakespeare's audience would have associated many of the languages of *Love's Labor's Lost* with the court, or courtliness, and it seems no accident that the play itself was presented before the royal courts of both Elizabeth and James. Navarre's court in *Love's Labor's Lost* is, like the play's linguistic texture, situated at a complex historical moment, which in some ways still remains obscure. The idea of making the court into "a little academe" (1.1.13) of contemplation and study derives from a noble humanist tradition (typified in the previous century by Cosimo de' Medici's Platonic Academy in Florence), most recently articulated by Pierre de la Primaudaye's *L'Academie française* (translated 1586). The historical king of Navarre had been the royal patron of such an academy in the early 1580s.[4] (The Princess's royal embassy has in the past also invited considerable speculation about the relation of Navarre's court to various models in Renaissance France.) Several of the characters' names reflect French prototypes, but convincing historical parallels go only so far, and in most cases persuasive evidence of specific connections is lacking. Other parallels have been argued that connect the court in *Love's Labor's Lost* to the court of Queen Elizabeth, particularly in the scene in which the Princess hunts the deer (4.1), a scene perhaps reminiscent of comparable moments in Elizabeth's royal progresses. Elizabeth's court also may be more generally suggested by the frustrated wooings, the petty rivalries, and the competitive displays of wit.[5]

Whatever its royal origins, however, the "little academe" of *Love's Labor's Lost* almost immediately collapses; it is revealed to be not "the wonder of the world" (1.1.12) but a ridiculous comic failure. The ends of study—the grand humanist aspirations to godlike knowledge—degenerate here to the tautological goal, "to know which else we should not know" (1.1.57), or in Berowne's mocking phrase, "Things hid and barred . . . from common sense" (1.1.58–59). Common sense, it turns out, is exactly what this academy lacks. The rigorous educational program of other academies becomes in Navarre a series of merely negative oaths, impossible prohibitions that are broken almost as soon as they are first enunciated: for three years' term, "not to see a woman in that term"; to fast once a week, and take only "one meal on every day besides"; "to sleep but three hours in the night," and not to close one's eyes during the day. Moreover, "no woman shall come within a mile" of the court, and no man shall "be seen to talk with a woman." The embassy of the Princess of France means that several of these prohibitions already have been, and others soon will be, violated, as anyone could have predicted.

The King of Navarre declares in his opening speech that he and his lords struggle against a powerful, cunning enemy—themselves. They are to be "brave conquerors, for so you are / That war against your own affections / And the huge army of the world's desires" (1.1.8–10). The specific objects of their affections, however, will be the ladies from France, and desire will be the power driving the turns and transformations of the plot. "Fame" may be one way to triumph over the "disgrace of death" (1.1.1–3), but so too is the desire to woo, marry, and reproduce, as many of Shakespeare's sonnets argue. Thus Navarre's foolish prohibitions are themselves life-denying, a fact underlined not only by the arrival of the desirable Princess, but also by that of the apprehended Costard, whom the constable Dull delivers, with a fantastic letter from Armado describing Costard's having "sorted and consorted, contrary to [the] established proclaimed edict and continent canon," with Jaquenetta, who is "a child of our grandmother Eve, a female; or, for thy more sweet understanding, a woman" (1.1.259–66). This comic allusion to the Fall in the garden, as in traditional misogynistic discourse, locates in women the source of male self-betrayal. The anxieties associated with the "world's desires"—as if the world, not men, were desirous—are evident in the comic uncertainty of Jaquenetta's exact status, always defined in sexual terms, as either a "wench . . . damsel . . . virgin . . . [or] maid" (1.1.283–97), otherwise known, in Armado's phrase, as "the weaker vessel" (1.1.272). At the end of the play, however, just before Marcade's entrance, we learn that Jaquenetta is already "two months on her way" (5.2.745–46), pregnant neither by the world, nor by Costard, but by Armado himself. In an ironic echo of Navarre's oaths at the beginning of the play, Armado ultimately vows to Jaquenetta "to hold the plow for her sweet love three year" (5.2.957–58), while the lords are being required to do various penances to their own ladies for "a twelvemonth and a day" (5.2.899). The Jaquenetta subplot thus more than demonstrates the "necessity" that will make all the lords "forsworn" (1.1.152). Costard puts it in oracular terms: "Such is the sinplicity of man to hearken after the flesh" (1.1.222–23); his coinage ironically strikes again the note of prohibition, according to which sexual desire is a *sin*. But the flesh won't be denied, as comedy is always reminding us, and the play suggests that the very establishing of a prohibition simultaneously produces a desire to transgress it.

The comic action with Jaquenetta reproduces the main plot in several ways. Hearkening after the flesh is one underlying level of the games and conventions of courtship being played out between the lords of Navarre and the French ladies. The uncertainties attending Jaquenetta's title, and her apparent receptivity to different partners, are replicated in the Masque of Muscovites scene (5.2.164–291): here the ladies wear masks and exchange the "favors" that the men had previously given them, so that the men woo the wrong ladies, after having offered a "penned speech" to an unreceptive audience. The lords' inability to "read" their lovers, to see their faces literally and figuratively, suggests how the men have idealized the female body, projecting upon it stale

Petrarchan clichés that serve both to distance and to control desire. Their use of such rhetoric continually stresses the eye, suggesting the superficiality of the lovers' vision—"My eyes are then no eyes, nor I Berowne"; "love, first learnèd in a lady's eyes, . . . adds a precious seeing to the eye"; "From women's eyes this doctrine I derive" (4.3.252, 321–27, 344). The play's repeated "I"/"eye" puns reveal the lords' fundamental narcissism, seeing what they want to see, otherwise blind (and deaf) to "necessity." When the lords finally understand how the ladies, with their masks and exchanged favors, have deceived them, they also (partially) understand how their own language has betrayed them, as Berowne observes in a stirring speech:

> O, never will I trust to speeches penned,
>   Nor to the motion of a schoolboy's tongue,
> Nor never come in vizard to my friend,
>   Nor woo in rhyme like a blind harper's song.
> Taffeta phrases, silken terms precise,
>   Three-piled hyperboles, spruce affectation,
> Figures pedantical—these summer flies
>   Have blown me full of maggot ostentation.
> I do forswear them, and I here protest
>   By this white glove—how white the hand,
>   God knows!—
> Henceforth my wooing mind shall be expressed
>   In russet yeas and honest kersey noes.
> And to begin: Wench, so God help me, law,
> My love to thee is sound, sans crack or flaw.
>
> ROSALINE
> Sans "sans," I pray you.
> BEROWNE   Yet I have a trick
> Of the old rage. Bear with me, I am sick;
> I'll leave it by degrees.   (5.2.438–56)

It is a wonderful speech, full of illumination, but, as
Rosaline observes and Berowne admits, it also still
bears more than a trace of the "old rage," a kind of
verbal infection. Further distinguishing the language
of the women from that of the men, this speech
suggests how the women's language in the play is more
critically self-aware. Berowne, by contrast, is forswearing linguistic affectation here in favor of plain
speech, yet doing so in a perfectly formed sonnet, thus
wooing "in rhyme" even as he swears not to. The
implication is that he could find some transparent,
"natural" language, but the play has shown, in a suggestive anticipation of modern linguistic theory, that language is always compromised, opaque, self-contained as
well as referential.

The language of the men, both high and low, misun-
derstands, misreads, and misappropriates the women in
the play. A comparable miscognition provides the very
occasion of the play, the dispute over the land of
Aquitaine, "a dowry for a queen" (2.1.8). Navarre claims
that the King of France did not pay the hundred thousand crowns he claims to have paid, and in any event still
owes an equal amount, as repayment of Navarre's father's support of France in his wars; thus he holds
Aquitaine as surety for the money. France not only
claims that he has paid, but asks for repayment, and the
return of the land; the Princess says that she has
"acquittances / For such a sum" (2.1.165–66) which
will prove France's contention, although they are not
with her at the moment. Navarre is willing to return
Aquitaine if she can prove her case, but, aside from the
Princess's enigmatic thanks for her "great suit so easily
obtained" (5.2.814), the issue is never resolved in the
play. With her father's death, the Princess herself inher-
its the disputed "dowry for a queen."

This fundamental conflict over property rights is but one instance of the play's continuing interest in the relations between property and gender. Navarre is partly dismissive of Aquitaine's value, "so gelded as it is" (2.1.152)—that is, reduced in value, or deprived of some essential part, but also emasculated, and therefore of less value. Property can serve as a gender marker in the play in other ways as well. As one critic has noted, the names of the lords in *Love's Labor's Lost* are inherited, and refer to the property passed down through the male in each family—Navarre, Berowne, Longaville, Dumaine— while the noble ladies have no surnames, and the Princess no name at all, only a generic title identifying her as a daughter.[6] As Aquitaine is said to be a "dowry," moreover, it is linked to the Princess and her marital status. In this respect, at least, Navarre's possession of it is premature and improper. Thus Aquitaine figures as a kind of substitute for possession of the Princess herself, as the men struggle throughout the play to appropriate and possess the ladies through courtship. Given the way in which such relations are usually resolved—by the woman delivering "property" (herself and the dowry) to the male—it is all the more surprising that the Princess rejects the "bargain" (5.2.866) being proposed, with her and her ladies returning to France unwed. It is so surprising an ending, so completely different even from the endings of Shakespeare's other romantic comedies, that Berowne remarks on it:

> Our wooing doth not end like an old play.
> Jack hath not Jill. These ladies' courtesy
> Might well have made our sport a comedy.

KING
  Come, sir, it wants a twelvemonth and a day,
  And then 'twill end.
BEROWNE   That's too long for a play.
                                      (5.2.947–52)[7]

Berowne's rueful self-consciousness returns us to the
notion of *Love's Labor's Lost* as a relatively sophisticated,
experimental play. Shakespeare is certainly well aware
here of the elements of his own artifice: the violation of
comic form in the non-marriages at the end is only one
of several self-consciously metatheatrical moments in
the play. The Masque of Muscovites scene, which we
have already considered from the perspective of male
misrecognition, should also be seen as an embedded
play-within-the-play. A typical courtly "entertainment"
—it may even be based on a real masque[8]—the Masque
reflects some of the transformations and semiotic confusions associated with wearing masks and performing
roles. A second scene that functions much like a
play-within-a-play is 4.3, in which each lord enters,
reads a foolish love sonnet that is overheard by the
previous lord, and is then mocked by him—and he, in
turn, is then exposed as guilty of the same hypocrisy.
Even Berowne, who takes the highest position on the
ladder, is exposed when Costard brings in his misdelivered letter. (Letters and words are always being misdelivered in *Love's Labor's Lost*, of course.) The sonnet-
reading scene also reflects ironically on the idea of
perceptive and imperceptive audiences and defeated
expectations.

The only formal play-within-the-play, however, is the
Pageant of the Nine Worthies—or the nine *wordies,* as it
was probably pronounced[9]—in the final scene. Here
irony and self-consciousness again work as elements

within the play as well as serving as a commentary on its own principles. The Worthies were legendary figures in a literary tradition dating back to the early fourteenth century. They were usually three pagans (Hector, Alexander, and Caesar), three Jews (Joshua, David, and Judas Maccabaeus), and three Christians (Arthur, Charlemagne, and Godfrey of Bouillon), but others were occasionally substituted, as Pompey is here. The Worthies were paragons of the heroic life, who had achieved all the "fame" and "honor" that the men of Navarre could ever dream of; they were truly "brave conquerors" and "heirs of all eternity" (1.1.1–8). Yet devices representing the Worthies had by this time also become overused, a little moth-eaten, turning the heroes into examples of falsely inflated worth. In this Pageant, they have also become further examples of linguistic instability and the shifting sands of poetic convention. Their speeches are comically inflated and archaic in style, and even their names are subject to the ravages of the pun: thus "Pompion [i.e., pumpkin] the Great" (5.2.553), "Ajax" (i.e., "jakes," or privy [5.2.645]), and "Jud-as[s]" (5.2.698).

The actors of the Pageant are ludicrously incapable of performing their heroic parts, just as the lords have been confounded and self-betrayed in their various attempts at securing fame or love. For the most part this dissonance between actor and role is figurative, but it is literal in the case of the boy Mote, who is playing the greatest of all heroes ("Great Hercules is presented by this imp" [5.2.655]). As comic reflections of Navarre's court, the Worthies expose the flawed and comic pretensions of the lords who overrate their own "worth" and engage in shallow "praise" of the ladies throughout. Yet Navarre and his men remain unable to "see" themselves. Their mockery of the Worthies' Pageant, almost

cruel at times, exhibits a condescension that has not
been earned.

The Pageant of the Nine Worthies does not have a
proper ending, just as *Love's Labor's Lost* does not. It
ends with a near-fight between Armado and Costard,
who has brought the news of Jaquenetta's pregnancy.
But at the moment that Armado backs away from
combat, Marcade enters with his stunning announcement, with what results we have already seen. The
play-within and the play that contains it remain parallel
even in their shattered forms, ending before their "natural" resolutions can occur. Instead, the lords are given
their twelve-month penances, extending beyond the
structural and chronological boundaries of the play
itself. As the chief possessor of an ungoverned wit,
Berowne is given the most difficult task: for the term of a
year to

> Visit the speechless sick, and still converse
> With groaning wretches; and your task shall be,
> With all the fierce endeavor of your wit,
> To enforce the painèd impotent to smile.

Berowne's response is quite logical: "To move wild
laughter in the throat of death? / It cannot be, it is
impossible" (5.2.924–29). But Rosaline wants him to
learn about decorum—learn when particular styles of
speech should be used and how different audiences
respond, as if Berowne were a playwright trying to write
a comedy for the most difficult audience imaginable.
Shakespeare himself has done something similar here,
moving laughter against the "disgrace of death."

This extraordinary self-consciousness evident
throughout *Love's Labor's Lost,* from ironic puns and
metadramatic self-references to the formal play-within-
the-play, which explicitly analyzes the customs and

conventions upon which all drama depends, indicates that Shakespeare must have had a very clear idea of the challenges, both verbal and dramatic, which he faced as a playwright.

The final songs of Spring and Winter offer a remarkable further step in the play's interrogation of style and artistic self-consciousness. They seem to embody a more "natural" poetics (associated with "the songs of Apollo"), yet they are very carefully crafted. They offer a vision of natural sexual completion ("When turtles tread, and rooks and daws, / And maidens bleach their summer smocks"), but this completion is attended by all too familiar projections of male anxiety ("The cuckoo then on every tree / Mocks married men . . . O word of fear, / Unpleasing to a married ear"). The songs offer images and rich associations that link them to various elements of the play, yet they remain elusive, suggestive, even mysterious. In performance, the effect of the songs on the audience can be profound. They seem to be exactly the right ending for *Love's Labor's Lost*, even if—or especially because—they are not the one an audience expects. This deliberately "open" ending seems especially modern in its suspension of form and certainty. The final line of the play—"You that way; we this way"—may divide the members of the cast into their separate exits, but it may also serve as an ultimate distinction between the audience ("you") and the actors, sending the audience back into the world where "cormorant devouring time" is not always countered, or transformed, by the seasonal time of Spring and Winter.

———

1. On aspects of language in the play, see James L. Calderwood, *Shakespearean Metadrama* (Minneapolis:

University of Minnesota Press, 1971); William C. Carroll, *The Great Feast of Language in Love's Labour's Lost* (Princeton: Princeton University Press, 1976); Keir Elam, *Shakespeare's Universe of Discourse: Language-Games in the Comedies* (Cambridge: Cambridge University Press, 1984); Malcolm Evans, *Signifying Nothing: Truth's True Contents in Shakespeare's Text* (Athens: University of Georgia Press, 1986); and Patricia Parker, "Preposterous Reversals: *Love's Labour's Lost*," *MLQ* 54 (1993): 435–82.

2. E. K. Chambers, *William Shakespeare: A Study of Facts and Problems* (Oxford: Clarendon Press, 1930), 1:335

3. Berowne's, Longaville's, and Dumaine's poems appeared in *The Passionate Pilgrim* (1599), which also included a poem by Marlowe; Dumaine's poem also was printed in the well-known collection *England's Helicon* (1600), which included such authors as Sidney, Spenser, Drayton, Greene, Surrey, and Marlowe, among others. Both collections were nostalgic in tone, and must have seemed faintly archaic when they appeared.

4. See Frances Yates, *The French Academies of the Sixteenth Century* (London: The Warburg Institute, 1947).

5. See Graham Holderness, Nick Potter, and John Turner, *Shakespeare: Out of Court. Dramatizations of Court Society* (New York: St. Martin's Press, 1990).

6. Katharine Eisaman Maus, "Transfer of Title in *Love's Labor's Lost*: Language, Individualism, Gender," in Ivo Kamps, ed., *Shakespeare Left and Right* (London: Routledge, 1991), pp. 210, 216.

7. As if to make amends for the fractured ending here, Shakespeare has Puck promise, in *A Midsummer Night's Dream*, "And the country proverb known, / That every man should take his own, / In your waking shall be shown. / Jack shall have Jill; / Naught shall go ill; / The

man shall have his mare again, and all shall be well" (3.2.487–93).

8. Performed at a somewhat notorious revels at Gray's Inn in the 1594–95 Christmas season, at which *The Comedy of Errors* was also performed; see Chambers, *William Shakespeare*, 1:336.

9. The *th* sound was apparently sounded as a *t;* thus "Moth" was probably pronounced "mote."

Further Reading

Love's Labor's Lost

Asp, Carolyn. *"Love's Labour's Lost:* Language and the Deferral of Desire." *Literature and Psychology* 35:3 (1989): 1–21.

Asp uses the theories of Lacan (especially his ideas of Imaginary and Symbolic and intra- and interpersonal development) to explain the play's rejection of the conventional comic ending: marriage. Navarre and his courtiers, in pursuit of "an idealized image of ego unity," defer their natural desires "into linguistic displacements [of] pedantic knowledge and courtly rhetoric." The Princess and her ladies succeed in decoding this male behavior. At the end of the play, however, it is the women who defer desire by imposing "ascetic tasks" upon the men.

Barber, C. L. "The Folly of Wit and Masquerade in *Love's Labour's Lost.*" In *Shakespeare's Festive Comedy: A Study of Dramatic Form and Its Relation to Social Custom,* pp. 87–118. Princeton: Princeton University Press, 1959.

In this anthropological reading, Barber applies to *LLL* the formula "through release to clarification" that he finds in the "native saturnalian traditions" (of Elizabethan holidays and the popular theater) lying behind Shakespeare's early comedies. Clarification—the "heightened awareness" of man's relationship with nature—comes with the "movement between the poles of restraint [responsibility] and release [playful liberation]." The unconventional ending is appropriate, Barber argues, given what is released by the preceding festivities: ". . . the folly of acting love and talking love, without being in love." Moreover, the final songs, in their celebration of the rhythms of holiday and everyday, remind us of the "going-on power" of life.

Berry, Ralph. "The Words of Mercury." *Shakespeare Survey* 22 (1969): 69–77. Rpt. in *Shakespeare's Comedies: Explorations in Form*, pp. 72–88. Princeton: Princeton University Press, 1972.

The form of *LLL* can best be described as a "movement toward reality," reality being defined as "all those phenomena of life that are symbolized by the entrance of Mercade"—"the key fact" of the play. Berry reads the play as "a sustained inquiry into the nature and status of words" and their relationship to reality. The tidings Mercade brings of mortality "dissolve the world of illusion and announce the presence of a reality that must be mediated by words."

Bevington, David. "'Jack Hath Not Jill': Failed Courtship in Lyly and Shakespeare." *Shakespeare Survey* 42 (1990): 1–13.

Agreeing with Alfred Harbage that *LLL* is the most Lylyan of Shakespeare's plays, Bevington compares it to Lyly's *Sappho and Phao* (1584), which also ends without romantic union—Phao falls in love with Sappho but at the end, realizing that she is impossibly beyond his reach, leaves her court in disappointment. Bevington makes no claim for Lyly's text as a source for *LLL;* his interest lies, instead, in probing the plays' shared emphasis on "the hazards and uncertainties of courtship" and their implications for the "larger pattern of patriarchal control" operative in both.

Breitenberg, Mark. "The Anatomy of Masculine Desire in *Love's Labor's Lost*." *Shakespeare Quarterly* 43 (1992): 430–49.

Breitenberg begins by citing Montaigne's "Upon Some Verses of Virgil" (a "meditation" on masculine desire and its side effect of cuckoldry anxiety) and the male-empowering tenets of Petrarchanism to argue that the Petrarchan tradition underlies the "economy of masculine desire that structures [*LLL*] and shapes its action." His probing of this economy's fissures, paradoxes, and contradictions centers on the play's pervasive cuckoldry anxiety, most pronounced in the final song of Spring. In *LLL*, "Shakespeare anatomizes masculine desire by reproducing and parodying its effects, providing an anatomy that exposes the very same limitations and contradictions it cannot fully escape."

Burnett, Mark Thornton. "Giving and Receiving: *Love's Labour's Lost* and the Politics of Exchange." *English Literary Renaissance* 23 (1993): 287–313.

Burnett counters the traditional reading of *LLL* as a light and witty courtly entertainment with the argument that it is "as much concerned with a contest over power, property, and financial debt." Drawing upon cultural materialist and new historicist studies of Shakespeare, he examines the play as a series of exchanges, beginning with the central issue from which everything else springs: Aquitaine and the dispute over tribute payments. "The play manifests a range of responses toward money from cautious uncertainty to philosophical curiosity and excitement . . . and broaches but does not resolve a conflict between, on the one hand, exchanges that benefit donor and recipient and, on the other hand, naked self-interest."

Calderwood, James L. *"Love's Labour's Lost:* A Dalliance with Language." In *Shakespearean Metadrama: The Argument of the Play in "Titus Andronicus," "Love's Labour's Lost," "Romeo and Juliet," "A Midsummer Night's Dream," and "Richard II,"* pp. 52–84. Minneapolis: University of Minnesota Press, 1971.

Calderwood traces the dynamic of the play's verbal action through three phases: the scholars' aggrandizement of words in the formation of the academy, their debasing of words in its abandonment, and, with the entrance of Mercade, their growing awareness—thanks to instruction from the ladies—of language as a valid, reliable, and even moral "medium of exchange." As for the metadramatic implications of his analysis, Calderwood declares that *LLL* "embodies Shakespeare's discovery that drama is the literary form of true liberality and that drama achieves fulfillment when verbal celibacy and verbal prodigality give way to a genuine marriage of words to action."

Carroll, William C. *The Great Feast of Language in Love's Labour's Lost*. Princeton: Princeton University Press, 1976.

In this full-length study of the "radical instability" of the play's language, Carroll explores *LLL*'s central strategy: the setting of multiple perspectives in conflict to encourage "debate on the right use of rhetoric, poetry, and the imagination." The first three chapters identify three distinct kinds of style: that of the prose passages belonging to the six low characters, the theatrical style of the three plays-within-the-play (the eavesdropping scene in 4.3 and the Masque of the Muscovites and Pageant of the Nine Worthies in 5.2), and the poetic style of the lunatics and lovers turned sonneteers. Chapter 4 takes up the play's Ovidian strain as manifest in the way characters through their fantastic imaginations transform reality. Chapter 5 locates the schematizing structure that comprehends the whole in the basic dualism of art and nature. The final chapter discusses the closing songs as an emblematic resolution of all the contrarieties previously disclosed.

Donawerth, Jane. *"Love's Labor's Lost:* Creative Words." In *Shakespeare and the Sixteenth-Century Study of Language*, pp. 141–64. Urbana and Chicago: University of Illinois Press, 1984.

Instead of focusing on the thematic dimension of language in *LLL*, Donawerth concentrates on the dramatic implications of its ideas *about* language: i.e., the ways in which such ideas define the world of the play and the kinds of people inhabiting it. As befits the artificial world of Navarre's court, the emphasis in *LLL* is on the patterning of language as written rather than on its greater naturalness as spoken. Beginning with the entry of Mercade, however, Donawerth observes a significant shift in terms as "language" and "words" are replaced by "tongue" and "breath." This abandonment of the graphic (artificial) aspect of language for the oral (more natural) dimension parallels "a growth in humanity in the characters."

Elam, Keir. *Shakespeare's Universe of Discourse: Language Games in the Comedies*. Cambridge: Cambridge University Press, 1984.

Although *LLL* receives no chapter-length analysis in this study of the "self-consciousness" of Shakespeare's discourse—the playwright's general word for "language in *use*" and his favorite linguistic term in the comedies —the play serves as a major point of reference, weaving in and out of Elam's discussion of different kinds of linguistic games and frames: theatrical, world-creating, semantic, pragmatic, and figural. The author provides an eight-page glossary of terms derived from the "modes and instruments of contemporary linguistic enquiry" brought to bear on the plays: semiotics, philosophies and sociologies of language, speech-act analysis, conversational decorum, and rhetorical theory.

Evans, Malcolm. "The Converse of Breath." In *Signifying Nothing: Truth's True Contents in Shakespeare's Text*, pp. 41–67, esp. 50–67. Athens: University of Georgia Press, 1986.

Like Donawerth (see earlier citation) but from a poststructuralist perspective, Evans examines the triumph of breath (speech) over letters (writing) in *LLL*; this victory, however, is ironically overturned when the "modern encounter" with the play is with something printed in book form. Evans frames his discussion of the play's structural opposition of writing and speech—letters and sounds—within a commentary on the "postscript" significance of the 1598 Quarto's printing of the lines "The Words of Mercury / Are harsh after the songs of Apollo." Set without speech headings and in larger type than the rest of the play, the lines assume a "Delphic ambiguity and portentous tone," calling attention to the central conflict between Mercury (the "inventor of letters" and patron of solitary learning) and Apollo (the god of rhyme and speech).

Gilbert, Miriam. *Love's Labour's Lost*. Shakespeare in Performance Series. Manchester and New York: Manchester University Press, 1993.

The story underlying Gilbert's study of selected productions is "how scholars, directors, actors, and audiences have come to appreciate the play after more than three centuries of neglect, and what qualities they have found to appreciate." Gilbert considers productions directed by Samuel Phelps (1857), Tyrone Guthrie (1936), Peter Brook (1946), Hugh Hunt (1949), John Barton (1965 and 1978), Michael Kahn (1968), David Jones (1973), Elijah Moshinsky (1984), Barry Kyle (1984), and Terry Hands (1990).

Goldstien, Neal L. *"Love's Labour's Lost and the Renaissance Vision of Love." Shakespeare Quarterly* 25 (1974): 335–50.

Goldstien reads the play as a satire on the two major components of the Renaissance love theory informing its dramatic situation, dialogue, imagery, and theme: namely, Petrarchanism and the Florentine Neoplatonism associated with Marsilio Ficino. Both Petrarch and Ficino were instrumental in effecting the spiritualization of love and beauty in the Renaissance: the first insisting upon the spiritual nature of womanly beauty; the second establishing the spiritual nature of love itself. In its strong sensual bias and its iconoclastic treatment of the conventions of the English vision of love and the spirituality underlying those conventions, *LLL* is part of a major poetic tradition in sixteenth-century English poetry. Yet what finally emerges is the realization that neither pole—sensuality or spirituality—is completely satisfying.

Granville-Barker, Harley. *"Love's Labour's Lost."* In *Prefaces to Shakespeare*, 2:413–39. Princeton: New Jersey: Princeton University Press, 1947, 1978.

Describing *LLL* as a "fashionable play; now, by three hundred years out of fashion," Granville-Barker brings his practical experience as a director to this discussion of staging, methods of acting, costumes, casting, music, and textual cuts (especially as relating to witty lines and jokes that pass over a modern audience's head and confusing/redundant passages in 2.1, 4.3, and 5.2).

Hunter, Robert G. "The Function of the Songs at the End of *Love's Labour's Lost*." *Shakespeare Studies* 7 (1974): 55–64.

Hunter sees the concluding songs of Spring and Winter as "more than pretty lyrics." Taking his cue from C. L. Barber (see earlier citation), he argues for their "definite thematic relationship" to the central conflict between Lent and Carnival informing the play: the songs ultimately resolve this conflict by "strik[ing] a balance" between the devouring forces of linear Lenten time and the renewing powers of circular Carnival time. The result is an "alliance that will combine the seemingly irreconcilable strengths of both." Lent may appear to return in the arrival of Mercade, but the songs deny its view as being the whole truth: Spring will come again.

Lamb, Mary Ellen. "The Nature of Topicality in 'Love's Labour's Lost'." *Shakespeare Survey* 38 (1985): 49–59.

In spite of critical opinion to the contrary, the author argues that *LLL* "was no more or less 'aristocratic' in its appeal than Shakespeare's other earlier plays . . . [and] that what topicality it possesses was available to a wide audience." The false identification of the play as an obscure piece of coterie drama stems from its intrinsic topicality: i.e., the fact that each of its major male characters has an historical counterpart against whom similarities and differences can be measured. Lamb does not "disparage topicality as a valid field of inquiry" but advocates a more evenhanded approach that insists on the *locus* of meaning in the play itself and not in its relation to topical sources; by way of illustration, she looks at the significance of the historical Navarre's adulteries at Nerac for the play's iterative pattern of oath-breach. Despite the usefulness of topical source hunting as a tool, the author concludes that "the topicality of *Love's Labour's Lost* is dead . . . It stands on its own, as recent directors and audiences have shown." (For examples of such productions, see the Gilbert citation.)

Maus, Katharine Eisaman. "Transfer of Title in *Love's Labor's Lost:* Language, Individualism, Gender." In *Shakespeare Left and Right*, ed. Ivo Kamps, pp. 205–23. New York and London: Routledge, 1991.

In a reading that combines feminism and formalism, Maus contends that linguistic issues informing the play —especially naming and reference—are "inseparable from its generic, comic concerns with sexual politics and with the construction of a gendered identity in a social context." Navarre and his courtiers seek permanence by stabilizing their (aristocratic, paternally inherited) names in a way that "close[s] the gap between signifier and signified . . . word and world." The arrival of the ladies, whose strategy of self-assertion involves "subverting the clarity and permanence" of such essentialist thinking, "confront[s] Navarre with everything he had tried to repress: the involvement of women in the title transfer, the dependence of the present generation upon the action of its predecessors, and the possibility that the title itself may be ambiguous, subject to conflicting claims." The conceptual differences between the sexes are most evident at the end of Act 5; there the men's view of truth as a masculine-authorized exercise of intellect is starkly set against the women's understanding of it as "disciplined will," as something social, contractual, and behavioral: "the keeping of a marital vow that demands submission to a patriarchal order."

Montrose, Louis A. "'Sport by sport o'erthrown': *Love's Labour's Lost* and the Politics of Play." *Texas Studies in Literature and Language* 18 (1977): 528–52.

In *LLL*, "playwright, actors, and audience are engaged in the purposeful playing of a play whose fictional action is generated almost entirely by characters at play"—the various dimensions of which include dressing up, songs, entertainments, flirtations, puns and conceits, allusions to specific children's pastimes, and the game of the chase. Montrose's treatment of the drama's ludic quality is informed by the distinction between two species of play "related by inversion": game and ritual—the former disjunctive in its effects, the latter conjunctive. One reason for the play's failure to end in the weddings generically associated with comedy derives from the men's turning the "ritual goal of union with the beloved into a game" which they must win.

Parker, Patricia. "Preposterous Reversals: *Love's Labor's Lost*." *Modern Language Quarterly* 54 (1993): 435–82.

As evidence for her reading of *LLL* as "bodily or 'obscene'" rather than bookish or esoteric (lowbrow rather than highbrow), Parker focuses on the excremental and scatalogical aspects of the comedy's wordplay. From the opening scene, "the language of the 'high' . . . is contaminated . . . by the 'low matter' of the bodily and sexual." On several levels—verbal, structural, generic, and genderic—the play is "a series of . . . 'preposterous' inversions—of male and female, high and low, prior and posterior, and their bodily counterparts."

Roberts, Jeanne Addison. "Convents, Conventions, and Contraventions: *Love's Labor's Lost* and *The Convent of Pleasure*." In *Shakespeare's Sweet Thunder: Essays on the Early Comedies*, pp. 75–89. Ed. Michael J. Collins. Newark: University of Delaware Press, 1996.

Suggesting that *Love's Labor's Lost* "cannot be read by us as either a precociously feminist or a specifically satirical drama," Roberts claims that it can be read as "at least a forerunner of feminism." In support of this claim, she offers a comparison of Shakespeare's play to *The Convent of Pleasure*, a play published in 1668 by Lady Cavendish, Duchess of Newcastle, which may have been inspired in part by Cavendish's reading of *Love's Labor's Lost*. Roberts shows how Cavendish's play begins by defying patriarchy's assumption of the inevitability of marriage for women and then concludes with marriage, while *Love's Labor's Lost* appears from the beginning to be destined to end with marriages and then does not because of the control exerted by the play's women.

Roesen, Bobbyann (Anne Barton). "*Love's Labour's Lost*." *Shakespeare Quarterly* 4 (1953): 411–26.

This seminal essay is called by Montrose—see earlier citation—"a landmark in the critical revaluation" of *LLL*. Focusing on the play's fundamental opposition between art and nature, the author describes the dramatic movement as one from illusion to reality. In the artificial world of Navarre's court, the reality of Death is introduced only to be forgotten in the program of the Academy, which will yield immortal fame against the ravages of "cormorant devouring Time." With the arrival of the ladies, through whom "the voice of Reality speaks," death is reintroduced, albeit in ritualized form, in the Princess's killing of the deer (Act 4). Finally, Death's "tremendous reality" is personalized in the entrance of Mercade: "In the space of four lines [5.2.793–

96] the entire world of the play, its delicate balance of reality and illusion, all the hilarity and overwhelming life of the last scene has been swept away and destroyed as Death itself actually enters the park, for the first time. . . ." (See the Berry, Calderwood, Montrose, and Carroll citations for examples of Roesen's influence on the art-nature debate.)

Turner, John. *"Love's Labour's Lost:* The Court at Play."
In *Shakespeare: Out of Court. Dramatizations of Court Society,* by Graham Holderness, Nick Potter, and John Turner, pp. 19–48. New York: St. Martin's Press, 1990.

Turner's focus (unlike Barber's, see earlier citation) is not courtly pleasures but the dissonances and anxieties of court life as mirrored in *LLL*. Seizing upon the Renaissance double meaning of "competitor" (2.1.84) as partner or rival (and, by extension, the contrary feelings it evoked of exhilaration and entrapment), the author explores the threefold competitiveness structuring the play's "unstable mixture of rivalry and fellowship": the internal competition in Navarre's court, the international competition between the court of Navarre and the court of France as represented by the Princess and her attendants, and ("most interestingly perhaps") the pastoral competition between the court of Navarre and the country it rules.

Shakespeare's Language

Abbott, E. A. *A Shakespearian Grammar.* New York: Haskell House, 1972.

This compact reference book, first published in 1870, helps with many difficulties in Shakespeare's language. It systematically accounts for a host of differences between Shakespeare's usage and sentence structure and our own.

Blake, Norman. *Shakespeare's Language: An Introduction.* New York: St. Martin's Press, 1983.
This general introduction to Elizabethan English discusses various aspects of the language of Shakespeare and his contemporaries, offering possible meanings for hundreds of ambiguous constructions.

Dobson, E. J. *English Pronunciation, 1500–1700.* 2 vols. Oxford: Clarendon Press, 1968.
This long and technical work includes chapters on spelling (and its reformation), phonetics, stressed vowels, and consonants in early modern English.

Houston, John. *Shakespearean Sentences: A Study in Style and Syntax.* Baton Rouge: Louisiana State University Press, 1988.
Houston studies Shakespeare's stylistic choices, considering matters such as sentence length and the relative positions of subject, verb, and direct object. Examining plays throughout the canon in a roughly chronological, developmental order, he analyzes how sentence structure is used in setting tone, in characterization, and for other dramatic purposes.

Onions, C. T. *A Shakespeare Glossary.* Oxford: Clarendon Press, 1986.
This revised edition updates Onions's standard, selective glossary of words and phrases in Shakespeare's plays that are now obsolete, archaic, or obscure.

Partridge, Eric. *Shakespeare's Bawdy.* London: Routledge & Kegan Paul, 1955.
After an introductory essay, "The Sexual, the Homo-

sexual, and Non-Sexual Bawdy in Shakespeare," Partridge provides a comprehensive glossary of "bawdy" phrases and words from the plays.

Robinson, Randal. *Unlocking Shakespeare's Language: Help for the Teacher and Student.* Urbana, Ill.: National Council of Teachers of English and the ERIC Clearinghouse on Reading and Communication Skills, 1989.

Specifically designed for the high-school and undergraduate college teacher and student, Robinson's book addresses the problems that most often hinder present-day readers of Shakespeare. Through work with his own students, Robinson found that many readers today are particularly puzzled by such stylistic devices as subject-verb inversion, interrupted structures, and compression. He shows how our own colloquial language contains comparable structures, and thus helps students recognize such structures when they find them in Shakespeare's plays. This book supplies worksheets— with examples from major plays—to illuminate and remedy such problems as unusual sequences of words and the separation of related parts of sentences.

Shakespeare's Life

Baldwin, T. W. *William Shakspere's Petty School.* Urbana: University of Illinois Press, 1943.

Baldwin here investigates the theory and practice of the petty school, the first level of education in Elizabethan England. He focuses on that educational system primarily as it is reflected in Shakespeare's art.

Baldwin, T. W. *William Shakspere's Small Latine and Lesse Greeks.* 2 vols. Urbana: University of Illinois Press, 1944.

Baldwin attacks the view that Shakespeare was an uneducated genius—a view that had been dominant among Shakespeareans since the eighteenth century. Instead, Baldwin shows, the educational system of Shakespeare's time would have given the playwright a strong background in the classics, and there is much in the plays that shows how Shakespeare benefited from such an education.

Beier, A. L., and Roger Finlay, eds. *London 1500–1800: The Making of the Metropolis*. New York: Longman, 1986.
Focusing on the economic and social history of early modern London, these collected essays probe aspects of metropolitan life, including "Population and Disease," "Commerce and Manufacture," and "Society and Change."

Bentley, G. E. *Shakespeare's Life: A Biographical Handbook*. New Haven: Yale University Press, 1961.
This "just-the-facts" account presents the surviving documents of Shakespeare's life against an Elizabethan background.

Chambers, E. K. *William Shakespeare: A Study of Facts and Problems*. 2 vols. Oxford: Clarendon Press, 1930.
Analyzing in great detail the scant historical data, Chambers's complex, scholarly study considers the nature of the texts in which Shakespeare's work is preserved.

Cressy, David. *Education in Tudor and Stuart England*. London: Edward Arnold, 1975.
This volume collects sixteenth-, seventeenth-, and early-eighteenth-century documents detailing aspects of formal education in England, such as the curriculum,

the control and organization of education, and the education of women.

Dutton, Richard. *William Shakespeare: A Literary Life*. New York: St. Martin's Press, 1989.
Not a biography in the traditional sense, Dutton's very readable work nevertheless "follows the contours of Shakespeare's life" as he examines Shakespeare's career as playwright and poet, with consideration of his patrons, theatrical associations, and audience.

Fraser, Russell. *Young Shakespeare*. New York: Columbia University Press, 1988.
Fraser focuses on Shakespeare's first thirty years, paying attention simultaneously to his life and art.

De Grazia, Margreta. *Shakespeare Verbatim: The Reproduction of Authenticity and the Apparatus of 1790*. Oxford: Clarendon Press, 1991.
De Grazia traces and discusses the development of such editorial criteria as authenticity, historical periodization, factual biography, chronological development, and close reading, locating as the point of origin Edmond Malone's 1790 edition of Shakespeare's works. There are interesting chapters on the First Folio and on the "legendary" versus the "documented" Shakespeare.

Schoenbaum, S. *William Shakespeare: A Compact Documentary Life*. New York: Oxford University Press, 1977.
This standard biography economically presents the essential documents from Shakespeare's time in an accessible narrative account of the playwright's life.

Shakespeare's Theater

Bentley, G. E. *The Profession of Player in Shakespeare's Time, 1590–1642*. Princeton: Princeton University Press, 1984.

Bentley readably sets forth a wealth of evidence about performance in Shakespeare's time, with special attention to the relations between player and company, and the business of casting, managing, and touring.

Berry, Herbert. *Shakespeare's Playhouses*. New York: AMS Press, 1987.

Berry's six essays collected here discuss (with illustrations) varying aspects of the four playhouses in which Shakespeare had a financial stake: the Theatre in Shoreditch, the Blackfriars, and the first and second Globe.

Cook, Ann Jennalie. *The Privileged Playgoers of Shakespeare's London*. Princeton: Princeton University Press, 1981.

Cook's work argues, on the basis of sociological, economic, and documentary evidence, that Shakespeare's audience—and the audience for English Renaissance drama generally—consisted mainly of the "privileged."

Greg, W. W. *Dramatic Documents from the Elizabethan Playhouses*. 2 vols. Oxford: Clarendon Press, 1931.

Greg itemizes and briefly describes many of the play manuscripts that survive from the period 1590 to around 1660, including, among other things, players' parts. His second volume offers facsimiles of selected manuscripts.

Gurr, Andrew. *Playgoing in Shakespeare's London.* Cambridge: Cambridge University Press, 1987.
Gurr charts how the theatrical enterprise developed from its modest beginnings in the late 1560s to become a thriving institution in the 1600s. He argues that there were important changes over the period 1567–1644 in the playhouses, the audience, and the plays.

Harbage, Alfred. *Shakespeare's Audience.* New York: Columbia University Press, 1941.
Harbage investigates the fragmentary surviving evidence to interpret the size, composition, and behavior of Shakespeare's audience.

Hattaway, Michael. *Elizabethan Popular Theatre: Plays in Performance.* London: Routledge & Kegan Paul, 1982.
Beginning with a study of the popular drama of the late Elizabethan age—a description of the stages, performance conditions, and acting of the period—this volume concludes with an analysis of five well-known plays of the 1590s, one of them (*Titus Andronicus*) by Shakespeare.

Shapiro, Michael. *Children of the Revels: The Boy Companies of Shakespeare's Time and Their Plays.* New York: Columbia University Press, 1977.
Shapiro chronicles the history of the amateur and quasi-professional child companies that flourished in London at the end of Elizabeth's reign and the beginning of James's.

The Publication of Shakespeare's Plays

Blayney, Peter. *The First Folio of Shakespeare.* Hanover, Md.: Folger, 1991.

Blayney's accessible account of the printing and later life of the First Folio—an amply illustrated catalog to a 1991 Folger Shakespeare Library exhibition—analyzes the mechanical production of the First Folio, describing how the Folio was made, by whom and for whom, how much it cost, and its ups and downs (or, rather, downs and ups) since its printing in 1623.

Hinman, Charlton. *The Printing and Proof-Reading of the First Folio of Shakespeare*. 2 vols. Oxford: Clarendon Press, 1963.

In the most arduous study of a single book ever undertaken, Hinman attempts to reconstruct how the Shakespeare First Folio of 1623 was set into type and run off the press, sheet by sheet. He also provides almost all the known variations in readings from copy to copy.

Hinman, Charlton. *The Norton Facsimile: The First Folio of Shakespeare*. New York: W. W. Norton, 1968.

This facsimile presents a photographic reproduction of an "ideal" copy of the First Folio of Shakespeare; Hinman attempts to represent each page in its most fully corrected state.

Key to
Famous Lines and Phrases

. . . make us heirs of all eternity. [*King*—1.1.7]

. . . the huge army of the world's desires
[*King*—1.1.10]

Fat paunches have lean pates . . . [*Longaville*—1.1.27]

Small have continual plodders ever won,
Save base authority from others' books.
[*Berowne*—1.1.88–89]

Berowne is like an envious sneaping frost
That bites the firstborn infants of the spring.
[*King*—1.1.104–5]

At Christmas I no more desire a rose
Than wish a snow in May's new-fangled shows,
But like of each thing that in season grows.
[*Berowne*—1.1.109–11]

A man of fire-new words . . . [*Berowne*—1.1.182]

. . . a child of our grandmother Eve, a female; or, for
thy more sweet understanding, a woman . . .
[*Armado*—1.1.264–66]

. . . sit thee down, sorrow. [*Costard*—1.1.315]

Love is a familiar; love is a devil. There is no evil
angel but love . . . I am for whole volumes in folio.
[*Armado*—1.2.172–85]

This wimpled, whining, purblind, wayward boy,
This Signior Junior, giant dwarf, Dan Cupid . . .
                              [*Berowne*—3.1.189–90]

On a day—alack the day!—
Love, whose month is ever May,
Spied a blossom passing fair,
Playing in the wanton air.   [*Dumaine*—4.3.105–8]

But love, first learnèd in a lady's eyes,
Lives not alone immurèd in the brain . . .
For valor, is not love a Hercules,
Still climbing trees in the Hesperides?
Subtle as Sphinx, as sweet and musical
As bright Apollo's lute strung with his hair.
                              [*Berowne*—4.3.321–37]

For wisdom's sake, a word that all men love
                              [*Berowne*—4.3.351]

They have been at a great feast of languages and
   stolen the scraps.   [*Mote*—5.1.38–39]

. . . in the posteriors of this day, which the rude
   multitude call the afternoon. [*Armado*—5.1.89–90]

The tongues of mocking wenches are as keen
As is the razor's edge invisible . . . [*Boyet*—5.2.281–82]

Taffeta phrases, silken terms precise,
Three-piled hyperboles, spruce affectation . . .
                              [*Berowne*—5.2.442–43]

He speaks not like a man of God his making.
                              [*Princess*—5.2.579]

. . . a foolish mild man, an honest man, look you, and
  soon dashed. He is a marvelous good neighbor,
  faith, and a very good bowler.

[*Costard*—5.2.648–51]

A time, methinks, too short
To make a world-without-end bargain in.

[*Princess*—5.2.865–66]

When daisies pied and violets blue . . .

[*Spring*—5.2.968–85]

When icicles hang by the wall . . .

[*Winter*—5.2.986–1001]